The CSS *Albemarle*
and William Cushing

ALSO BY JIM STEMPEL

The Battle of Glendale: The Day the South Nearly Won the Civil War (McFarland, 2011)

The CSS *Albemarle* and William Cushing

The Remarkable Confederate Ironclad and the Union Officer Who Sank It

JIM STEMPEL

McFarland & Company, Inc., Publishers
Jefferson, North Carolina, and London

LIBRARY OF CONGRESS CATALOGUING-IN-PUBLICATION DATA

Stempel, Jim, 1948–
    The CSS Albemarle and William Cushing : the remarkable Confederate ironclad and the Union officer who sank it / Jim Stempel.
        p.   cm.
    Includes bibliographical references and index.

    ISBN 978-0-7864-6529-3
    softcover : 50# alkaline paper ∞

    1. Cushing, William Barker, 1842–1874.   2. Albemarle (Confederate ironclad)   3. United States — History — Civil War, 1861–1865 — Commando operations.   4. North Carolina — History — Civil War, 1861–1865 — Commando operations.   5. United States — History — Civil War, 1861–1865 — Riverine operations.   6. North Carolina — History — Civil War, 1861–1865 — Riverine operations.   7. Roanoke River Valley (Va. and N.C.) — History, Military — 19th century.   8. Ship captains — United States — Biography.   9. United States. Navy — Officers — Biography.   I. Title.
E467.1.C98S74 2011
973.7'58092 — dc23   2011030522
[B]

BRITISH LIBRARY CATALOGUING DATA ARE AVAILABLE

© 2011 Jim Stempel. All rights reserved

No part of this book may be reproduced or transmitted in any form or by any means, electronic or mechanical, including photocopying or recording, or by any information storage and retrieval system, without permission in writing from the publisher.

On the cover: (top) Sepia wash drawing of the CSS *Albemarle* by R.G. Skerrett, 1899; (bottom) portrait of Lt. Cmdr. William B. Cushing by A. Bradish, 1865 (both images from the U.S. Naval Historical Center)

Manufactured in the United States of America

McFarland & Company, Inc., Publishers
  Box 611, Jefferson, North Carolina 28640
    www.mcfarlandpub.com

Table of Contents

Preface — 1
Prologue — 5

1. The Mosquito Fleet — 13
2. A Close One, Sir — 20
3. We Are About to Build a Large Number of Gun Boats — 26
4. When Fought as Gallantly as That — 34
5. For Want of This Iron Our Work Has Been Going Backward — 41
6. Wrong Wharf, Wrong Boat — 47
7. In High Favor — 53
8. In a Cornfield at Edward's Ferry — 60
9. A Presidential Compliment — 65
10. Magnificent, Grim, Irresistible — 70
11. The Good Ship *Albemarle* — 79
12. Shokokon to Monticello — 85
13. Winter Offensive — 91
14. The Essence of Impudence — 96
15. All Ahead, Full — 102
16. Plymouth Is Ours — 108
17. Heaven Has Crowned Our Efforts with Success — 114
18. A Terrific Grand Waltz — 119
19. Four Miles from Wilmington — 127

20. Captain Cushing's Exploits in the Cape Fear River	134
21. Captain Cooke	140
22. David against Goliath	147
23. To Prevent an Impending Calamity	151
24. Send the Boats On	156
25. I Have Undertaken a Great Project	160
26. You Must Not Hope to Return	166
27. Pick Your Men	170
28. An Example of Coolness and Skill	176
29. The Fixed Determination to Escape	182
30. No More Gallant Thing	188
31. Dead Gone Sunk	193
32. It Is Done	198
33. Cheer Ship	202
34. Thanks of Congress	207
35. The Cost of the Nation's Unity	211
36. Blind to the Facts	218
Epilogue	225
Chapter Notes	227
Bibliography	237
Index	239

Preface

THE PURPOSE OF THIS BOOK is twofold. The first goal is to recapture one of the most compelling stories of the American Civil War, a story that involves great skill, intelligence, ingenuity, fortitude, and courage. The second goal is to place that story within the natural context of the times, to understand it through the eyes and words of the many contemporaries whose lives both shaped and drove the events described.

Cast as one of the lead characters in this tale — and an extraordinary story in its own right — is the formidable Confederate ironclad CSS *Albemarle*. Conceived and built by the young Southern shipbuilder, Gilbert Elliott, an accomplishment as much of persistence as it was genius, the *Albemarle* was constructed in a cornfield bordering North Carolina's Roanoke River without the necessary and appropriate tools, or labor, or finances, and with precious little in the way of governmental assistance. Despite these innumerable and ongoing difficulties — obstacles surely that would have stymied far lesser men — Elliott completed his ironclad, and in so doing fashioned a vessel that would ultimately take its place in the high pantheon of Confederate accomplishments.

So successful would the *Albemarle* become on the inland waterways of North Carolina that the Federal government feared it would regain all the waters of the outlying sounds, thus opening a new supply route to Richmond and a supply route that might radically alter the course of the war. The destruction of the *Albemarle* thus became a Federal objective of the highest priority, but the means to that end remained elusive, for the Confederate ironclad so overwhelmed all Union waterborne efforts to destroy her that the *Albemarle* quickly took on the aura of invincibility. The Federal Navy had ironclads aplenty, but none that could operate in the shallow waters of the coastal sounds; thus the CSS *Albemarle*, like a wolf with no natural predator, continued to roam free.

Ultimately, and in sheer desperation, the Federal Navy would hitch its star to the coattails of a mere twenty-one-year-old lieutenant whose storied career is every bit as fascinating as that of the *Albemarle*. Tossed out of the Naval Academy just weeks prior to graduation (for supposedly dumping a bucket of water on his Spanish professor's head), William Barker Cushing would nonetheless fashion over four years of Civil War one of the most accomplished records in the history of the naval service.

While the South would have the swashbuckling deeds of men like J.E.B. Stuart, John Mosby, and Nathan Bedford Forrest to gloat over, Cushing was one of the very few who would display the same sort of dash, ingenuity, and utter fearlessness in service of the Northern cause. During the course of the war, his name would become as celebrated in the North as it would become feared along the southeastern coast of the Confederacy; thus was Cushing specially selected to lead the almost suicidal mission against the Confederate ironclad.

This book has been carefully researched using a range of modern and original sources in order to provide the most historically accurate presentation while at the same time losing none of the powerful, dramatic nature of the confrontation between the two principal players. The official records of the war have been heavily relied upon, along with numerous biographies and texts long out of print that fortunately recapture a range of incidents, quotations, attitudes, and sensibilities that well reflect the flavor of the times. While the principal document regarding the construction of the *Albemarle* was crafted by her builder, Gilbert Elliott, a number of years after the war, William Cushing's exploits attracted a number of postwar biographers, some who knew him personally. These sources offer an intimate glimpse of the evolving dynamic that would one day place Cushing and the *Albemarle* on a collision course of historic significance.

Author and historian Robert L. O'Connell once observed that "while it is not exactly accurate to say that military systems emerged full-blown at the dawn of history, a remarkable amount was finalized very early, with the details being worked out, forgotten, and periodically rediscovered over a span of five thousand years."[1] And what is true of war in general is true of particular conflicts as well. The tale of the *Albemarle* and Cushing's exploits have been largely lost to history over the last one hundred years, yet it is a story of such significance and power that it deserves a more permanent home in the American chronicle.

The ultimate confrontation between the young naval lieutenant and the

CSS *Albemarle* combine to form one of the most compelling stories in the history of naval warfare; a literal reenactment of the tale of David and Goliath, played out in deadly earnest on the inland rivers of North Carolina. It would simultaneously require an effort of immense daring and yet of the coolest of calculation to find and sink the *Albemarle.* Indeed, William Cushing's mission to destroy the formidable Confederate ironclad and his extraordinary escape and return to the Federal fleet surely ranks as one of greatest accomplishments in the history of American arms and — fortunately for the student of history or the lover of great drama — a story as engrossing as it is consequential.

J.S.

A swooping falcon
Breaks the back
Of its prey;
Such is the precision
Of its timing.

Sun Tzu
The Art of War

Prologue

THE SMALL BOY HAD WALKED quite a few city blocks to the wharfs that bordered Lake Michigan that day on a mission of serious intent. He was alone but untroubled, indeed had run-off with his father's best top hat to proclaim his worldly sophistication to any and all onlookers he might encounter. Sadly, the hat did not fit and instead drooped down over his eyes like a milking pail or flour sack, generally making it impossible for him to see. It was Chicago 1845, and the boy had cleverly slipped away from Rowena, his half sister, who had been charged with the almost impossible task of watching him.[1]

The city streets teemed with carts and wagons laboring with their loads of produce and meats and wares all bound for market; the wharfs were cluttered with the masts of sailing vessels of every description, and the boy had to hold his hat above his head with both hands just to take it all in as he ambled along. The clamor and bustle of the city did not appear to bother him, however, and he made his way straight for a dock where a boat was turning out into the vast open blueness of the Great Lake that stretched that morning far out and beyond his vision. The boy moved with sudden swiftness, for he had made up his mind that morning that there was a whole wide world out there that had to be seen, and he was heading off that day to see it. The boy, by the way, was all of three years old.[2]

As the boat pulled away from the dock, the boy broke into a run, convinced, apparently, that this was the one and only boat that might spirit him away to that far and unseen realm beyond Chicago, and he ran straight off the end of the dock as if he might simply walk across Lake Michigan unaided, only then to sink like a stone into the dark blue water that had claimed many a life before him. Men screamed and men pointed, yet fortunately there was a sailor standing nearby who saw the whole thing and dove straight away off the dock and found the boy as he sank toward the bottom and pulled him up to safety, apparently none the worse for wear. The small boy had been saved, and a curious link between boy, audacity, and water perhaps forged that day in 1845.

Not recognizing the boy at all, the sailor took him home, dried him off, and tried to discern just who he had saved from a watery grave. The boy promptly took his hat back — which had also miraculously survived the plunge — and placed it on his head. "Will Coon," he answered, using the play name his older brother had once bestowed upon him.[3]

The sailor shook his head. He didn't know any Coons in that part of Chicago. "Where do you live, boy?" he asked.[4]

The boy could not answer the question with any certainty — he had in fact wandered far from home — but was sure that he was now hungry and in need of sustenance. The sailor proved a good man, and he gave the boy some food, told him to stay put, and went off to try and locate his family. The sailor returned at nightfall, tired and unsuccessful in his attempts to locate the Coon family, and the small boy was content to remain with the good sailor for the evening.

Meanwhile the boy's family was frantic to find him and began a desperate search of every possible avenue in Chicago, asking if anyone had seen a small boy with a large top hat wandering off of late. It would take thirty-six hours to locate him, but finally Rowena tracked him down to the sailor's home, content and asleep, still answering to the name Bill Coon. Admonished fiercely, he was yanked from his comfortable bed, marched back home, and no longer allowed to wear his father's hat — a terrible punishment and loss of dignity for one so small.[5]

The boy remained unfazed, however, when it came to both his desire to travel the globe and the requisite pluck necessary to accomplish such a task. A year later, and now a mature four years old, the boy determined that he would set off once again on his journey around the world, this time on horseback. His father, a doctor in Chicago, had recently purchased a colt which he stabled in a barn in rear of the house; but the horse was unbroken and none too tolerant of anyone, not to mention small children. This did not faze the boy. He "crept silently into the building and examined the horse, and was horrified to discover that it had no shoes. He had spent the previous summer watching a blacksmith, whenever he could get away from Rowena, so he fetched a hammer and four shoes and some nails from his father's workbench and approached the horse again, opening the door of the stall and going in. The horse reared and kicked."[6] The boy was knocked clear across the stall into the wall, where his nurse later found him that day, unconscious but alive.

The boy had been born on November 4, 1842, in far off Wisconsin in a log cabin not far from the present day town of Waukesha. It was virgin country then, frontier in reality, but the family had moved to Chicago in 1844 due to his father's poor health. The family lived near the waterfront, the doctor's business thrived, and the small boy seemed to almost all who encountered him an almost ungovernable and inexplicable mixture of intelligence, energy, and remarkable self-confidence.

But there was, of course, a wider world out there beyond the narrow boundaries of Chicago, and in that world events were taking place that would one day greatly affect the future of the United States, and as a consequence, the fate of the young boy with the insatiable wanderlust. In 1842, for instance, the same year as the boy's birth, in Washington, D.C., Congress, grasping the emerging viability of ironclad ships, appropriated the first funds for the construction of an armored, steam-powered, seagoing vessel. Named the *Steven's Battery*, construction began that year in Hoboken, New Jersey, by ship builder Robert L Stevens; but the vessel proved unreliable and unworkable and the effort was later abandoned.[7] Regardless, work continued in Europe on ironclad designs, as it did in the United States, to a lesser degree, and it slowly became clear that the age of the wooden fighting ship was coming to an end. The day of the iron battleship was fast approaching; and those evolving efforts had unknowingly and unwittingly placed the small, unconscious boy left lying on the floor of the Chicago stall and the world of naval design on a violent collision course of historic importance.

Ill health stalked the family, and in 1846 the boy's father, at the age of only forty-six, passed away, leaving his mother with little money yet with many children to feed. In 1847 the family, therefore, left Chicago for Fredonia, New York, where they had relatives who might help.[8] The small New York town proved a far cry from the city bustle and congestion of Chicago's docks. "Fredonia, New York, was a pleasant little town with tree-shaded streets, good water, substantial houses, and a relaxed air owing to the fact that the great wave of migration had passed it by and was, in the 1840's, breaking against the wilder country to the west. The population of the town was about three thousand; the soil was sandy, the sun hot in the summer; it was a good place for grapes, and they were grown there as early as the beginning of the century."[9]

The boy's family moved into a nice home on Green Street,[10] but there was little money to go around, and soon his mother, who had been well educated herself, opened a finishing school in her home. The school did well; and while the family hardly prospered, they did not want for necessities, so long as all the children pulled together and did their fair share of the work. The boy was only five years old when all this took place, and he leaned on his older brother for support through it all; and over the years the two grew incredibly close as often only young siblings can do.

His brother's name was Alonzo and the boy's name was William. "All the children had inherited their father's charm. They were all slender, graceful and good-looking; they were popular in the community, and jobs were always available. They were aware that they were poor relations; they knew that their mother did not buy new dresses, that they must practice economy in household matters, that the students living in the house were a necessity; but if their characters were affected it was mostly for the good, for they grew up feeling that they must make their own way."[11]

Despite the various, disruptive moves and the death of his father, Will's confidence seemed not the slightest diminished, but rather enhanced by the adversity of life. At the age of only seven, for instance, his mother sent him off on the train for Silver Creek to visit his aunt. She provided him enough money for the fare, but only enough for that; and Will, rather than buying a ticket for the train as he'd been instructed, instead spent it on a present for his aunt. He got on the train anyway without even a penny to pay for his ticket, but with a good idea how best to handle the situation. "Entering the car, he sat down next to a benevolent-looking gentleman in a checked vest with a silver watch chain. The man was sleepy but Will soon had him interested in the duck eggs which he and Allie [Alonzo] had found the day before. They struck up a conversation, and the man was charmed by his young traveling companion. Out of the corner of his eye Will saw the conductor enter the car, and talked even more briskly. When the conductor was three seats away he reached in his pocket as though to pay the fare, but the man insisted that he should pay it himself, since he had received more than the fare was worth in entertainment. Will said that he guessed he ought not to let the man do it, but the latter, thankfully, was adamant."[12]

Allie and Will grew both together and up in Fredonia, and by 1855 both were reasonably mature and educated young men. In the summer of that year his uncle, who had won a seat in Congress the year before, returned to Fredonia with good news. He was near securing an appointment as a cadet for Allie at West Point, and for Will he had already found a position as a page in the House of Representatives.[13] Both were to complete their studies, and leave the following year. Over the years Allie had grown to be the cautious, thoughtful one, while Will had emerged as the energetic, daredevil, as quick to settle any argument with his fists as Allie was through reasonable compromise. At the age of fourteen Will was bound for the capital of the United States, Allie for West Point on the Hudson River; and despite their excitement, it broke their hearts to lose one another's company.

Will worked hard as a page, quickly acclimated to the urban environment, sent his meager pay home to his mother, and while in Washington had the opportunity to meet a number of distinguished personalities who seemed to take a shine to the youngster from Fredonia. "Among the important people whom he came to know was Commodore Joseph Smith, who had been since 1846 the chief of the Bureau of Navy yards and Docks in Washington and in control of all naval construction. Commodore Smith was Will's mother's cousin, and though he was a solidly built man with iron-gray hair and 'a rather frighteningly serious demeanor' the two relatives became friends. Will met him at Christmas, and it was not many months later that the boy was informed that, owing to the efforts of his Congressman uncle and Commodore cousin, he had been accepted at the Naval Academy in Annapolis, to enroll in the class of 1861."[14]

Meanwhile, on the other side of the globe, the nations of Europe had become embroiled in the Crimean War, and as a consequence the evolution of the ironclad was in the process of taking another leap forward. While the Spanish navy had tinkered with iron designs for over 150 years, the French during the Crimean conflict had turned to the inclined armored casement for use in several floating batteries with success. These designs were in turn studied world wide, and would become the rudimentary forerunner of American prototypes during the upcoming Civil War.[15]

Will reported to the Academy — which had been founded in 1845 — in September 1857 at the tender age of fifteen. Over the next several years he would patch together a fairly unremarkable record, his high energy level and devotion to horseplay often getting the better of his academic pursuits and repeatedly landing him in trouble with the administration. This trend would come to a boiling point in March 1861, just weeks prior to his graduation, when he finally pushed the wrong people too far, and was forced to resign from the Academy. Officially Will was found deficient in Spanish, but the precise reason for his dismissal remains to this day unclear. "It certainly was an unusual proceeding to dismiss a first classman, standing high in his class, for being unsatisfactory in Spanish, and one is forced to conclude that some personal resentment entered largely into the motives for prompting summary action in his case."[16]

Will was crushed by the dismissal. His mission in life had been to become a naval officer, and now that dream appeared to have been yanked out from under him. For days he paced and pouted, then decided to try and do something about it. He traveled to Washington to try and marshal some friends on his behalf. Meanwhile the Naval Academy was coming apart at the seams due to the secession of Southern states. "The Academy was almost an armed camp. No one was entirely sure on which side Maryland would jump; if it did choose the Confederate cause, the Naval Academy, with its big guns and large store of ammunition, would be a rich prize. Academy personnel went into Annapolis armed; at night the gates were guarded by details of armed men, soldiers as well as future sailors."[17] In Washington Will met with Commodore Smith and also Lieutenant Charles Flusser, a former teacher at the Naval Academy and a friend of Will's who took up his cause and suggested he meet with Gideon Welles, then Secretary of the Navy.

On April 12, 1861, as Will doggedly pursued his reinstatement to the Academy, the guns in Charleston Harbor rang out, Fort Sumter was bombarded, and the American Civil War became a bitter reality. The Confederate Navy had already been established in February 1861 in Montgomery, Alabama, and on February 21 Stephen Mallory was appointed Secretary of the Confederate States Navy Department — a department, by the way, that boasted not a single ship.[18] Mallory had grown up in Key West, Florida, and had managed to teach himself maritime law in his spare time. Bright and energetic, Stephen Mallory was elected Town Marshal in 1832, then U.S. Senator in the 1850s.[19] With his thorough understanding of maritime matters, he was selected in 1853 to chair the Senate's Naval Affairs Committee, where he instituted a number of sensible reforms to the then stagnated Federal Navy. In particular, "he showed an early interest in experiments with ironclad ships; indeed, he was one of the very few congressmen who recognized the coming revolution in naval construction."[20]

For the Confederate government Stephen Mallory handled the difficult job of running a department with very limited resources with vision and skill. "Throughout the conflict he managed the Navy Department and conducted the war afloat with virtual independence. Davis [Jefferson Davis] went through six secretaries of war, but Mallory was his only navy chief, and the only member of the Confederate Cabinet to serve the same office for the duration."[21]

Gideon Welles, Secretary of the Federal Navy (Library of Congress).

At the war's very inception, Stephen Mallory had a clear vision as to the direction the Confederate Navy ought to move, and he was a strong advocate for armored sea power. "He dispatched officials to the Northern states, across the borders to Canada, and to Europe in search of vessels equipped for military use or for conversion to such use."[22] In April 1861, just as the smoke from the guns at Fort Sumter began to drift away, he wrote, "I propose to adopt a class of vessels hitherto unknown to naval service ... a combination of the greatest known ocean speed with the greatest known floating battery and power of resistance."[23] Mallory pointed out the most recent successes the French had obtained with ironclad floating batteries during the Crimean War, and urged strongly that the fledgling Confederacy pursue this new design to its optimum benefit. To Mallory the ironclad represented a breakthrough weapon, and one that might immediately render obsolete the entire Federal wooden fleet. "Such a vessel," Mallory wrote, "could traverse the entire coast of the United States, prevent all blockades, and encounter, with a fair prospect of success, their entire Navy."[24]

Thus, as Will was immersed in efforts to obtain his reinstatement to the Naval Academy, the seeds were being sewn in the infant Confederacy for a number of ironclad vessels, however many the South could either afford to purchase or marshal the requisite material to build. Will went directly to the navy department and presented himself humbly, requesting a position — it did not matter at what grade — in the service. He eventually met the Secretary of the Navy, Gideon Welles, and made a sincere case for his reinstatement, and Welles was good enough to hear the boy out. A few days later Welles called again for Will and gave him his decision — he would not be reinstated to the Academy, but would be provided an appointment in the service at the rank of master's mate. For William Barker Cushing, that appointment was to be the first step on the road to a career of extraordinary adventure, daring, and success.

The country was devolving into civil war. Will was assigned to the USS *Minnesota*, a forty-seven gun, wooden frigate, and one of the principle vessels that would comprise the navy's North Atlantic Blockading Squadron; and in late April Will Cushing hustled to Boston to join his shipmates. His brother, Alonzo Hersford Cushing, was scheduled to graduate from West Point that June, and the two would, over the coming years of civil strife, carve out exceptional records of valor and service.

Meanwhile in the South, Stephen Mallory was aggressively pursuing his agenda for the acquisition or construction of ironclads. At the burned out remnants of the former Federal Navy yard at Norfolk, Virginia, the charred remains of the frigate *Merrimack* had been discovered, and the decision made to raise and convert the ship over to the ironclad design. Soon other contracts would be dolled out to contractors across the South, and the collision course between William Barker Cushing and the dawning era of the ironclad battleship, which had been put in motion in 1842, began to accelerate rapidly.

As the *Minnesota* sailed from Boston's harbor in early May, Will took the time to pen a letter to his cousin. "I am an officer aboard the *Minnesota*," he wrote proudly. "We have just left our moorings, and as I write we are moving under steam and sail out of Boston harbor. I am going to fight under the old banner of freedom. I may never return, but if I die, I shall be under the folds of the old flag that sheltered my infancy and while striking a blow for its honor and my own."[25]

Many daring and remarkable missions would await the young master's mate, then only eighteen years old, indeed one on the Roanoke River in North Carolina that is considered to this day one of the most daring and heroic in American naval history. The boy who at only three had set off to see the world in Chicago was finally sailing off from Boston Harbor. He would leave his mark on the history of the United States. Writing years later, Gideon Welles would recall William Cushing fondly, and note, "I may add that the great chief of the American Navy, Farragut, who was endowed with like heroism, and for whom *alone*, the office of admiral was created and its honors intended, said to me that while no navy had braver or better officers than ours, young Cushing was the hero of the War."[26]

CHAPTER 1

The Mosquito Fleet

FOR SEVERAL DAYS WIND AND rain had lashed the North Carolina shoreline, coming and going in blustery bursts, making operations unpredictable, visibility difficult. It was February 7, 1862, and the small collection of refitted tugs and paddleboats, called affectionately the Mosquito Fleet by the Confederate sailors and soldiers who manned them, had taken up a defensive position along a pile line near Roanoke Island to try and stop the oncoming Yankee flotilla. The men were cold, hungry, outmanned and certainly outgunned; but they were game, nevertheless, and determined to make the best showing they could manage in the face of unforgiving odds.

The previous summer the Federal fleet had appeared off Hatteras Inlet, North Carolina, and simply pummeled the Confederate defenders huddled in their meager redoubts into submission. For the Yankees it had been an impressive operation, a combined sea and land assault, the army's forces under General Benjamin Butler, the Navy's North Atlantic Blockading Squadron commanded by Flag Officer Stringham aboard his flagship *Minnesota*. The pounding of the Confederate defenses and the taking of Hatteras Inlet represented the first significant Federal victory of the war, and news of the triumph had been greeted across the North with jubilation. "A White House watchman woke the President to give him the news. Still in his nightshirt, Lincoln ran into the Cabinet room, and literally danced a jig around Gus Fox, who had come from the Navy Department across the street bringing the official word."[1]

By closing Hatteras Inlet the Yankees had managed to block one of the most significant avenues of entry and egress to the inland waters and rivers of North Carolina, all used by enterprising blockade runners as a back door to Richmond and Norfolk for resupply. But unfortunately for the Federal cause, that critical success had not been immediately and properly followed up. With the fall of the Confederate defenses at Hatteras Inlet, the door had been left wide open for Federal forces to take control of the North Carolina sounds, and the numerous rivers that fed them; but the moment had not been seized, and the Confederates left to reinforce the area at their leisure. Thus what could have been taken by maneuver alone during the course of the previous summer could now only be taken by force.

The key to the position was Roanoke Island sitting smartly between Pamlico and Albemarle sounds. Whoever controlled the island controlled the avenues of water transportation; but more importantly, it became Burnside's objective "because permanent possession of Albemarle Sound would greatly facilitate the task of the blockading fleet, but chiefly because he hoped to be able to strike a blow at the Weldon Railroad after the capture of Newbern."[2] Realizing the strategic mistake the Yankees had made by not taking the island when it had been essentially unoccupied and indefensible, Confederate authorities moved quickly to fortify the area. Three thousand troops were sent to Roanoke Island, a string of shore batteries put in place, and a line of piles driven into the channel between the island and the mainland to impede any unwanted water borne traffic through the channel.[3] These defenses were sufficient to give any small Federal flotilla second thoughts of advance, but entirely inadequate when it came to preventing another large-scale operation — such as the one that had opened Hatteras Inlet the preceding August — from succeeding.

Unfortunately for Confederate aspirations, such a large-scale operation had been marshaled to the task, and was in fact now approaching. Thus it was that the Mosquito Fleet had deployed behind the pile line near Roanoke Island awaiting the first salvos from the swiftly closing Federal flotilla. On the short line of bobbing Confederate craft that morning was the small tug *Ellis*, drawing some six feet of water, measuring about 100 tons, and mounting small rifled artillery pieces both fore and aft.[4] Commanding the *Ellis* that day was Lieutenant James Wallace Cooke, an officer of the old U.S. Navy who had resigned his commission in 1861 and joined what was then the Virginia Navy in May, only to be commissioned a lieutenant in the Confederate Navy the following month. Born in Beaufort, North Carolina, in 1812 to Thomas and Esther Cooke, James had lost both parents to illness, and by the age of four was living with his uncle, Colonel Henry M. Cooke.[5] Receiving an appointment to the U.S. Navy at only sixteen, in 1828 he was assigned to the USS *Guerierre* as a midshipman, and promoted lieutenant in 1841. At the outbreak of hostilities, Cooke had been living on a farm near Fairfax, Virginia; but that had now been taken over by the Federals, his orchards cut down, and his property vandalized. It was a loss he could neither forget nor forgive.[6] Thin and feisty, James Wallace Cooke was prepared that morning to do battle with "the vandal horde of the North,"[7] his own uncomplimentary description of those Federal gunboats that were at that moment rapidly closing on the *Ellis* and the remainder of the Mosquito Fleet.

The Yankee force that was approaching was, like its successful predecessor that overwhelmed the Confederates at Hatteras Inlet, a combined sea and land operation. The officers in charge, however, had changed from the previous summer. The ships of the North Atlantic Blockading Squadron were now under command of Flag Officer Louis M. Goldsborough, the land forces under Brigadier General Ambrose Burnside.[8] It was Goldsborough's plan to first take Roanoke Island, and with that piece of the puzzle secure, move up the Carolina sounds. Burnside, thinking well and in advance of the operations unique needs, "suggested raising an amphibious or 'coastal' division from the Northeastern states. Burnside knew that among its men, 'should be found a goodly number of mechanics to fit out a fleet of light draught steamers and barges ... to transport the division, its armament and supplies, so that it could be rapidly thrown from point to point on the coast.' It was a far-reaching idea, much ahead of its time."[9]

The Federal expedition was gathered at Hatteras Inlet, Burnside with a division of almost 15,000 men, and started off for Roanoke Island on the morning of February 5, 1862. Bad weather blew up, however, hampering operations, and it would not be until the morning of the 7th before the assault could be commenced in earnest. The landing areas selected for Burnside's division were scouted and found free of Confederate opposition; and as the landing force chugged off toward Ashby's Harbor on Roanoke Island, the navy's gunboats prepared to make a dash at the Rebel batteries, and the Mosquito Fleet, spotted just behind the pile line. In moments only the sky filled with smoke, and the air resonated with the relentless booming of artillery fire.

The Federal Fleet moved in on the Confederate positions and began pummeling the Confederate redoubts with heavy fire. The Flag Officer's official report indicated that "at 1:30 P.M. the effect of our firing caused the barracks behind the fort at Pork Point to burst into flames, and at 2:15 P.M. they were burning furiously, entirely out of control. About this time, our vessels being placed by their respective commanders as advantageously as circumstances would permit, the firing was the hottest."[10] The combat raged for hours, the Confederates giving as well as they took, but the odds were decidedly in favor of the "vandal horde of the North" that day; and by late afternoon the Mosquito Fleet and the accompanying Confederate land batteries had been shot nearly to pieces and were near wreckage. As daylight began to fade,

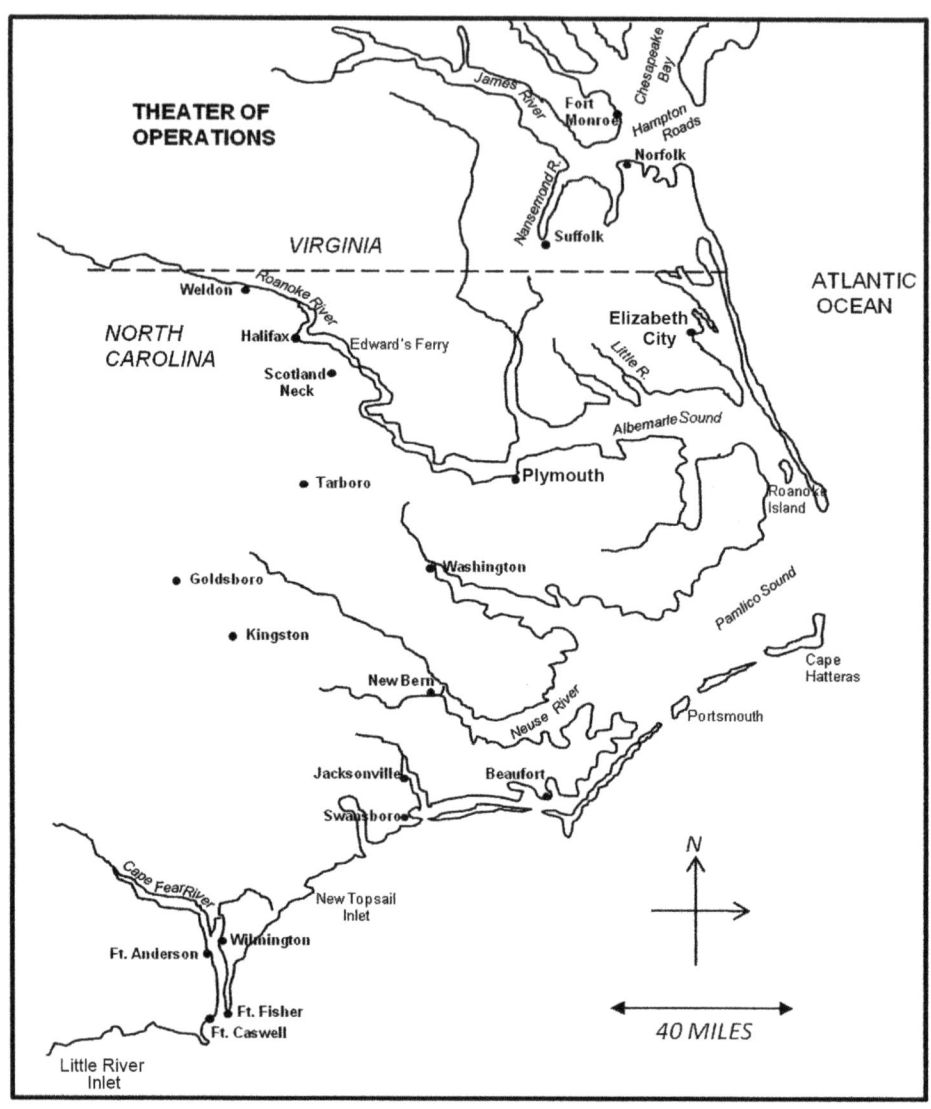

Theater of Operations (created by author).

and now nearly out of ammunition, the commander of the Mosquito Fleet decided to move what remained of his battered flotilla — only six boats surviving — back to Elizabeth City where they could hopefully resupply and renew the effort the following day.

Meanwhile at Ashby's Harbor the Federal troop landing was proceeding without incident or opposition. Here again, General Burnside had thought the effort through in advance, and his planning was reaping dividends. For "over the weeks and months Burnside had worked out a clever method for getting his men from boat to beach. The transports each came fitted with specially designed ladders, down which the troops climbed into large surfboats. In strings of twenty they were towed inshore by a steamer, cast off and rowed the final yards over the surf. In concept and practice, it pointed a direct evolutionary line to the United States' amphibious assaults of World War II."[11] By late evening a force of over 6,000 Federal infantry was ashore, prepared to begin the assault at dawn.

At first light the infantry moved out, brushing aside the Confederate skirmish line, and assaulting Fort Bartow from the rear as the Federal gunboats again renewed their bombardment from the water. For a period the fight raged anew, but soon the return fire from the fort slowly dwindled, then trailed-off to nothing. In the late hours of the afternoon the bewildered Confederates finally marched off, abandoning the position. At 4:30 P.M. the Stars and Stripes were observed flying over Fort Bartow by the boats of the Federal flotilla, and shortly thereafter the navy successfully breeched the pile line — effectively compromising the entire Rebel defensive arrangement. Having little in the way of options, the Confederate commander surrendered his entire command, consisting of 2,500 men and three thousand stands of small arms. At a cost of only 41 dead infantry and sailors, the combined operation had proved a complete success.[12]

The Federal victory, while accomplished with remarkable ease and swiftness, was still one of critical importance. At the moment the Stars and Stripes were raised over Fort Bartow, there was precious little organized opposition to Burnside inland in the Carolinas; and if Yankee forces moved rapidly, Burnside's division might well be able to seize the railroads feeding Richmond from the south. Such a rapid thrust into central North Carolina would cut off the Confederate capital from its vital southern supply line, and as a consequence the main Rebel army operating in Northern Virginia.

Additionally, all Confederate opposition on the waters of North Carolina would of necessity be forced to retreat to the inland rivers and sounds if, indeed, further Federal advances were to be resisted. The region was not one well suited to large-scale operations. "Swamps line the western side of the sounds, and are pierced by slow, meandering rivers, over which the thick, almost jungle trees nearly close in summer, to drop their leaves into the muddy, dark currents. Sailing is out of the question up these creeks and rivers; sometimes the only means of water transportation is poling."[13] This sort of environment would entail the deployment of an entirely different class of smaller, more maneuverable craft that could operate in the shallow bays and rivers, boats that would have to be newly designed or fitted out for operations.

Meanwhile, in Elizabeth City the Mosquito Fleet had been cut off from any potential escape. The locks operating the inland canals had been jammed, thus there was no way out except a suicidal dash back toward the Federal flotilla. Such a dash, however, would prove unnecessary, as on Sunday, February 9, a Federal flotilla of fourteen gunboats was spotted approaching in the channel. For what remained of the Mosquito Fleet, it was fight or surrender. They chose not to surrender.

The remains of the battered Mosquito fleet valiantly, if forlornly, took up positions in the channel opposite—*Fanny, Beaufort, Raleigh, Ellis, Sea Bird,* and the *Appomattox*[14, 15]—and awaited the Federal advance. It came the following morning as six of the fourteen Yankee gunboats, commanded by Stephen Rowan, came steaming north. "When three quarters of a mile from the battery, Rowan's signal floated out in the morning breeze, 'Dash at the enemy.' Commanding officers shouted for full speed, and their coal heavers maniacally threw shovelfuls into the glowing fireboxes."[16] Black smoke poured from the Federal's smokestacks as the gunboats picked up speed and closed on the Confederate defenses, blasting away with their guns, intent ultimately on ramming the Rebel craft, then boarding and having it out with pistol and cutlass.[17]

The *Fanny* was run aground and scuttled, the *Sea Bird* rammed and sunk, its crew diving for dear life into the river. Aboard the *Ellis* James Cooke was determined to make a fight of it no matter what the odds, and for this he had rigged a charge in the hold to blow both he and the Federal gunboat *Ceres* to pieces as it closed on his hapless craft. But the charge failed, the Yankees leaped onto his tug, and Cooke went down fighting, cutlass in hand. Cooke was wounded and taken prisoner in the fracas, but he would be paroled only days later, and recover from his wounds. The feisty rebel officer would be heard from again.

But the Mosquito Fleet had sailed its last, and the back door to Norfolk and Richmond slammed shut by the successful Federal operation. Burnside then moved to the mainland in early March, and quickly took the towns of Newbern, Beaufort, and Morehead City. Suddenly the Federals controlled much of the sounds and inland waters of North Carolina.[18] Burnside telegraphed General George McClellan, the overall Federal commander at Washington, frantically asking for cavalry enough to rush inland and cut off the Rebel railroads; but McClellan, marshaling strength for his anticipated campaign on the Virginia Peninsula near Yorktown, refused. Regardless, the initial victory on the North Carolina coast had gone to the Federals, and as the Confederates scrambled to prepare suitable water craft to resist, the scene had been set for a bitter confrontation on the rivers of Virginia and North Carolina for control of the region.

Writing in her journal at her plantation home near Edward's Ferry, NC, Catherine Edmondston grasped instantly the magnitude of the loss. "Ah what trouble that neglect of the defences at Roanoke Island has cost us! ... We have the *stern present* & the uncertain future before us. God grant us strength to meet them with a determined will and a cheerful spirit."[19]

The resistance would require all that and more.

CHAPTER 2

A Close One, Sir

ON EXPEDITION FROM ALBEMARLE SOUND up the Blackwater River, the gunboat *Commodore Perry* with her crew of twenty-nine was in serious trouble. The three boat Federal flotilla had started upriver on October 2, the *Perry* in the lead followed by the *Whitehead* and *Hunchback*; but the journey had been plagued from its inception, and was now on the brink of disaster. It was designed to be a joint land and naval operation, the two elements to rendezvous at Franklin, Virginia, on the 3rd, where the Confederates were reported to be gathering a sizeable force for an assault north toward Norfolk.[1] The night before the small flotilla had reached a point roughly three miles below Franklin where they dropped anchor, and after a quick breakfast the following morning, started upriver again in hopes of contacting the Yankee infantry.[2]

But the Rebels had gotten wind of the flotilla's approach, the banks of the river were narrow and high, and Confederate infantry and militia had been dogging the boats all morning, pouring a terrific rifle fire down upon the decks at almost every opportune location, or turn in the river. The three gunboats had managed to come within shouting range of Franklin without suffering too many casualties, but a narrow, sharp bend in the channel had spelled danger. In attempting to run the bend without stopping to tie lines to trees along the shore to help swing the boats about — a task that would have been impossible under the constant Rebel fire — the *Commodore Perry* had temporarily lost control, drifted wide, and run aground on the southern bank of the river.

Now masses of Confederate infantry, grasping the Yankees' desperate predicament, had gathered on the bank, and with a yell were storming straight toward the vessel. There was not a second to lose if the *Commodore Perry* was going to be kept from falling into enemy hands.

William Barker Cushing leaped into action. He screamed for his men to follow, and without hesitating to see if any one of them had actually followed his lead, dashed toward the field howitzer on the afterdeck of the gunboat. Six good men swarmed the gun suddenly right behind him, and with their help Cushing quickly loaded the tube with canister, and swung the howitzer about.[3] Bullets filled the air, cracking off the *Perry*'s sideboards, thumping into flesh. Cushing's men were cut down around him, falling and screaming. Blood pooled on the afterdeck, and as Cushing looked up, he realized suddenly that every one of his six mates had been gunned down.

With only seconds left before the Rebels would be upon him, Cushing wheeled around, saw the Confederates now only thirty or forty yards away, a mass of butternut and grey running straight toward him. They were shouting and screaming, waving their guns overhead as they ran. He calmly sighted the gun down the barrel, then pulled the lanyard. The gun exploded with a resonant crack, and a burst of canister ripped through the grey infantry like an enormous shotgun blast. The howitzer shot stopped the infantry dead in its tracks, men stumbling over their fallen comrades, but the officer in front had miraculously survived and came on all on his own, as Cushing would later recall, a "splendid looking fellow with long curly hair."[4]

The officer, waving his sword, came straight on, and Cushing grabbed frantically for the revolver at his side, only to suddenly realize that in the excitement of the moment he had inadvertently dropped it somewhere on the deck. Just as the Rebel officer neared the boat, and as William Cushing stood helpless to defend himself, a rifle barked, and the officer flopped, face-forward in the mud. "Cushing looked down, astonished, to see that one of the wounded sailors had risen-up to his knees and was leaning on the rail, his smoking weapon in his hands. The wounded sailor looked up at Cushing. 'Close one, sir,' he said, and winked. Cushing winked back, then ran to the pilot-house."[5]

Since his maiden voyage as master's mate aboard the *Minnesota* the previous year, William Barker Cushing had had a busy and impressive number of months at war. In July he had volunteered for a raid up the Back River to seize reported Confederate ships and building facilities inland. In all nine boats departed Fortress Monroe on the Virginia peninsula, five naval launches, and four carrying Federal infantry. The expedition located and burned ten Confederate vessels, and captured a schooner which was then confiscated for Federal use. It was just the sort of daring, behind enemy lines type of mission that Cushing, over time, would develop a remarkable talent for handling.

Then in August Master's Mate Cushing had been aboard the flagship *Minnesota* when that vessel took part in the bombardment of the Confederate works at Hatteras Inlet. Cushing had been commanding officer of an eight-gun section on the quarterdeck that day, and was heavily involved in the action. The sound of the guns and the thrill of combat he'd found almost intoxicating. "This was a great moment for me," he wrote, "a youngster who had never been fairly under fire — and I shall never forget or again experience the wild pleasure and excitement that I felt, as the stern challenge and response passed over the blue water on that sunny August day."[6] His calm, professional bearing had not gone unnoticed by naval command. For his good work Cushing had been "warranted a mid-shipman on October 19, 1861, the warrant to be dated from June, 1, and ordered to the *Cambridge*." Thus William Cushing would be listed as having graduated from the Naval Academy in the class of 1861 after all, twenty-first in a class of twenty-six,[7] his calm under fire having regained what his laxity in the classroom had previously lost.

Throughout the winter the *Cambridge* performed blockade duties off the Virginia coast. Then in March 1862 the boat was in the waters near Fortress Monroe at the mouth of the James River when the feared Rebel ironclad *Virginia* (called *Merrimack* by both friend and foe alike) steamed from its berth out to challenge the wooden ships of the blockading squadron on its maiden voyage. Thus William Cushing had a front row seat to history in the making. The *Cambridge*, with only five guns, was hardly a worthy opponent for the massive Rebel ironclad, and was thus deployed alongside the frigate *St. Lawrence*; and a good thing it was, for the contest proved entirely lopsided. When the *Virginia* had finished with the Federal fleet that day, the *Cumberland* had been sunk, the *Congress* shot to pieces and captured by the Rebels, and both the *Minnesota* and *St. Lawrence* run aground. The encounter had been a complete disaster for the Federal Navy.

That evening, however, the Yankees' own ironclad *Monitor* had completed its maiden voyage from New York, and eventually took up a blocking position near the *Minnesota*. The following day, March 9, 1862, history would be made as the two ironclad battle ships fought to an essential draw. The *Virginia* ultimately withdrew to her berth near Norfolk, and the *Monitor* remained behind in the waters near Fortress Monroe.

While in defense of the stranded *St. Lawrence*, the *Cambridge* had come under fire, and Will Cushing had been wounded when a shell burst directly overhead; his first wound of the war. Theron Wilber Haight, an associate of Alonzo's in the infantry, writing of Will's presence at the famous encounter, wrote that "he was a spectator [March 9, 1862] of the battle in Hampton Roads between the *Monitor* and the *Merrimac*, wherein the destiny of wooden ships was settled for all time."[8]

Appreciation for Will Cushing's daring and ability leaped as a result of his efforts that day, and his stock immediately rose at the Naval Department in Washington City. In July Will was selected to accompany the new commander of the North Atlantic Blockading Squadron, Flag Officer Louis M. Goldsborough, on a trip up the James River to Harrison's Landing, where the Federal Army under the Young Napoleon, George McClellan, had encamped after its failed campaign on the Virginia peninsula. It gave Will an opportunity to visit with Alonzo and meet many of the officers in the army. Abraham Lincoln had come down to try and get McClellan to take action with his ponderous but inactive Federal force, and a review of the army was ordered by the commanding general. Will Cushing was selected to ride with the president's staff, and he had been deeply honored by the opportunity. "I went up the James River on the 5th of July, and remained for several days with Alonzo, in General McClellan's camp," Cushing would later write. "While there, President Lincoln reviewed the troops. I had the honor of riding on his staff. I was introduced to the most noted generals and saw every regiment in the army. I had a fine time in every way."[9] Cushing adored the president, and would never forget the experience.

In July 1862 Will Cushing was jumped two grades to the rank of lieutenant—a very rare occurrence, and unheard of for one so young—and as a result allowed to pick whoever he wished to serve under. The answer for Will was a simple one. He would serve only under Lieutenant Commander Charles Flusser, the man who had stood by him during his travails at the Naval Academy, and a man Cushing respected enormously.

In just that manner, then, had William Cushing come to the afterdeck of the *Commodore Perry* that October 3, second in command to Charles Flusser on their expedition up the Blackwater River. The brave Confederate officer now lay dead before him in the mud, and as the smoke from the rifle shot that had saved Cushing's life drifted off into the swampy air, he realized somewhat to his surprise that the enemy infantry had been utterly stunned by the howitzer blast. That shot seemed to have represented a harsh message of the grim nature of war, and a bloody message for which the inexperienced Rebels were entirely unprepared. They had expected an easy and glorious success, only to be torn to pieces for their misconceptions. But the fight raged on. Will wrote, "For four hours we fought them at the barricade, and in that time routed them five times. Once they tried to board us, but the terrible canister mowed them down at a twenty-yard distance, and the charge failed."[10]

Cushing dashed back to the *Perry*'s pilot house where he encountered Commander Flusser berating the man who had inadvertently steered the ship onto the riverbank in the first place, and desperately trying to get the vessel to reverse both its engines and its plight. Fortunately for all hands, Flusser's actions worked; and before the Confederates could again gather themselves, the *Commodore Perry* had been backed off the bank safely and was free in the channel again. The small gunboat churned slowly upriver, cleared the nearest bend, then turned and opened with its four artillery pieces on the pursuing Confederates. The Rebels, still grouped in the woods nearby, were in turn forced to dive for cover. Canister ripped the trees and bushes to shreds, and it became quite clear that the advantage had suddenly and radically shifted. The *Commodore Perry*, once the hunted, had flipped the order of battle, and was, with its four guns belching metal, now the hunter.

Under the withering covering fire of the *Commodore Perry*, both the *Hunchback* and the *Whitehead* were able to maneuver successfully around the river bend; and once joined, all three started upriver again. Slightly below the objective at Franklin, the small flotilla dropped anchor and waited for the sound of the anticipated Federal land assault, which they had reason to believe was soon to be, if it had not already been, initiated. But they heard nothing, and hours passed unproductively. Moreover, Rebel infantry and militia had followed along the riverbank and again began an incessant fire on the three boats. Over time it became too hot to remain stationary in the river. The three gunboats could not waste all their ordnance chasing off the enemy marksmen; and when no sound of a Federal advance could be discerned from near Franklin, Flusser ordered the flotilla back downriver to its original base.

The trip back was just as hot and hazardous as the one upriver had been, clearing obstructing trees felled by hordes of Confederates along the riverbanks; but it was accomplished nevertheless in good order and with minimal loss. The reality, unfortunately, was that the junket had all been for naught, communications between the land and naval forces disjointed, as the Federal infantry had never been able to make proper contact with the flotilla. Thus the expedition had proved a dismal failure for Federal aspirations, but not necessarily so for William Cushing.

When Commander Flusser filed his official report of the Blackwater River operation, he described William Cushing's heroic actions during the expedition, and especially on the afterdeck in such glowing terms, that naval command took immediate notice. The navy was desperate for daring officers, and in that category William Cushing's name seemed to keep popping up. The Federal blockade was at that time expanding and good, aggressive ship's captains few and far between, thus Will Cushing was soon offered command of his own vessel.

Cushing, taking command of his own gunboat, would enter a naval enterprise far different from anything he had trained for at the Academy, or for which his experience aboard the *Minnesota* had prepared him. This was not the navy of white sails and high seas, of thunderous broadsides and flapping pennants, but rather of swampy rivers in snake-infested lowlands.

But to William Barker Cushing it hardly mattered. Cushing swelled with pride when his orders were received, and Commander Flusser had him taken to the New Bern dock in the *Perry*'s launch where both his first crew and ship awaited. For Cushing it seemed both a royal send-off and a royal welcome. "It was with a feeling of great pride that the young lieutenant was piped over the side of his first command. Her crew of twenty-eight was lined upon the foredeck when he came aboard, and though they seemed surprised to have a boy — so one, at least, later called him — for a captain, they snapped smartly to attention while he read them his orders."[11] At the age of only nineteen, Will Cushing had been given command of his own ship, and he looked her over adoringly. "She was of iron," he recalled later, "three-eighths of an inch thickness, measured about one hundred tons, and mounted an eighty-pounder rifle forward, and a twelve-pounder rifle howitzer aft."[12] The boat had recently been refitted, indeed had been captured from the tiny Confederate Navy earlier that year when the Mosquito Fleet had been defeated near Elizabeth City,[13] its combative Confederate captain wounded and taken prisoner during the melee. Now the pride of William B. Cushing and his small crew of Federal sailors, the gunboat's name was the *Ellis*.

CHAPTER 3

We Are About to Build a Large Number of Gun Boats

WHILE CONFEDERATE SECRETARY of the Navy Stephen Mallory had devised a forward thinking and strategically sensible plan for the projection of naval strength that fit both the Confederacy's needs and meager capabilities, that plan was nevertheless dogged over the years by limited facilities and material, along with a profound sense of indifference on the part of the Rebel government itself. Jefferson Davis' experience in the Federal government as Secretary of War had not prepared him for a naval concept of warfare, and his views of the war thus remained "strictly continental and landlocked."[1] Funds and material were consistently diverted to the land armies, while the navy's needs of iron for its ironclads and funds to support its shipbuilding efforts went begging. Indeed, as hostilities erupted and the Confederate government struggled to meet its wartime goals, Matthew Fontaine Maury, an officer of high caliber in the Office of Orders and Detail wrote, "It is evidently no part of the plan of the Administration to have a navy at present or even to encourage one."[2] This mind-set, coupled with the South's paltry shipbuilding, transportation, and industrial facilities in place at the onset of the conflict, crippled even Mallory's vision of a roughly equal seaborne competition with the vastly larger Federal Navy by means of a smaller fleet of ironclad design. The result ultimately produced a hodgepodge of local or even "backyard" projects, many of questionable design, others that went either under funded or unsustained.

Yet even if the Confederate government had been entirely committed to the construction of a modern navy for its defense, the internal problems it faced were staggering. "In 1860, the South produced barely a tenth of the manufactured goods in the United States. Of industrial works it had less than a tenth (in fact, the entire South had less manufacturing capacity than New York City). It forged no steel, nor had it the facilities to construct machine tools. Many of the South's foundries and mills were little better than village smithies, and those along the banks of the Tennessee and Ohio rivers quickly fell to Union forces. Of the eleven rolling mills of any size, only Richmond's Tredegar Iron Works was fitted for heavy production and had experience casting naval guns."[3] In the short run, there was no way to rectify these systematic deficiencies; thus over time even a small flotilla of seaworthy ironclads, as Mallory had originally envisioned, was reduced to little more than a fantasy.

As far as the construction of ironclads was concerned, the simple lack of iron proved the most problematic. The South did not have the requisite ore deposits, the capacity to mine what little they had, the foundries to smelt the ore into iron, nor the rail lines necessary to ship the finished product to the local shipyards for final application. The Confederate Navy was desperate to emulate European naval designs, but had virtually no capacity to do so. "The French and English ironclads had been clothed only with solid armor-plates. Four and a half inches ... had been fixed upon as the standard thickness. In Europe there were foundries provided with the means of rolling such plates. Nothing of the kind existed in America. These plates could be produced here only by the slow process of forging."[4] But the South was almost hopeless to produce such forged plates. So critical did the situation become that the Confederacy literally began to cannibalize itself to try and reach even the most meager of these goals, tearing up miles of non-military rail lines to feed its few meager foundries. But even this desperate tactic proved insignificant when it came to meeting the Confederacy's military needs, on both land and sea. "At least ten ironclads had to be broken up, incomplete for want of plate. In late 1864, the navy's chief constructor reported a dozen vessels on the stocks awaiting their armor, 'but the material is not on hand.'"[5]

Nowhere was the Confederate government's psychological and material indifference to the navy's needs felt more keenly than in North Carolina, where the local defenses, due to early Federal inroads, had been backed westward into the inland waterways. After Roanoke Island fell to Federal forces in February 1862, the need for smaller, lighter draft vessels that could maneuver and fight on the inland waters skyrocketed; but the facilities for their construction were almost nowhere to be found, nor men who could expertly craft them.

But even before the eventual demise of the Mosquito Fleet, the Confederate Navy had been casting about for people and facilities in the Carolinas; men who could build boats, and shipyards where they might be crafted. One individual the Confederate Navy turned to was Gilbert Elliott, then only eighteen years old. Born in Elizabeth City, North Carolina, in 1843, Elliott was familiar with the water, but by no means a shipbuilder of any reputation in the latter months of 1861. Elliott was in fact a young lawyer at the outbreak of hostilities, and worked for a local shipyard owner by the name of William Martin.[6] When Martin moved off to serve as an officer in the war, Elliott remained behind to supervise the shipyard. Neither man had extensive experience in shipbuilding, but Martin arranged for Elliott to meet with Stephen Mallory, and contracts were soon discussed. Martin, aware of both his own and Elliott's limitations wrote, "I feel some hesitation to undertake a regular contract not knowing anything about the business & suggest that you be very careful in your calculations & allow for contingencies. I am inclined to think it would be safer to rent the yard & hire the hands to the government."[7]

John Luke Porter was at the time the chief naval constructor for the Confederate Navy, and through his office all plans for naval construction in North Carolina flowed. Having few boatyards to work with and fewer quality craftsmen, Porter eventually turned to Martin's shipyard in Elizabeth City as a potential site for contractual work. "Feeling secure with the knowledge that timber was available for a price, Elliott was pleasantly surprised when summoned by Flag Officer Lynch to his flagship *Sea Bird* off Roanoke Island. He was being invited to discuss an agreement, whereby he could be awarded a shipbuilding contract."[8] A contract was then negotiated and signed on October 22, 1861, for the construction of a gunboat "of the *Chattahoochee* Class with twin screws, and mounting five to six guns."[9] Overnight, it seemed, Elliott and Martin were in the shipbuilding business; and with contract in hand, Gilbert Elliott began receiving inquiries from qualified craftsmen for positions at the shipyard. Like a collapsing line of dominoes, for Elliott and Martin everything seemed to be falling into place.

Material and workmen then became the problem for Gilbert Elliott. It seemed he could never really corner enough of either. Elliott wrote one of his new agents: "I am sorry to hear that there are not as many trees as Snell counted. However one must be satisfied. I am trying to hire Frank Duke from Isaac Pritchard and William Berry from Thomas Berry. They are both good sawyers. You can put them to doing anything which you please. Horatio Dozier, who is hired by Thos Roton, will see you tomorrow. Put him to work. You are authorized to make any bargain with him which suits you. When he is done give him an order on me for amount which you owe him. In the same way you can hire hands if any come to you."[10]

Despite the problems, things moved along reasonably well, and the agent responded to Elliott's note, if not with Shakespearean eloquence, at least with a positive frame of mind. "I hav had Gregory stews 3 days this weak. We have got along first rate ... this weak. We hav got a new road thru the field ... you wll let me hear from you."[11]

Work on the contract moved slowly. Accounts were drained to pay for supplies of timber and iron, not to mention the cost of transporting everything to the shipyard by means of a system that was constantly late and unreliable. In particular, iron was extremely difficult to come by, a fact that put the costs continually on the rise, and a fact that constantly skewed estimates for the completed work. It became extremely difficult to bid for contracts when costs could not be confidently projected. Still, the Confederate Navy maintained high hopes of constructing a substantial number of boats despite all the delays and difficulties, and Gilbert Elliott and the shipyard at Elizabeth City increasingly played into those hopes. In late November Elliott received a confidential note from William Williamson, the navy department's chief engineer, who had recently visited with Elliott to inspect the Elizabeth City facilities. "We are about to build a large number of gun boats to carry 2 guns each," he wrote confidentially," and shall probably get you to build several. Don't speak of this to anybody, not even your foremen, as it is only known as this time to the Secy and myself. They will be about 100 or 120 ft. long and 18 or 10 ft beam."[12]

The contest to design and build ironclad warships was to prove a struggle, not only of industrial and ship making capacities between the North and South, but also of nautical philosophies between Great Britain and the United States. "The U.S. Navy preferred the monitor style with the huge fifteen-inch guns; the British idea was to plate the sides of a faster ship with iron and outfit her with smaller rifled guns."[13] Thus over time this contest became a version of the race between the tortoise and the hare, the British opting for the hare, the Federal Navy opting for the tortoise; but a tortoise with a serious kick.

The Confederacy adopted a version of the British model, and Stephen Mallory had specific ideas as to the qualities he wanted all Rebel ironclads to embody in addition to the ship's speed and lighter ordinance. The first of these was a vessel covered in four-inch armor, angled at such a degree that would make the ship impervious to traditional broadsides; and secondly Mallory wanted each craft to sport a sharp iron ram at the bow, a weapon that — harkening back to the age of Greek and Roman seacraft — would make fair game of any traditional wooden vessel. But the Secretary had far more than those two design features in mind. "Mallory strongly embraced three additional innovative decisions that were to become standard specifications for Confederate ironclad gunboats. Those were the use of rifled cannon; solidly reinforced ship's bows, ironclad for ramming; and exposed surfaces above water to be covered with armor plates."[14]

The first test of these two competing designs came with the clash of the original prototypes, the *Monitor* and the *Merrimack* in March 1862. That test would prove indecisive, however, as neither craft was able to land a lethal blow, or seriously incapacitate the other, as the two fought essentially to a draw. The *Merrimack* was eventually scuttled by her own crew, but that was a desperate necessity born of the political decision to abandon Norfolk — the *Merrimack*'s home port — and nothing at all to do with her fighting prowess.

The true and final test would not come until the spring of 1863 in the waters off Savannah, Georgia, when the Federal monitor *Weehawken* faced off with what was then considered the Confederacy's most advanced ironclad, the *Atlanta*. In late 1861 the British steamer *Fingal* had run the Federal blockade into Savannah with military equipment for the Confederacy, but had as a result become instantly trapped by the same blockading force. Unable to escape, the ship was eventually sold to the Confederate government and converted into a fighting ship of the British model. "Her armament consisted of two 7-inch Brooke rifles fore and aft, two 6.4 inchers on the broadside, and a spar torpedo in her bow."[15] She was commanded by Lieutenant William Webb, who had a fighting reputation in the Confederate Navy.

The vessel had been used for a number of months successfully on the inland waters where Federal ironclads could not negotiate the shallows, and in June of 1863 the Federal blockade got wind of reports that the Confederate ironclad, now renamed the *Atlanta*, had its sites on the Union wooden flotilla in Wassaw Sound. The Federal monitors *Weehawken* and *Nahant* were subsequently shifted into the sound to bolster the Union flotilla in that area, and the scene was set for a showdown of consequence. In the early hours of June 17, the *Atlanta*, accompanied by another smaller gunboat, began her trip toward the sound, Webb and his crew believing inherently that they had the strongest fighting vessel ever produced in the Confederacy.

The *Atlanta* started down river early, hoping to take the Federal flotilla by surprise, but the Union ships were ready and waiting, confidently commanded by John Rodgers aboard the *Weehawken*. The *Atlanta* and her sister ship were spotted, and the commands given for general quarters. The officer of the watch had spotted the Rebel ironclad and both Union monitors prepared to give battle at full speed ahead. The *Atlanta*, maneuvering in the shallows, ran aground on a sandy bar, then, spotting the closing Federal ironclads, opened fire at long range, but all to no effect.

The two Union monitors continued to close rapidly to a range of only 350 yards, from where the *Weehawken* opened fire. "The 400-pound, steel-cored shot struck the *Atlanta*'s casemate abreast the pilot house, driving in the armor and ripping away a swath of woodwork three feet wide along its full length."[16] The entire port side gun crew was hurled to the deck, many wounded, and everything in the ship not bolted down flung across the open decks. The *Weehawken* fired again and again, tearing the pilot house to shreds, and rocking the Rebel boat to its core. Unable to maneuver, and now facing the two monitors on its flanks, positioned where the *Atlanta* could not bring its guns to bare, the Rebel vessel, then the pride of the Confederate Navy, had little choice but to surrender.

With that surrender the question of design superiority was finally settled once and for all. "In a way, this battle was a double victory for the U.S. Navy. It ended the career of a potentially formidable Confederate vessel before it even began, and it sent a message to Great Britain: the United States had a naval force that was not to be trifled with."[17] Indeed, so pleased was Federal Navy Secretary Gideon Welles with the result of the engagement, that he would later write, "The guns of the *Weehawken* have knocked the breath out of the British statesmen as well as the crew of the *Atlanta*."[18] But it would take a few years for that clash to finally unfold; and as Gilbert Elliot began his work in North Carolina during the winter of 1861-1862 the ultimate result was far from a foregone conclusion.

Shipping delays, late payments, and a general shortage of every material imaginable continued to plague Elliot's efforts at the yard in Elizabeth City. Slowly the fall of 1861 dissolved into winter, with little in the way of progress being achieved. In mid–December Elliott received another note from his miller, H.L. Hinds, and could at least be thankful that wood was still being cut, stacked, and readied for use. "We have got along vary well this weak sawing and carrying out the plank and timber and also hewing with the exception of an accident of my son. Cut his foot last evening wich will confin him some tim. I think I have hiard the boy Edmund of Mrs. Willis for 75c per day and he finds himself he is quiet good hand he has work 1½ days this weak all the trees are down but 4 and 2 of them are dug up."[19]

In January Elliott made a proposal to Stephen Mallory suggesting the construction of an additional three boats. He received a response from the Secretary on January 4, and also the first payment on his original contract, which finally allowed some bills to be paid and the work to move forward. Mallory agreed in concept with Elliott's proposal, and wrote back saying, "Your letter of the 1st instant offering to build three gun boats according to the specifications furnished in four months for the sum of $10,000 each has been received. You can proceed at once with the work under your offer and the contract will be drawn and sent to you ... to begin from the day your receive this letter. The Department further offers you a bonus of one thousand ($1,000) dollars on each boat if completed within three months and of five hundred ($500) dollars if delivered within three and a half months."[20]

It seemed a windfall for both Martin and Elliott, but new contracts alone could not alter the delay in payments or the shortage of proper material for the boats. Hence work continued to putter along until February 1862 when disaster struck along with the successful Federal assault upon Roanoke Island. With the fall of Pamlico Sound, Elizabeth City also fell almost immediately into Union hands, and Confederate ship building at the yard instantly became a thing of the past. "The dark clouds of impending disaster looming over city and harbor interests brought more anger than panic to the citizens. Many decided to remain, while some left for destinations further west. Among those who remained was Gilbert Elliott. He did what he could to secure the business and personal affairs of Colonel Martin since he managed Martin's various rental properties."21

After awhile Elliott removed what he could manage of the shipbuilding facilities and equipment to a location near Norfolk, but that soon proved untenable as well. For Norfolk lay essentially cut off from the remainder of Confederate Virginia after McClellan had landed his army on the tip of the Virginia peninsula, and could neither be defended nor sustained by the government in Richmond. It was decided, therefore, to abandon the city, and all Confederate efforts in the area; and despite his contracts, Elliott was once again left bereft of a shipyard.

Elliott, now out of work and out of facilities, enlisted with Colonel Martin in the Confederate infantry on May 16; but his ship building abilities made him a unique individual, and those abilities had hardly been forgotten by Secretary Mallory, who summoned the young man to his office in Richmond. Elliott "had not long been in camp at Petersburg when he was urgently solicited by Secretary Mallory, of the Confederate Navy Department, who had formed a very high opinion of Elliott's business capacity and energy, to undertake the building of another gunboat, this time to be an ironclad ram, as the career of the *Virginia* [*Merrimack*] had revolutionized naval warfare.

"Upon Mr. Mallory's request the Confederate States War Department granted Lieutenant Elliott two years' furlough, and he was relieved of the duties of Adjutant, returned to North Carolina, gathered up the tools and carpenters, and began his new venture at Tarboro on the Tar River."22

Thus had Elliott come to have three fresh contracts in hand, yet no facilities in which to get started building a single boat. It was at this time as well that Federal incursions up the North Carolina rivers began to cause alarm across the state, the most prominent of those incursions conducted by the Federal Lt. Commander Charles Flusser. In response to the increasingly bold and damaging raids on the part of the Union Navy, a number of shallow draft, yet powerful ironclads were conceived as essential for the defense of eastern North Carolina. Elliott, now on leave, wrote Mallory in September 1862 suggesting "to construct for your Department one ironclad gunboat and ram at Tillery's Farm on the Roanoke River in North Carolina, seven miles below the town of Halifax, upon the same terms and conditions as are expressed and stated in the contract under which we are now working. Said boat and ram to be of the same plans and dimensions as the one we are now building at Tarboro, N.C."[23] Stephen Mallory promptly accepted Elliott's proposal, and advised the new Confederate naval liaison officer recently appointed to oversee contracts and naval construction in North Carolina of his decision.

In just that odd, circuitous manner had Gilbert Elliott been placed finally in the position where he would one day craft in a farm field on the banks of the Roanoke River what would become one of the Confederacy's most famous ironclad vessels. It would take much time and effort to finally accomplish the task, but with the help of the new liaison officer, a man of high reputation and naval experience, the work would eventually be completed, and the ironclad make its mark on the inland waters of North Carolina. The vessel, constructed on the British model, would eventually be known as the *Albemarle*, and the naval officer whose help Elliott would need to see the job through to completion, none other than the former Confederate captain of the *Ellis*, now recovered from his wounds and recently promoted Lt. Commander, the feisty James W. Cooke.

Lt. Commander James W. Cooke C.S.N. (U.S. Naval History and Heritage Command).

CHAPTER 4

When Fought as Gallantly as That

ON OCTOBER 19, 1862, AS Stephen Mallory was advising James Cooke via correspondence of the recent contract that had been executed between the naval department and Gilbert Elliott for an ironclad to be built on the Roanoke River in North Carolina, William Barker Cushing, now commanding the *Ellis*, was also penning a letter regarding the war, this to his cousin. "Three days ago," he wrote, "I left New Berne, steamed down the Neuse River, across the sound, and out to sea. I anchored at the city of Beaufort for one night, put to sea again and ran down here. I am alone, inside the outer bar. The nearest friendly vessel or citizen is forty miles away. Three miles off, up the inlet, is the rebel town of Swansborough [North Carolina]. ...You see that I am on a sort of roving commission," he continued, "and can run around to suit myself. For the present I am my own master. If under these circumstances I cannot stir the rebels up in more places than one it will be strange indeed."[1]

Cushing's intentions were set, and they were, to say the least, aggressive. First he intended to steam up the inlet the following morning, take the town, and put the clamps on whatever trade or blockade running he might discover in the area. The day before he had fired a shot near the village, only to observe a white flag quickly run-up the flag pole by the good citizens of Swansborough. Cushing was then at Bogue Inlet, NC,[2] but a few days of close observation uncovered no Rebel activity to speak of, so Will, exercising his independent command and venturesome spirit, shoved off for New Topsail Inlet further south along the coast, not far from the busy port of Wilmington on the Cape

Fear River. His hunch was well rewarded as he spotted a Rebel schooner taking on cargo upriver. Cushing steamed straight for the prize, only to ground the *Ellis* a hundred yards or so from the schooner. But the Confederate crew was so spooked by Cushing's sudden appearance that they panicked and fled the vessel, leaving behind the boat and its large cargo of turpentine, tobacco, and cotton. The schooner proved to be the *Adelaide*, and she represented a fine haul.[3]

Will Cushing was initially determined to tow his prize back out to sea, but the schooner drew far more water than did the *Ellis*, and as a result constantly ran aground in the shallows. After a day of fruitless towing, Will finally decided to scuttle the *Adelaide* along with its cargo. The turpentine was fired, and the boat went up in a ball of leaping red flames and billowing black smoke, the spiraling black cloud visible for miles around. It had been a simple success, born far more of aggressiveness than cunning, but it represented exactly the type of action Naval Command was desperate to see from its officers. When word of Cushing's venture got back to his commanding officer, he was promptly rewarded with an order to "act in accordance with the dictates of your best judgment."[4] For a young, combative officer such as William Cushing, the new order represented nothing less than an official carte blanche for him to put in play his every hunch or scheme, and it was not long before the *Ellis* was steaming up New Topsail Inlet once again in search of Rebel prey.

This time he slipped inside the Inlet to the shallows where presently the smoke from what appeared to be some sort of factory was spotted rising above the treetops by the lookouts above. Once again, Cushing simply rushed the objective, dropped anchor, then led a party ashore on smaller boats. What they discovered was a large Confederate salt works, large enough to furnish salt for the entire city of Wilmington, and much of the area surrounding. The local workers had all run off as Cushing and his landing party approached, and for the time being at least, Will had his run of the factory. As Cushing later reported, the landing party then "destroyed their large copper and iron kettles and pans, cut holes in their flatboats and lighters, cut through the cisterns and waterworks, and burned the buildings; 10 or 15 bushels of salt that had been made that morning I turned into the ditch."[5] Salt was a major ingredient for food and its preservation, and the destruction of so significant a works would no doubt put a crimp in the local economy.

But the Rebels returned while Cushing and his crew were still ashore, hot as hornets over what was going on, this time with infantry and artillery to support them. Suddenly, the tables had turned. Will raced his men back to their boats, and they were rowing for their lives as the Confederates unlimbered their field pieces nearby and began firing at the fleeing sailors. The

Rebel shells landed all around them, dousing the boats and soaking the landing party, but the Confederate artillerymen apparently had a hard time getting the range of a moving target, and the small party managed its way back to the *Ellis*, soaked but uninjured. Once back on board, Cushing immediately had the gunboat's rifles quickly trained on the Rebel gunners, and this time it was their chance to run, fleeing down the road toward Wilmington as the shells from Cushing's guns exploded amongst them. Outgunned by the larger naval pieces, they had little choice but flee. The quick expedition had proved a success; indeed, just the sort that the Federal Navy hoped would bring the secessionist population to its senses.

William Cushing then sailed back up the coast where he again dropped anchor at Bogue Inlet, hopeful of interdicting any Confederate traffic in the area, in compliance with his original orders. But three weeks of boring inaction were enough to prove to Will that Bogue Inlet offered little in the way of activity, and far less in terms of romance. Thus he hatched a new scheme, intent now on sailing south again to where he might cross over into the shallows and sail up the New River toward the village of Jacksonville. His purpose was "to sweep the river, capture any vessels there, capture the town of Jacksonville, or Onslow Court House, take the Wilmington mail, and destroy any salt works that I might find on the banks."[6] It was a bold plan, but then boldness had come naturally to William Cushing since the age of three.

In late November he set out, and five miles up the New River a boat was spotted approaching. Apparently spotting the *Ellis* even before Cushing could take action, the boat was fired by its own crew, and the Rebels quickly took to small craft and escaped unharmed. Will pulled close enough only to be sure that the vessel was totally engulfed — it too was carrying turpentine and cotton, as flammable a combination as could be imagined — and then pushed on. The *Ellis* finally came upon Jacksonville early that afternoon, November 23,[7] about eighteen miles from the sea, and there they dropped anchor, much to the shock and horror of the local citizenry, who could hardly imagine a Yankee ship so far inland. A party was sent ashore "which took possession of the public buildings and raised the American flag over the courthouse. It flew gaily in the wind, and the men remaining on the *Ellis* cheered."[8] Quite a few stands of rifles were seized in the courthouse, along with the mail and some small schooners tied up at the public dock. It was a substantial haul, and Lieutenant Cushing had every reason to be pleased with his work that day. His hunch had been well rewarded.

The *Ellis* remained in the river off Jacksonville for almost two hours before Cushing finally decided to shove off. Moreover, he was aware of the fact that a few Confederate officers had fled the town upon his arrival, and surely that meant eventual trouble. Cushing had little doubt they would return heavily reinforced, thus his time ashore was limited. With the two small schooners in tow, he decided to head back downriver, hopeful to gain the open sea without further event. In that he would be severely disappointed.

When they reached the spot where the schooner they had initially captured lay smoldering in the water, a heavy trail of black smoke still rising like steam into the air above the tree line, the *Ellis* suddenly came under severe artillery fire from the riverbank where the intrepid local defense had set a trap.[9] Cushing's crew jumped to the guns, however, and the heavy rifles aboard the *Ellis* began to boom, instantly overmatching the Confederate entrapment. The guns along the riverbank were quickly limbered up and withdrawn, the Rebels disappearing down the road again. Thus was the immediate problem solved, but another far more serious one immediately reared its head, and this could not be dispatched quite so easily.

Night was now falling, and even with the aid of a local pilot — which Will had made the effort to secure — it would be too dangerous to try and cross over the bar in the darkness. Thus were they trapped on the river for the night, no doubt to be assailed by the gathering Rebel forces come morning. It was not a pleasant proposition. Thus passed a very difficult night, with the sounds of an ever encroaching enemy nearby, Rebel campfires smoldering along the riverbank, and the prospect of immediate battle come morning. It was a nerve wracking experience, but come morning the sunlight revealed no Confederates nearby, and the *Ellis* again began its journey down river unmolested. The calm was merely a ruse, however, for when the boat neared a sharp bend in the river, two guns opened on them from the bank. Once again the crew scrambled to the guns and returned fire. The duel went on for over an hour, but eventually the larger and more accurate rifle the *Ellis* was armed with proved decisive, and the Rebels skedaddled for fear of being shot to pieces.

At that moment it appeared the *Ellis* had survived her foray into enemy territory, but that assessment would prove premature. For the pilots botched their job, and within a mere three miles of the Inlet the gunboat struck bottom, would not budge, and appeared utterly grounded at high tide. Desperate to avoid the receding waters — which would leave them high and dry and a virtual sitting duck for enemy artillery — Cushing tried to lighten the boat by every means possible, but all to no avail. The *Ellis* would not budge. The anchors were dropped and the engines reversed to try and get the gunboat to pull itself off the sand bar, but nothing worked. By now it was late afternoon, the tide was going out, and the water level surrounding the boat receding. Yet the two small schooners were still fastened to the rear of the gunboat, so Cushing ordered everything into them that could be carried. Still, it made no difference. The *Ellis* was stuck, and the tide was dropping. If they could not move the boat soon, it would be the following day before the tide would return enough to even hopefully float the gunboat again. That would surely be too late.

William Cushing had a tough decision on his hands. Unable to move, the *Ellis*, he knew, would be an easy target, and there would be no hope of escape come morning should the Rebels attack in force. He could fight to the finish, but that would be suicide; and while he might make such a choice for himself, he would not order his men to make such a suicidal stand. He thought the situation through, then called the crew together.

"Officers and men!" Will barked, bringing them to attention. "We will probably be attacked in the morning, and that, too, by an overwhelming force." Cushing let that thought sink in for a moment, then continued. "If we are attacked by the enemy in the morning and he overpowers us, either by boarding or otherwise, the only alternative left is to go up with the vessel or submit to an unconditional surrender." The crew stared at him. Not one man responded, yet Cushing had developed a plan of his own. "I wish all the men, except five or six — and these must be volunteers — to go on board the schooner. I wish the schooner to be dropped off down the river to a point without the range of the enemy's fire from the bluff. It is my intention," he explained, "with the five or six men who may volunteer to remain with me, in the event of an attack, to work the pivot gun in the morning, and fight her to the last. I will not surrender [to] the enemy, while a magazine or match remains on board."[10]

Cushing then turned away, allowing the men to mull his proposition over, expecting that those few who might volunteer would step forward for the choosing. When he turned back to face them he was at first taken by surprise as the ranks of sailors and officers appeared to remain the same. Then it dawned on him — they had all taken a few steps forward in unison. They had *all* volunteered to stay and fight with him to the last.[11] Will broke into an enormous grin. "By God!" he cried, "I won't forget that, men. I won't forget it as long as I live!"[12]

Cushing chose six men to stay behind with him, and the others were quickly loaded into the largest of the schooners. "Save yourselves if they get us," Will called out as the schooner disappeared downriver. "But don't leave us unless you're sure!"[13]

As dawn broke over New River, a ball struck the side of the *Ellis* with a sudden clang, and Cushing thought at first the assault was about to come down on them, but then everything returned to quiet. When the sun was finally up it became clear that the Rebels had installed two two-gun sections behind strong earthworks along the riverbanks, so posted as to give them a cross fire of the gunboat from behind their fortifications.[14] It was obvious that he could not beat both down simultaneously with the pivot gun, no matter how quick or accurate a fire he directed, but that did not matter. He had stayed to fight, and fight he would. Will and his crew slipped up to the pivot gun and prepared for the onslaught. It was not a long wait before the Confederate pieces began to belch metal, hot and accurate. Will returned fire as best he could, but soon it became apparent that the fight was useless. The boat was wrecked, and Cushing was soon running out of ammunition. With the *Ellis* shot to pieces there were few choices left. He could fight and die, or scuttle the boat and make a run for it, and while Will Cushing still had a lot of fight left in him, he saw no reason to die for nothing.

Will could see that the schooner with the rest of his crew was still laying at anchor a mile or so down river, so he decided to fire the gunboat and make a dash in the ship's boat. There was little question it would be a desperate attempt. They would be under Rebel artillery fire most of the way, but it was their only real shot at survival. But if he was going to scuttle his own ship, he was going, at least, to do it in fighting style. "The halyard to the flag was cut, insuring that the rebels would have to shoot the standard down if they wanted it down, and the ship was fired in five places. Before leaving the pivot gun, the piece was loaded and trained on the enemy with a slow match set."[15] The hope was that the *Ellis* might provide the crew some covering fire, and that, as Cushing later phrased it, "the vessel might fight herself after we left."[16]

Will and the six volunteers dove into the small boat, and the men took up the oars as if their lives depended on it—which, in fact, they did. The Confederates turned their artillery fire toward the escaping crew, and while the shells sent watery plumes soaring in the air, turned the river to foam, and came close to swamping the boat, Will and his men were never hit, and rowing hard with the current, were out of effective range in a few minutes only. When he was sure the shells could no longer reach him, Cushing removed his hat and held it high in a tribute to his exhausted crew.

But there was no joy in the words, nor joy in the escape. Will Cushing had lost his boat, had scuttled his first command, in fact, and the loss of the *Ellis* weighed heavily upon him. They rowed back out toward the schooner in silence. The schooner was named the *Home*, and while Will would eventually make good use of her, only a sense of loss pervaded the small party of men. But there was no time to lose or mourn. "It was low water on the bar and a heavy surf was rolling in, but the wind forced us through after striking several times. We were just in time, for about six hundred yards down the beach were several companies of cavalry trying to reach the mouth of the inlet in time to cut us off. We hoisted our flag, gave three cheers and were off."[17]

Cushing was concerned that he would be censured for the loss of the *Ellis*, but the opposite turned out to be the case. Boats were aplenty, gifted commanders who would fight them few, and the top people in the Naval Department thrilled to the story of how he had fought the Confederates on the New River, not to mention his daring escape. "We don't care for the loss of a vessel when fought as gallantly as that,"[18] was the official word that came back to him. Will Cushing had turned quite a few heads in the Federal Navy with his work on the New River, and more responsible commands along with more interesting and challenging exploits now awaited the young lieutenant.

CHAPTER 5

For Want of This Iron Our Work Has Been Going Backward

ON NOVEMBER 24, 1862, the very day William Cushing was trying desperately to float the *Ellis* off a sand bar in the New River, Gilbert Elliott began work on his gunboat contract, sending lumbermen out along the banks of the Tar River just east of Tarboro to cut timber for the framing and flanks of the numerous craft he now had under contract with the Confederate Navy. Tarboro was about 30 miles south of his selected building location at Tillery's Farm on the Roanoke River where the floating battery was under construction, and central to his ambitions.[1]

The truth of the matter was, however, that while timber was plentiful and the wooden framing little problem at any location for shipbuilding in the state of North Carolina, iron, on the other hand, represented a far different story, and ironclads without iron were like clipper ships without canvas — useless. The endless, fruitless quest for iron for Confederate gunboats was ongoing and endless. It began at the very top of the Confederate naval chain of command, and worked its way down that chain, web like, to the lowest shipbuilder, contractor, and merchant, most often to no profit whatsoever. Had the Confederate Navy aspirations of covering their gunboats with gold, it seems the task could not have been more difficult than in covering them with iron.

In late October, as an example, Secretary Mallory had written to James Cooke requesting that he look into the possibility of scavenging several miles of railroad in North Carolina for iron from lines that were considered nonessential for military use. "I learn from Mr. Elliott," he wrote, "that railroad iron has been collected by Messrs. Jno. and Nickolas Long, who live near Weldon, and that several miles of railroad iron may be secured from the tracks between Kinston and New Bern without detriment to public interest. See to this at once as iron to roll into plate is greatly wanted."[2] The request from Mallory seemed simple enough.

But nothing came of it. When that dispatch got apparently nowhere, the Secretary wrote directly to Zebulon Vance, then governor of North Carolina. "Sir:" he began, "Commander Cooke, sent by me to North Carolina to obtain iron for plating the gunboats being built for the defense of the State has returned without having accomplished this objective. He reports that you have the control of a quantity of railroad iron," Mallory continued, "and I therefore address myself to you upon the subject. To enable the boats to resist the guns of the enemy their armor must be at least 4 inches thick, placed at an angle of at least 36 degrees. This armor, from the limited power of our mills, we are compelled to roll into plate 2 by 7 inches and 10 feet long, and to put them upon the vessels in two courses. If you will let the Department have the rails and facilitate its transportation to Richmond they will be immediately rolled into plates for the vessels in question and for such other defenses as we may build in the waters of your state."[3] Mallory then went on to explain to the governor that Cooke would supervise the removal of the iron rails, and make the necessary arrangements to insure proper compensation. In concept the task seemed, once again, simple enough, but for a variety of reasons the request was to go nowhere.

Typically, weeks went by before Mallory received a response from Governor Vance's office, and this proved equivocating and unsatisfactory. "His Excellency Governor Vance," an aide to the governor replied, "has received your letter stating that he had control of the quantity of railroad iron and asking his consent to have the same rolled into plate to be used upon boats now being built in this State. His Excellency presumes that your informant, Commander Cooke, alludes to the iron of the Atlantic road. The State is but a stockholder in the road, a large portion belonging to private individuals. A meeting of the directors of the company has been called and your proposition will be submitted to them. Their decision will be made known to you."[4]

With that things finally appeared to be moving forward, and by late November Mallory had his answer. "Upon consultation with the directors of the Atlantic and North Carolina Railroad Company," the governor replied, "I have concluded to let you have the iron for the gunboat building on the Neuse River if you will get it from the torn-up portion of the road nearest the enemy. In consideration of the alarming condition of our main roads (the iron giving way, etc.), it is deemed advisable that the iron taken from the Atlantic road, which is nearly new, be exchanged with the other roads for their damaged rails, which I am told will answer for rolling as well as the others."[5] With that finally accomplished, it appeared that Gilbert Elliott was indeed on his way to a gunboat building career with contracts in hand, iron on the way, and land defenses along the rivers being arranged for the protection of the building sites.

But November turned into December, and soon the New Year was at hand, yet still there was no word on the railroad iron for the boats. On January 6, Secretary Mallory dictated an obviously exacerbated note to Cooke, who was clearly having his own difficulties trying to get the state government of North Carolina to cooperate. "The Department has heard nothing from you relative to the iron for completing the battery and boats," Mallory wrote. "No time is to be lost. If the iron can be obtained at all it must be sent here to be rolled out, at the earliest moment. You are requested to keep yourself in communication by telegraph with the Department and to keep it advised of your progress in getting iron."[6] But Commander Cooke, Mallory was soon to discover, was not the problem.

Meanwhile Gilbert Elliott had at least begun work at Tillery's Farm, yet conditions there were far different from those at Norfolk or even Elizabeth City. Elliott's shipyard was in fact little more than an open field bordering the river. When the railroad iron from North Carolina failed to appear, Elliott himself tried to help remedy the situation with a trip to Richmond. There he secured a car load of iron, then returned to his yard at Tillery's Farm in a glum state of mind. It seemed to the young shipbuilder at that time that things, like a poorly run carnival trick, were going in endless circles. He wrote to Colonel Martin: "I have not yet received any money in addition to the $3,000 [the initial payment] paid me by Tredwell in Tarboro. I shall go to Wilmington tomorrow or the next day after $5,000 which I have had an order for some time. Cooke is a decided humbug. I was delaying my visit to Wilmington expecting to receive an order, as I wrote you, for the additional $5,000 on the Tarboro boat when lo and behold here came a letter from Cooke stating that he had ordered Mr. Roberson to report upon it.

"Such a time as I have had for the last seven days," Elliott continued in frustration. "I went to Richmond last Sunday after one car load of iron, thinking that I would get back in a day or so. I have just gotten here, and have had the hardest week's work it has been my fortune to be charged with. For want of this iron our work has been going backward and for the last week our expenses will be sure to overreach the income."[7] Fortunately for Elliott, his trip the following day to Wilmington proved far more productive, as he was in fact presented with a payment voucher for the advanced payment of $5,000 for the gunboat. That payment represented a good step forward, and another came after Commander James Cooke inspected Elliott's work and reported back to Stephen Mallory that the third and fourth payment for the boat at Tarboro had been approved, and "upon the floating battery [the ironclad at Tillery's Farm on the Roanoke] two payments of five thousand each, making it all the sum of twenty thousand dollars due Messr. Martin & Elliott."[8]

Perhaps by this point in time Elliott was no longer so much inclined to refer to Commander Cooke as a "decided humbug," for what Elliott had not fully appreciated was the fact that Cooke was not only charged with procuring the iron for all naval construction in North Carolina, but with oversight of that construction as well. As far as the iron was concerned, Cooke was getting nowhere, but it was not from lack of effort. The entire question of naval use of the railroad iron was now in debate before the North Carolina legislature, this despite all the commander's efforts, and thus entirely out of his hands to influence one way or another. Exasperated, he wrote directly to Flag Officer Lynch, laying out the situation as clearly as he could. "As all the force is now concentrated on the Roanoke River on the battery [Elliott's floating battery at Tillery's], this work could soon be completed. All the timber could be transported by rail to Halifax and floated down to where we are now building, but if no iron can be obtained to clad these boats, I think the entire work ought to be abandoned.

"I have stated to you in a former letter that I think it is impossible to procure any railroad iron unless it is seized. The Petersburg Railroad agent says that he must have the old iron on the Petersburg road to replace the worn out rails on that road. The Kinston and Raleigh road requires the iron taken below Kinston to replace the iron on the Charlotte and N.C. road, and these roads are considered a military necessity."[9]

Iron was the problem, and iron would continue to be the problem as progress on the ironclad continued apace. All other construction issues could be dealt with and overcome, but no amount of money or effort appeared capable of producing the iron that was necessary to plate the gunboat, and this produced a high level of anxiety and frustration in all parties involved in the construction process. One day the government of North Carolina appeared ready and willing to give up the necessary rails, the next suddenly opposed. The state's response seemed as fickle as the weather, but far more discouraging.

In late January 1863, Stephen Mallory, determined to get an answer regarding the iron, decided to once and for all lay the matter at the feet of Flag Officer Lynch, and this he did in language that was both direct and unmistakable. In this correspondence, which was then directed to Governor Vance, Mallory pointed out, for instance, that "these vessels would not have been undertaken had the Department not had good reason to believe the railroad iron could be obtained in North Carolina to form the plate armor." Mallory then went on to point out the obvious fact that the vessels in question were being built solely to protect the waters of North Carolina, with the ultimate hope of literally ridding the rivers and sounds of Federal gunboats. But *iron* was the problem. "Convinced," Mallory argued, "that they would clean the waters of that State [North Carolina] of the enemy's vessels I have felt great anxiety to complete them. All the efforts of Commander Cooke however, to obtain the iron have failed and I commit the subject again to you." Wanting to leave no stone unturned or argument unspoken, Mallory then stated the issue as clearly as he possibly could. "Railroad iron, as you have doubtless learned from our private experiments with inclined surfaces covered with it here and from the vessels of the *Arkansas* affords but little protection against heavy shot. Whereas rolled into plate we can produce vessels that will run every gun boat out of North Carolina. The engines of these boats are ready and are delayed for iron alone."[10]

Ultimately the directors of the Atlantic & North Carolina Railroad proved supportive, at least to some degree, of the naval project, but remarkably, the North Carolina Legislature did not. Previous arrangements with the railroad thus collapsed, and Elliott found himself once again back at square one. When an agreement to remove a limited amount of iron from Besse's Station fell apart at the last moment, Elliott naturally became discouraged. "When the agent for the Department applied for transportation of iron," Elliott explained to Stephen Mallory in frustration, "the Quartermaster of the post at Goldsboro referred him to Mr. Jno. D. Whitford, President of the A & NC railroad. Governor Vance happened to be at Goldsboro at the time. Mr. Whitford became alarmed about his iron and induced Governor Vance to countermand the order which he had given us."[11] Elliott went on to explain that he was sure at this point that no iron recovered from the rail lines along the Neuse River, even if available, could be removed and transported in time efficient for the construction of the gunboat, or the completion of the floating battery, which was now ready for iron to be placed below the waterline; and then he simply threw-up his hands. Elliot wrote: "If the Department can furnish us forty tons of iron at once the work can go on. If you are unable to do this we respectfully ask for instructions in regard to the construction of the Battery. Vance says in his letter that the work must be stopped. Please address us at Halifax, whither we go immediately."[12]

Nothing seemed to work. The railroads needed to be maintained in any event for the ready transfer of troops and material if the Confederacy was to hold together, and this necessitated having ready spare rails for use whenever the lines either failed (a frequent occurrence on the often poorly constructed

Southern lines) or were struck by Yankee raiders. On the other hand, if the gunboats and ironclads were not completed soon, the Yankees would simply overwhelm the state's interior via waterborne routes, and the railroads would be taken and destroyed in any case. No matter which alternative was accepted, it appeared the Confederacy was simply robbing Peter to pay Paul, thus neither alternative a palatable choice. In that sense these two perfectly legitimate interests, like ropes pulling on the same wagon from different directions, failed to create movement or solutions, only stagnation. Typically in such situations, each interest ultimately guards its own, and nothing in the way of compromise can be achieved, and that is exactly the course of action the railroad owners embraced. Under the circumstances neither Elliott, Cooke, or even Stephen Mallory, for that matter, appeared capable of breaking the iron deadlock.

Foul winter weather soon bought construction of the floating battery at Tillery's Farm to a halt. Payments ran late, iron was impossible to locate, or what could be located proved immoveable. By early winter 1863 it appeared clear to all that efforts to build the needed ironclad on the Roanoke river or to complete the battery at Tillery's had been for naught, and there seemed no future in it. Then in early February James Cooke received specific orders to "proceed without delay to Kingston and make the best arrangements you can, for the speedy transportation of railroad iron below that point, using your best judgment in determining whether it shall be brought across the Neuse or conveyed by wagons to the Wilmington and Weldon railroad.... Spare neither labor or expense in having the iron conveyed to the floating battery near Halifax [the Tillery Farm location] employing Mr. Roberson in anyway wherein he can assist you."[13]

Whether this order simply represented one more leg in a never ending wild goose chase or a real possibility was unknown to both Cooke and Elliott during the gloomy days of February 1863, but at least it brought hope, no matter how slim. And slim hopes were better than none.

CHAPTER 6

Wrong Wharf, Wrong Boat

THE NEW YEAR BROUGHT William Cushing to Washington City on a well deserved leave after yet another daring venture, this time on North Carolina's Little River, not far from the state of South Carolina. Flushed with that success, Cushing had been granted a new command and a few days leave before heading out again. So in late in January he started off on a lark to try and visit his brother, Alonzo, in camp with the Army of the Potomac at Falmouth, Virginia.[1] Armed with bottles of sherry and a supply of fresh cigars, he "got a pass and early the next morning started off for the foot of Sixth Street, to take the boat for Acquia Creek, and to go by railroad from that point to the Army of the Potomac."[2] Will had not seen Alonzo since the spring of '62 when he had accompanied Flag Officer Goldsborough to Harrison's Landing on the James River in conjunction with President Lincoln's visit to the Federal Army. At that time "Will had the chance to see 'every regiment in the army,' and was introduced by General Sumner, Alonzo's patron, to Generals Sedgwick, Hooker, Couch and Peck, and to Colonel Hunt, later the great Union artillery commander, as well as to a number of other officers."[3] It proved a thrilling visit, and Will had been able to catch up on the ups and downs of Allie's career, a subject that, very much like his own, not surprisingly sported far more ups than downs.

Upon graduation from West Point in the spring of 1861, Alonzo had been given a position in the artillery with the rank of lieutenant. He was quickly sent off to Washington City where he was assigned to train the young volunteers who were soon to march off to war in basic gunnery drill. Like Will, Alonzo had grown into a tall, handsome man with a captivating air about him. There in Washington Theron Wilber Haight first met Allie, and recalled that "Alonzo's smooth, swarthy face and supple figure were to be seen wherever there was a volunteer battery in need of instruction or drill. Although he worked his pupils hard, they all loved him for his radiant smiles and frequent infectious laughter, which were potent factors in smoothing the grim front of grizzled war."[4]

Alonzo then moved out with the 4th United States Artillery, and was in the thick of the first major land battle at Bull Run in July. The following day his battery was selected to accompany several regiments of infantry near Fairfax Court House to determine the extent of the Confederate pursuit, which they found nonexistent; and they then returned to Washington with the thousands of other Yankee refugees that jammed the roads. That day the rains fell hard, the roads turned to mud, and the going was exhausting for the men in the artillery. It was a long, miserable slog as "the roadsides were strewn with knapsacks, blankets, and other impedimenta of the returning soldiers who plodded along towards Washington from the battle of the day before. Many of them had marched all night, and very few of them had taken more than short intervals of rest during their night exit from the vicinity of Bull Run."[5]

The routed Federal Army streamed back into the Washington defenses, fearful of a Confederate assault; but despite their victory, the Rebels were equally as exhausted, and the feared Confederate attack was not to come. Alonzo Cushing returned to his duties of drilling and local defense as the army, now under command of the Young Napoleon, General George McClellan, slowly pulled itself back together. As the writers at *Harper's* described it at the time: "The great uprising in April had brought to the capital a vast assemblage of *militia*; and these, not waiting for the mature results of discipline ... marched forth of a hot summer's day ... very much as the same number of men would have gone to a picnic or a fancy tournament, and with not half the regularity that would have marked an ordinary training day; and this mock army had been swept from the field, disorganized and useless. Following upon this disaster came a second uprising, which gave us, at length, an army of *soldiers*."[6] Alonzo Cushing was one of the few professionals who helped bring forth that new army of *soldiers*, and by September Allie had been promoted to captain.[7]

For months the Young Napoleon, despite constant demands from both Congress and the White House, did little if anything with his new army of *soldiers*; but come spring 1862, McClellan was under so much pressure to take action that he loaded his army onto a massive fleet and shipped it down the Chesapeake Bay to the Virginia peninsula where it debarked near Yorktown. McClellan's Peninsula Campaign had begun, and Allie, for the most part, was out front and in the line of battle. By then he had secured a position on the staff of corps commander, General Edwin Sumner, and at the battle of

Williamsburg Allie had a horse shot right out from under him while delivering orders. He was both uninjured and unfazed by the incident, however, and later at the battle of Fair Oaks Alonzo was struck in the chest by a ball, but spared serious injury when the bullet struck the handle of a pistol he had holstered in place.[8] He was quickly becoming a veteran. Indeed, when the fighting at Fair Oaks became furious, and as the light faded into evening, Allie witnessed what he conceived the spectacular scene of two combating lines of infantry blazing away at one another in the fading light. "Just as it was getting dark," he later recalled, "the muskets were much heated, there were two long parallel sheets of flame from the opposing lines, and I can conceive of nothing more grand than the spectacle presented.... I never expected to witness another so beautiful a fight, if I live to be as old as Methuselah."[9]

At Glendale, during the Seven Days battles during McClellan's retreat from Richmond toward the James River, Alonzo again had a horse shot out from under him while delivering messages for General Sumner, and the same occurred the next day at the battle of Malvern Hill, where Robert E. Lee's Army of Northern Virginia charged the Federal Army atop the heights, and suffered grievously for their effort. Throughout the entire campaign Allie had been in the thick of the fighting, his bravery had not gone unnoticed, and Alonzo was given the brevet rank of major. "It may incidentally be mentioned that in those days a presidential brevet was of more importance than it afterwards became under subsequent acts of Congress. Originally it entitled the officer, if he pleased, to wear the uniform of his brevet rank, to be addressed by his brevet title, and serve as his brevet rank when specially detailed."[10] Alonzo Cushing was fast receiving a great deal of recognition for his gallantry and unflinching effort, whether honorary or not, and his career appeared on a fast track to high achievement. One thing was certain, however; Alonzo's brother, William, was most impressed with his progress. Will wrote: "I don't know where he is going to stop in promotion. He ranks far above every man in his class. I am proud of his success, for I think such rapid promotion for a boy of twenty is entirely without precedent in the regular army."[11]

At Antietam Alonzo was in command of a battery of artillery, Battery A of the 4th United States Artillery, in Sumner's Second Corps, where his efforts received both "McClellan's and Sumner's high praise."[12] The Army of the Potomac was then reorganized, and Allie was transferred to the staff of General Darius Couch, commander of the Union Second Corps; and once more he performed his duties on the bloody battlefield at Fredericksburg with unflinching courage. There seemed little question that by late January 1863 Alonzo Cushing had become a highly respected young officer of noted ability, and would one day rise high in rank.

But Will Cushing had a story or two of his own to tell, and with sherry and cigars in hand, he made his way through the Washington muck and mud that January afternoon in hopes of meeting his brother in Falmouth soon. He recalled that "the hackmen were disposed to cheat me, so I got on my feet and dignity, and determined to walk. The farther I went, the deeper became the mud, but I swam along without much trouble until I reached the wharf." Despite the cold and mud, William Cushing was in high spirits, no doubt prepared to regale his brother with his own stories of adventure on the rivers of North Carolina. "On my way to the wharf," Will wrote, "the load, though heavy, was lightened by the thought that a jolly good time was ahead,"[13] perhaps recollections of his own most recent adventure still fresh in his mind.

Will's most recent mission had been impressive in its own right. He had set sail for the Little River in the *Home* on January 5. Will had hatched previously a plan to disguise the schooner as a blockade runner, and attempt to corner Confederate pilots by pretending to run the blockade with a few Yankee ships in fake pursuit, only then to grab any Rebel pilots who came to his assistance. It was a clever idea, but it backfired just outside the Cape Fear River when the winds suddenly diminished and the *Home*, now bobbing on a light chop, was not captured, although clearly chased by the blockading fleet, and all this within easy sight of Confederate spotters. But that didn't stop him from trying again.

Hearing rumors of a pilot location somewhere near the mouth of the Little River, Cushing was off again in hopes of bagging his prey with the same shrewd gambit. He sailed south, then sat off the mouth of the river until darkness fell. Cushing and twenty-five handpicked men then piled into three navy cutters and began the trek upriver. They had not gone far when they were greeted with a sudden blast of musketry, and Will quickly ordered all three boats to the riverbank. "Follow me in!"[14] he called out, and the three cutters headed in toward the thick growth that overhung the river. Will had no idea in what strength the enemy might be posted, but that really did not matter. The boats were pulled up along the riverbank, and the twenty-five sailors deployed in a short line of battle.

"Forward; double quick; charge!"[15] Cushing ordered, and the sailors rushed forward behind him, rifles in hand, screaming at the top of their lungs. Coming through the thick undergrowth unseen, the screaming sailors apparently made such a hostile impression that they spooked the Confederate defenders, and the Rebels simply turned and ran, abandoning the position. "The enemy thinking that at least a regiment was upon them, turned and fled—escaping over one side of the fort, as Cushing entered the other. He never fired a shot."[16] What the small contingent of sailors discovered was a strong fortification, designed of earthworks, enclosing arms, ammunition, and food for a large garrison — indeed, a fort that could easily have withstood an assault ten times the size of Cushing's small force.

They had found no pilots, however, nor evidence of pilots; thus Cushing set about destroying all the property that could not be carried off, and had that loaded into the cutters. Unfortunately, while this was ongoing shots suddenly rang out, and it became clear that the Confederate defenders had returned, this time intent on serious business. The Union sailors promptly jumped to the blockhouse and began firing back at the Rebels, and this exchange was kept up until their limited ammunition began to run low. With that it was most definitely time to leave; and it appeared the sooner the better. So they gathered their weapons and headed off at the double quick, running for the beached cutters on the riverbank below. Quickly they boarded, and quicker still they set out to sea, returning to the *Home* with only one man wounded, and that but just slightly.

But Will Cushing was not yet out of the woods. Not knowing the channel, he decided to remain anchored at the mouth of the Little River until dawn, but overnight a strong storm blew up from the south, and this spelled serious trouble. The *Home*, after all, was only a small schooner, and no match for a furious storm at sea. A hard rain began to fall, the winds came up out of the south, and it was not long before it became apparent that the schooner would break anchor and be washed up against the rocks in the darkness if he remained where he was. What to do?

Cushing could surrender his command, or they could head out into the thirty miles of storm and, allowing for all the drift from the wind, make a desperate attempt to strike the small channel that lead through the breakers out to sea. Instantly rejecting even the notion of surrender, Will opted instead for escape. But he knew it would not be easy. "We are gong to go out," he said. "If we missed our way by a hundred yards in the fog, there was a certainty that we would be dashed in pieces."[17]

For a few hours the trip went well enough, although the storm continued to pick up in intensity. Dawn came finally, hard rain and a dark grey sky frowned down upon the now desperate mission, when suddenly Will spotted the quartermaster turn and yell. "Breakers ahead! For God's sake, sir, go about!" Large, menacing breakers were also spotted on both the lee and weather bows; and then, as Cushing recalled, with hardly a moments notice "we were into them." The *Home* struck the huge waves and was rocked furiously from side to side. It did not seem as though the small craft could withstand the pounding. "All seemed over now," Will remembered; "but it was only for a second, and she fairly flew through the great white breakers. Again and again she struck, but never hard. She had found the channel, and in twenty minutes we were safe, and scudding for Beaufort."[18]

Will Cushing did not look favorably upon the prospect of reporting yet another failure, for in fact his scheme to snatch a few Confederate pilots had come up short again, but his superiors proved so impressed with his guts and seamanship, that he was once again complimented on his efforts, and given a new, more significant command. Boldness, it seemed, had its own rewards.

And surely it was that adventure on the Little River — among many others — that Will looked forward to sharing with his brother, Allie, late that January afternoon; but sadly it was not to be. For the local provost marshal had provided him the name of the boat that supposedly sailed for Acquia Landing, but that information proved incorrect. "I went on board and made it my first business to get rested," Cushing later recalled, "but I had not been seated long, when I was informed that if I proposed to go to the tents of the wicked at Falmouth, I would have to make tracks for the next wharf, as I was on the wrong boat, and the right one was there."[19] Will jumped to his feet, and raced for the next wharf as directed, but the boat had pulled away just prior to his arrival. Will Cushing would not see his brother that January in '63, and he had little choice but to turn and make the glum, three mile hike back to his quarters, arriving mud splattered and miserable.

More than once Will had considered applying for a commission in the land forces in order to be closer to Alonzo, whom he missed terribly; and no doubt his failed trip that January was emotionally devastating. He had always feared for his brother. "I so long to be near Allie," he'd written. "It seems as if I might be some protection to him in the hour of action. If the rebels should kill him I don't think I would be a man any longer. I should become a fiend. I love that boy better than I do my own life, and I would not live without my brother."[20]

What Will did not know, of course, and what he would not wanted to have know, was that in a few short months Alonzo would in fact be gunned down in a hail of Rebel bullets while working his guns to the very last at a stone wall in a small Pennsylvania town named Gettysburg, and that he would never see his brother again.

CHAPTER 7

In High Favor

FROM ACROSS THE SANDBAR William Barker Cushing watched in dismay as the *Mount Washington* came under an increasingly devastating cross fire from concealed Confederate artillery.[1] It was late afternoon, April 14, 1863, and Cushing decided that he'd seen enough. Will gave prompt orders to maneuver his new gunboat, the *Commodore Barney*, along with the converted river ferry *Stepping Stones,* as close to the shallow bar as they could manage in order to engage the enemy's guns. Things were already hot, but they were about to get much hotter.

Upon completion of his short leave in Washington City, Cushing had met with Gideon Welles and been given command of the *Commodore Barney*, a relatively slow but robust steamer of 512 tons carrying "five one-hundred pounder smoothbore guns, a one-hundred pounder Parrott rifle and a twelve-pound howitzer."[2] Those weapons represented a substantial upgrade in fire power over his old vessel, the now scuttled *Ellis*, and with a crew of thirteen officers and one hundred and twenty-five men, a vessel generally commanded by an officer of higher grade than William Cushing. But the powers that be in the Naval Department had seen something far beyond the normal flamboyance in the young lieutenant from Fredonia, New York; and in Cushing's own words, his superiors "are pleased to think that I have earned the distinction — of course I am proud as a peacock at being the only Lieut. in the regular Navy who has been given a command."[3]

For most of March and February the *Barney* had sailed the relatively docile waters of the Chesapeake Bay in search of Rebel shipping that, by and large, did not exist. It had been a slow, sleepy, boring assignment, but spring had come with a burst of warmth, and right along with it came a new, and far more demanding, assignment on Virginia's Nansemond River, some thirty miles below Fortress Monroe.

In early April the First Corps of the Army of Northern Virginia under General James Longstreet had been detached from Lee's army and moved into the southeastern corner of Virginia on a forage mission to try and produce much needed supplies for the rest of Lee's army. Moreover, it was feared in Richmond the Yankees might well initiate an offensive from that quarter come spring, and the movement of a large Confederate force into the region was seen as a check to just that sort of an operation. "Virginia's southeastern coast, her 'deepwater corner,' had long been held by the Yankees, causing the Davis government constantly to cast nervous glances over its shoulder. It was well and good that McClellan's 1862 campaign on the Peninsula had been beaten off, but McClellan had left behind a sold base — Fort Monroe and Newport News at the tip of the Peninsula, Norfolk and Suffolk just to the south — from which the Yankees might launch another advance on the capital, or perhaps open a new front in North Carolina."[4] Thus for the Confederacy Longstreet's movement made strategic sense, but for the local Federal garrisons it had created new and immediate problems.

The Federal garrison at Suffolk, for instance, was placed in immediate danger by Longstreet's sudden appearance, and the commanding officer there became desperate for naval support. William Cushing had been selected for the job, and provided a small flotilla by the Navy Department to handle the task. While hardly a serious fleet of impressive throw weight, the *Commodore Barney*, *Stepping Stones*, *Cohasset*, *West End*, and *Alert*—all converted tugs, river steamers, and ferries — nevertheless represented a force to be reckoned with, most certainly so far as Confederate infantry movements along or near the river were concerned. The Navy's job was to help in holding the extreme right flank of the Union position which rested near the Nansemond River, and attack any Rebel movements observed in the area. Will Cushing, of course, almost burst with pride over his nomination, and promptly advised his mother of his appointment. "Who," he asked, "do you suppose was selected to perform the dangerous task of guarding the rear and preventing the crossing of ten thousand of the flower of the Southern army? Who but your son! That ex-midshipman, ex-master's mate, hair-brained, scapegrace, Will Cushing! Yes, it is even so."[5]

Naval Lieutenant R.H. Lamson was in command of the *Mount Washington*, and while Will was in charge of the entire flotilla, he was quick to strike a friendly, working bond with Lamson, who was also a graduate of the Naval Academy. While the *Commodore Barney* drew far too much water to work effectively in the shallows inside the bar, a number of the other vessels did not. Thus it was that on April 13 Lamson headed up the Nansemond in the *Mount Washington*, the *West End* and *Stepping Stone* trailing dutifully behind. The flotilla took some fire from sharpshooters concealed in the trees along the bank which amounted to a trifling; but the next day, as the small group approached Norfleet's Point, the Rebels opened on them with several well placed pieces of artillery. The Rebel artillery fire was heavy, and a shell struck the *Washington*'s engine room, scalding the crew, and sending hot steam whistling into the air. The vessel lost power as the crew jumped to the guns. The fight was on.

Unfortunately, the *Mount Washington*, now disabled and incapable of maintaining steam, drifted off uncontrollably, and grounded on the riverbank. In the confusion of battle, and perhaps trying simply to avoid the drifting *Washington*, the *West End* also ran aground not far away, thus offering two perfect targets for the Confederate artillerists. At a range of only three hundred yards, they could hardly miss.[6] Desperately, Lamson called for the *Stepping Stones* to come and try to tow the *Washington* to safety, and the little steamer finally accomplished this, but was shot to pieces itself during the effort, and many casualties were suffered amongst the crew. So too was the *West End* freed from the riverbank, and all three vessels started back downriver as best they could manage. When they finally reached the bar, the *Mount Washington* attempted a crossing, but once again ran aground, and the Rebels took the vessel immediately in a vicious cross fire. Without help, it was painfully apparent that all three would be stranded until the tide rose again, and like sitting ducks, simply shot to pieces.

It was precisely at this moment that Will Cushing, observing the action from aboard the *Commodore Barney*, decided to take action. "I had but two vessels afloat," Will later recalled, "but I silenced their fire in an hour."[7] But the Rebels weren't finished. Within a few minutes they had another battery in action, this at only a distance of five hundred yards; and from this new position the battery could sweep the channel, wrecking any craft trying to enter or exit. Cushing realized at once that, unless silenced, the new Confederate battery would pound the *Mount Washington* to splinters. "It was impossible to get our disabled steamer off from the bar until high water, five hours ahead," Will wrote, recalling the tense situation, "and I determined to fight on the spot as long as the *Barney* was above water."[8]

Cushing moved in closer, and the *Barney* began to draw fire from the Confederate artillery, The battle raged unrelenting for hours with the Rebel guns "which he at last silenced, though with the loss of ten of his crew."[9] Years later Will could still remember the contest vividly: "Up goes the battle flag," he wrote, "and at once the air is filled with the smoke of furious battle, and the ear thrills with the unceasing shriek and whistle of all the shell and rifled bolts that sinful man has devised to murder his fellow-creatures. *Crash!*

Crash! Splinters are flying in the air; great pools of blood are on the deck, and the first sharp cry of wounded men in agony rises upon the soft spring air."[10] The muzzle was blown off the *Barney*'s finest rifle, the carriage shattered. Ashes were sprinkled over the bloody deck for traction, new men jumped to the guns where the wounded had fallen out, and the fighting went on. The guns continued to thunder. Smoke filled the air. Every shot was made to count. Three hours of horrific combat turned to four, then four to five, and still the guns hammered away at one another in unrelenting fury. But after five hours the tide began to rise again, and at last the possibility of rescuing the *Fort Washington* beckoned. Cushing had a signal sent to the *Stepping Stones* to move in and try and tow the stranded steamer off the bar again as the *Commodore Barney* continued to draw the enemy's fire. The small steamer responded immediately. Almost miraculously the crew from the *Stepping Stones* made fast the lines under a withering fire, and the stranded *Fort Washington* was towed away from what just hours before had appeared its final resting place.

Defiantly, Will Cushing assessed the outcome. "My vessel is riddled with cannon balls and bullets, and I have lost three killed and nine wounded—four of them mortally—men who lost arms and legs. The loss on the other vessels is proportionately severe. I am no braggart, but I challenge the world to furnish a more determined fight or a victory more richly earned. The enemy *shall* not cross here. I will not give way one inch."[11] J.T. Headley reported of this severe clash that Cushing "received eight raking shots in this fierce contest, but fortunately his engine was not injured, and he [Cushing] reported 'I can assure you, that the Barney and her crew are still in good fighting trim, and will beat the enemy, or sink at our post.'"[12]

Yet in victory Will Cushing remained gracious. "And here let me pause to give credit to one who will never earn more glory than he grasped in our desperate combat then. Lieutenant Lamson is one of the class next below me, and commanded the disabled steamer.... I fought within a hundred yards of him and we are sworn friends for life. Well, I silenced the battery, and anchored at night where I had fought all day."[13]

Cushing lauded Lamson, and later Lamson would respond in kind, each appreciating the other's coolness and courage under fire. The situation at the mouth of the Nansemond remained essentially unchanged, although over the next few days it seemed the Confederates had not replaced their batteries, and that resistance was slightly diminished. What did it mean? Cushing had an idea to push some of his gunboats further upriver to try and find out; and Admiral Lee, now in charge of the North Atlantic Blockading Squadron, sent him four fresh vessels to aid in the effort—*Yankee, Primrose, Teaser,* and the *Coeur de Lion.* But problems with the river and the draft of the boats persisted.

The vessels that were most adequately armed could not traverse the bar, while those that could cross with ease would be shot to pieces by the Confederate artillery. No combination seemed to work, although Lamson took small flotillas upriver on more than one occasion, but to no substantial profit. What were the Confederates doing inland? No one could say for sure.

Thus remained the status quo until late April, when an unfortunate incident sent William Cushing into a rage. Will received a report that while patrolling the river on April 21 the *Stepping Stones* was signaled from the river's edge by someone waving a white flag. A boat was sent out to see what was wanted, and while approaching the bank took rifle fire from the shore. It appeared that one of the sailors was killed, and the other crew members captured.[14] Convinced the Confederates had deliberately lured his men toward shore by use of a false flag of truce, then criminally ignored this long established convention of war to foul advantage, Cushing erupted in anger, and railed like a caged lion in his cabin all night (it was much later discovered that the Confederates had opened fire when several of the Yankee sailors, sensing a trap, had raised their rifles first). He could not allow such a breech to go unchallenged. The next day he hatched a plan of retribution, to push ashore with a large party, and attempt to find his captured sailors, or at least stir up some trouble in the bargain.

From the crews of the *Commodore Barney*, the *Stepping Stones*, and the *Yankee*, Will selected a party of ninety choice men, made sure they were all well armed, included in his landing party fifteen soldiers, and insisted the infantrymen drag along behind a small howitzer for good measure. Will Cushing meant business. The transgression would not go unpunished.

The party shoved off in seven small boats, and rowed directly for the area where the sailors had been ambushed the day before. Once ashore Cushing immediately established a perimeter, and sent out a party of skirmishers to reconnoiter the area. In the rushes along the riverbank the small boat from the *Stepping Stones* was located, along with the body of the sailor who had been shot to death. The others were nowhere to be seen. So Will left a few men behind to guard the boats, then put the others in formation and started off down the road toward the small village of Chuckatuck, a few miles distant. It was not long before they struck a group of Confederate pickets, and the sailors spread out and drove the Confederates in, capturing one of the Rebels as they did. The captured picket spoke freely of the situation ahead, and advised Cushing that some four hundred cavalry were stationed ahead at Chuckatuck; that the escaped pickets would surely alert them to the Yankees presence, and that Will and his party were soon to be in for far more than they had bargained for.

Will Cushing was unimpressed by the Rebel picket's tale, however, and had no intention of curtailing his search. He could spare no men to guard the Rebel, so he had him tied to a tree by the road, and the landing party started off again. At a crossroads just outside of the village, Cushing divided his command in half, leaving one part behind as either a reserve or a fallback position — whichever circumstances dictated — and with the remainder pressed on toward the town at the double-quick. "As we entered the streets of the town, a rebel cavalry company came charging around the corner, two hundred yards away, with drawn sabres and horses at the gallop."[15] It was a mismatch by any standard, as trained cavalry could surely ride right over Cushing's men, slashing them to pieces as they did, but such conventions were meaningless to William Cushing. He had come for a fight and, cavalry or no cavalry, a fight he was going to have. "Something had to be done — so I ordered a charge and the novel sight ensued of sailors charging and beating cavalry."[16] Cushing yelled, racing ahead, and his men began to scream right behind him, sweeping down the road straight toward the Confederate riders, rifles in hand.

This was not supposed to happen. The Yankee sailors fired as they ran, unhorsed a few of the Rebels, and continued their screaming charge as if they were three hundred, not thirty-five. The Confederate horsemen, utterly shocked and confounded by the sight of the charging Federal sailors, pulled quickly to a halt on the dusty road. Then "they turned, called for the retreat, did not stop for the dead, and galloped out of town"[17] in the opposite direction. The Yankee sailors raced after them as fast as they could run, but they could hardly catch the fleeing horses. But they were now, at least, the proud possessor of Chuckatuck, for all that was worth, and they laughed at how fast the Rebels had ridden out of harm's way. But there was no doubt that the stampeded cavalry would be back, and when they returned they would come in force, so there was no time to waste. The sailors had a quick look around, then gathered up the loose cavalry horses, and started back for the boats.

Yet one thing of great importance had been made manifestly clear by Will Cushing's little expedition — Longstreet's position had clearly shifted away from the mouth of the Nansemond toward Suffolk, and what little force that remained deployed near the mouth of the river was obviously little more than a screen to confuse the Federal defenders. Cushing realized that he could not possibly have waltzed as he did into Chuckatuck were this not true, and he also realized that this was extraordinarily valuable information. As soon as he returned to the *Commodore Barney*, Will Cushing got off a message to headquarters explaining the situation; and later he returned to shore, grabbed one of the cavalry horses, and rode through a terrible rain nine miles to report the facts directly to General Peck, the Federal commander at Suffolk.[18]

What Peck did not know, however, was that both General Lee and Longstreet had determined that a bloody siege of Suffolk was not worth the price it would require in lives, and thus the Confederate movements in that portion of Virginia had become both hesitant and indecisive.[19] Lee wanted two of Longstreet's divisions held in a ready reserve, and this greatly compromised Longstreet's ability to accomplish the task of foraging he had marched south in the first place to complete. Longstreet would require every last man in his division to take Suffolk and complete his foraging operation for the Army of Northern Virginia; but Lee, while desperately in need of the stores of food, could not allow it. "Longstreet put the dilemma clearly in a dispatch to Lee on March 19. He could only collect the necessary supplies, he said, 'If I can use my forces; but if the two divisions are to be held in readiness to join you, or even one of them, I can do nothing.'"[20] Thus the stalemate that ensued around Suffolk, Peck weary of being overwhelmed and Longstreet unwilling to pay the price in men's lives it would require to overwhelm the town and move successfully into that quadrant of lower Virginia.

But for William Cushing the strategic paralysis did not matter. He had fought hard and valiantly along the mouth of the Nansemond River, had provided the Federal authorities with invaluable information, and had risked his neck on more than one occasion to do so. His daring had once again been rewarded, and he received well deserved plaudits from Secretary Welles on down to Admiral Lee and General Peck. "I have since received some very handsome letters," Will wrote proudly, "from the Secretary of the Navy, and the admiral, in acknowledgement of my services. I am in high favor with the department."[21] High favor, indeed.

As spring warmed and the weeks passed, Longstreet's division was ultimately withdrawn from the area and returned to Lee's army along the Rappahannock River, and the threat to Suffolk naturally diminished accordingly. The *Commodore Barney*, however, was so cut to pieces from all the action it had seen that the ship had to be taken to Baltimore for repairs and a full refitting. William Cushing then dutifully reported to the Navy Department in Washington where a very pleased Secretary of the Navy was anxious to see him.

CHAPTER 8

In a Cornfield at Edward's Ferry

WHILE HOPES OF PROGRESS had started off high that winter for Gilbert Elliott, reality soon brought him promptly back down to earth. In what seemed to becoming a never ending cycle of wasted correspondence and even more wasted effort, the construction of his vessels for the Confederacy had stalled once again due to a lack of iron. In early February Confederate President Jefferson Davis had himself become involved in the situation, sending Lt. John Wood to North Carolina on a mission to uncover the facts. Wood was expected to report back to Davis on "the status of ironclad construction, and make recommendations how best to defend bays and rivers in the Wilmington area."[1]

The Federal blockade was having its intended effect upon the Southern states, as imports of everything from weaponry and ammunition to foodstuffs and silks had dwindled off to a trickle. Many ports of entry had been sealed off entirely. Wilmington remained one of the few key open ports for the Confederacy on the Eastern Seaboard, and if the Confederate government was going to survive, the port of Wilmington on the Cape Fear River had to be maintained at all costs. That would require effective vessels to accomplish, for the Yankees were becoming far bolder on the inland rivers of the state; yet effective vessels meant ironclads, and for lack of iron, these boats were not being completed. Indeed, as far as construction was concerned, Wood reported back to Jefferson Davis that, among other things, "two others of lighter draft were commenced some time ago; one on the Roanoke River at Halifax, the other on the Tar at Tarboro, but owing to the want of iron the work on them is partially suspended."² Wood had discovered what Elliott and Cooke had known for months — there was no iron to be had for the ironclads under construction, and all reports, letters, and efforts to procure it had produced nothing but futility.

As spring approached Elliott moved his shipbuilding location from Halifax to a farm field about twenty-two miles below on the Roanoke River, not far from his other building facility at Tillery's Farm. As Gilbert Elliott later explained, "A point on the Roanoke River, in Halifax County, North Carolina, about thirty miles below the town of Weldon, was fixed upon as the most suitable for the purpose. The river rises and falls, as is well known, and it was necessary to locate the yard on ground sufficiently free from over-flow to admit of uninterrupted work for at least twelve months. No vessel was ever constructed under more adverse circumstances."³

Elliott had befriended one William Ruffin Smith and his son, Peter, both of whom owned large tracts of land along the banks of the river, and both of whom were interested in aiding the Confederate cause. The move from Halifax was made by Elliott to acquire more room for building, and as such clearly was one that was predicated upon his hope of soon acquiring an adequate iron supply. "Elliott and Smith rode their horses over those fields along the river searching for a place that would, in their collective opinion, make a suitable shipyard. The spot they chose was a field gently sloping north towards the river while nestled between slightly higher banks. It was near the river crossing called Edward's Ferry."⁴ Near a fine stand of oak and pine a sawmill was erected, capable of cutting the needed ship's beams, timbers, and planking. Here also was a sizeable forge for tool making, and plenty of labor to construct the vessels. Elliott moved in with the Smith's on their plantation, and work soon began on the ironclad.

These arrangements for the new Edwards Ferry shipyard were made in March, and that month Elliott wrote as well to General D.H. Hill, the new commander of Confederate forces in North Carolina. Elliot attempted to explain the seeming endless promises he had received for iron, as well his endless failures to procure it. He told of the fruitless pursuit of iron at Besse's Station, of his failed attempts to secure iron from a short line near Tarboro, and finally of iron sitting uselessly at Laurensburg. Elliott concluded by stating what was becoming increasingly obvious to all involved in the effort to construct gunboats in the state. "Old iron will answer my purposes as well as new," he said, "and I shall readily exchange bar for bar at this place, but iron must be had or the further construction of the gunboats discontinued. I have only enough iron for one of the two gunboats building here, that designed for one of them having been diverted to Charleston. The rails sent on can be rolled in Richmond, at the rate of thirty tons per day, and if expeditious, we may yet be prepared to close the Cape Fear against invasion. It is time that we should work together," the young shipbuilder pleaded, "and I am well aware as any one of the importance of our railroads, but how diminished in usefulness would the Wil.& Weld. R.R. be were this place to fall into the hands of the enemy. And to what avail would the iron at Laurensburg then be?"[5] Elliott's point was well taken — what possible use could the railroad men have for their iron once their lines, yards, and locomotives were all in Yankee hands? But that point, of course, had been made many times before, all to no avail.

Work began at Edward's Ferry, in a cornfield, of all places, and the conditions were primitive to say the least. "None of the usual facilities were available. There were no engines, no derricks and pulleys, no power tools — nothing but men, who were willing enough, and saws and hammers."[6] To try and make work more efficient, it was decided to move the floating battery, still at Tillery's, to the new site at Edward's Ferry to have what iron was available affixed; but this proved almost disastrous, for the helmsman aboard the small steamer that was towing the battery failed to properly adjust for the river's own current, causing the battery to float directly into the steamer, damaging both considerably. Catherine Edmondston, matron of a nearby plantation, described the accident with a dose of venom in her journal. "Last week the Battery constructed above us was taken in tow by a steamer to be carried down to a landing below us to be ironed. From some mismanagement they allowed her to drag the boat then underway of steam past the landing & attempting to turn she ran afoul of the boat crashing her wheel and damaging her greatly.

"Shameful conduct somewhere & conduct which will be felt in the Army, for this is one of the two Steamers upon which we depend to carry our supplies to Weldon. One boat was lost from the drunkenness of the person in charge last summer ... now this from incapacity."[7]

In an open cornfield, bereft of all but the most primitive tools and machinery, work on the new ironclad progressed at little more than a snail's pace, yet still it progressed. Years later Gilbert Elliot described how the craft slowly took shape. "The Keel was laid and construction was commenced by bolting down across the center a piece of frame timber, which was of yellow pine eight by ten inches. Another frame of the same size was then dovetailed into this, extending outwardly at an angle of 45 degrees, forming the side, and at the outer end of this the frame for the shield was also dovetailed, the angle being 35 degrees, and then the top deck was added, and so on around to the other end of the bottom beam. Other beams were then bolted down to the keel, and to the one first fastened, and so on, working fore and aft, the main-deck beams being interposed from stem to stern. The shield was 60 feet

8. *In a Cornfield at Edward's Ferry* 63

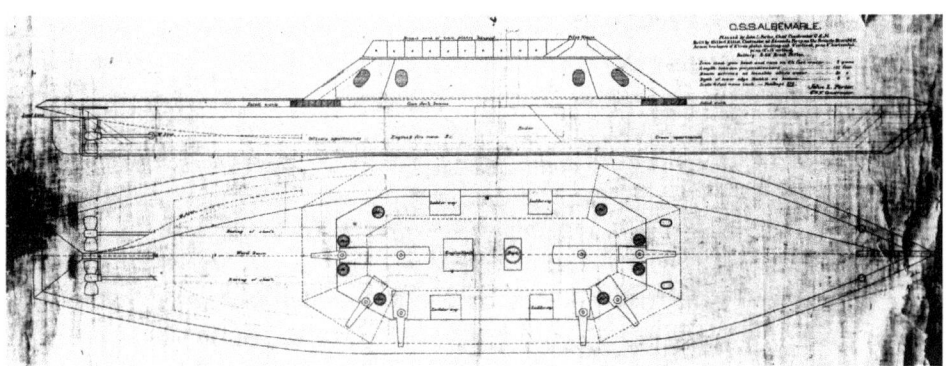

General blueprints for the CSS *Albemarle* (U.S. Naval History and Heritage Command).

in length and octagonal in form."[8] The job was an enormous test of the craftsmen's skill and patience, working at such a disadvantage, but piece by piece the ironclad slowly took shape.

The ironclad's specifications had been carefully thought out and provided by John Porter, the Chief Naval Constructor for the Confederate Navy. The plans, as described by Gilbert Elliott, called for a vessel that was "152 feet long between perpendiculars; her extreme width was 45 feet; her depth from the gun-deck to the keel was 9 feet, and when launched she drew 6½ feet of water, but after being ironed and completed her draught was about 8 feet."[9] On her bow she was to be fitted out with a strong, sharp ram for obvious purposes.

Building a reasonably sophisticated vessel from scratch in a field of corn was no easy assignment. Much innovation and substitution had to be thought through, the delays in payments and supplies constantly worked around. Elliott explained how the work continued after the beams were in place. "When this part of the work was completed she was a solid boat, built of pine frames, and if calked would have floated in that condition, but she was afterwards covered with 4-inch planking, laid on longitudinally, as ships are usually planked, and this was properly calked and pitched, cotton being used for calking instead of oakum, the latter being very scarce and the former almost the only article to be had in abundance."[10]

In May it was discerned through various sources that the Yankees at Plymouth, south of Edward's Ferry on the Roanoke, were installing torpedoes and pilings to prevent the approach of any Confederate ironclads from upriver, and a small detachment of Rebel infantry finally arrived to take up a position in defense of the shipyard. With some satisfaction Catherine Edmondston made note of each in her journal. "To our pleasure we hear that the Abolitionists are blockading the River just above Plymouth in order to keep the Gun Boat which we are building at Edwards Ferry from attacking them. I hope that their barricade will be effectual against themselves also. Yesterday a company of Infantry passed here on their way to the Ferry, with orders to guard it and to picket the River from Norfleet's to Pollock's Ferry."[11] Both of these occurrences undoubtedly pleased Gilbert Elliott no end, as he had been constantly fearful that a Yankee attack up the essentially unguarded river could destroy in a single stroke everything he had worked so long and hard to accomplish. The company of infantry might also hold off a small Federal flotilla, at least for awhile, while the news of the somewhat extravagant precautions the Yankees were taking in the river near Plymouth for their own protection led one to believe that, for the time being at least, defense rather than offense, was their goal.

So as the air warmed, and as spring slowly meandered toward summer, the ironclad at Edward's Ferry began to take shape. Iron remained the critical problem, of course, but at least now there was room to work, men enough to do handle the labor, and some meager protection from any Yankee incursions. It was hardly everything Jim Cooke and Gilbert Elliott could hope for, but with the future cooperation of one or more of the railroads in North Carolina, and just a little good luck, the ironclad might be finished by winter. Yes the crucial shortage of iron remained a daily headache, but both hope and cotton were to be had in abundance.

"On Friday, July 3 Cooke and Elliott left the construction site and rode over to neighboring Hascosea [the plantation home of Mrs. Edmondston] to visit Patrick Edmondston and his father-in-law, Thomas Pollock Devereux, but found them both away. Catherine Edmondston graciously invited both friends 'to remain for dinner, so they might not be disappointed on the object of their visit.'"[12] What Elliott, Cooke, or Mrs. Edmonston could not have known as they exchanged pleasantries on that hot July afternoon, however, was that a few hundred miles north of Hascosea at the Pennsylvania town of Gettysburg, one of the most decisive battles of the war was coming to a dramatic and bloody conclusion that very afternoon, and a conclusion that would have far reaching consequences for the course of the war.

CHAPTER 9

A Presidential Compliment

For William Barker Cushing the early summer proved a wonderful respite from the war on the rivers of Virginia and North Carolina. The damage inflicted to the *Commodore Barney* allowed for a layover in Washington for weeks, and a chance for Cushing to unwind. Cushing's handling of the flotilla on the Nansemond River had been splendid, and if it had not played a critical part in preventing Longstreet from assailing Suffolk, his actions certainly had not helped Confederate aspirations in the area. Reputation greatly enhanced, Cushing, between trips to Baltimore to check on the progress on the *Barney*, had called upon Secretary Welles at the Navy Department where he had been very well received.

Indeed, so pleased had Welles been with Will Cushing's actions in Virginia, that after a discussion of the facts, Welles "cleared his throat and asked the young officer, 'Would you like to be presented to the President? I have spoken to him about the good work you and Lieutenant Lamson have done for us and I think that he would be pleased to meet you.'"[1] Cushing was thunderstruck by the suggestion, and could not even frame a response, but Welles surmised the answer, and set about making the arrangements.

A few days later Will Cushing, a mere twenty-year-old naval lieutenant, was brought in by Secretary Welles for a private meeting with the president of the United States. Will had memorized a speech with which to regale Mr. Lincoln, but he found the president in a melancholy mood, and in no frame of mind for windy, patriotic orations. They talked for about an hour, and the president complimented Cushing warmly on his exploits. But Mr. Lincoln seemed somewhat remote to the young lieutenant, as he would comment years later. "The President was pleased to compliment me on my success. He seemed rather subdued and sad — and did not talk about the war. It is said that Chancellorsville was a blow to everyone here, and that the President was very depressed by it."[2]

President Lincoln had good reason for sadness — the land war continued to go poorly. The preceding summer General John Pope had been in command of the Federal Army of Virginia, and had been seriously defeated by Lee on the old Manassas battleground, sending the Federal Army once again reeling into the Washington defenses. Lincoln was virtually forced to turn to McClellan again after that debacle; and McClellan had fought Lee's army to a draw along Antietam Creek in Western Maryland in September of 1862, only to return to his old habits of overestimating the enemy and refusing to budge. So Lincoln then promoted General Ambrose Burnside, who had showed such pluck during the combined land-naval operations in North Carolina, to command the Potomac army. But command of a major army proved beyond Burnside's depth, and he virtually wrecked the Army of the Potomac in December of 1862, hurling it again and again against an almost invulnerable position taken up by Lee on the heights overlooking the Rappahannock River at Fredericksburg. So Burnside was replaced with Joe Hooker, and Hooker had talked big but failed to deliver in early May 1863 at the small Virginia crossroads of Chancellorsville, where the army had been flanked and almost destroyed by Stonewall Jackson.

Initially the reports from the front at Chancellorsville had been positive, and Lincoln had reason to believe Joe Hooker would back up his braggadocio with success, but as the hours wore on the reports began to turn. "Lincoln could not believe this. How could Hooker retreat when his was supposed to be the attacking force? May 3 brought even worse reports. Though outnumbered two to one, Lee had divided his army and struck Hooker with frontal and flank assaults, and a titanic battled roared around Chancellorsville. A cloudburst interrupted the telegraph for a time. But on May 6 came the awful news that Hooker had quit fighting and pulled back to Falmouth. Another defeat then? Yes, another defeat. Fighting Joe Hooker had let a smaller force whip the Potomac Army and had lost seventeen thousand casualties in the process. In the White House, Lincoln paced back and forth with his hands behind his back. 'My God!' he told Noah Brooks. 'What will the country say! What will the country say!'"[3]

After the debacle at Chancellorsville, Lincoln hardly knew where to turn. He did not want to replace Hooker — who had earned a good reputation as a hard fighting corps commander prior to that defeat — but Hooker's handling of the army certainly seemed questionable, and was in fact being challenged secretly by a number of the general's subordinates. It was a terrible situation with no easy answers. The merry-go-round of command changes had yet to produce the desired results, and while Lincoln did not want to judge or dismiss Hooker prematurely, he could not help but to question his abilities — he had seen too many well-qualified corps commanders fail miserably when promoted to higher command. The intriguing behind Joe Hooker's back had begun in earnest, and the president was forced to telegraph his general the uncomfortable news. "I must tell you," Lincoln wrote, "I have some painful intimations that some of your corps and Division Commanders are not giving you their entire confidence."[4] Thus was the country dissatisfied with the course of the war, the president dissatisfied with the situation surrounding his principle army, and it was no small wonder that Mr. Lincoln had met William Cushing in such a blue and somber mood.

Repairs to the *Commodore Barney* continued to drag in Baltimore, thus was Will provided an additional three weeks leave until the work could be completed. This he was pleased to make quick use of. Having already made the rounds in Washington, and as his mother was at the time in Boston visiting relatives, Cushing decided to take the train north and visit her there. The trip turned into a splendid three week vacation. "I must say," he wrote a few days after returning to Baltimore, "I have never enjoyed myself before as I did there. I had a dozen different engagements a day, laughed, talked, smoked, enjoyed the society of ladies, and had some grand rides, good fishing, and some splendid dinners on the sea beach."[5] It was well that Will Cushing had enjoyed himself as thoroughly as he had, for when he returned the repairs to the *Commodore Barney* had been completed, and she was once again fitted out for action. Cushing looked her over and offered his approval. "My vessel is in good repair, and my crew is replenished, my battery is heavier than before; and I am prepared to pay upon sight all that I owe the rebels in the shape of shell, grape, and canister."[6]

By late June the *Commodore Barney* was off again on offensive actions, this time plying its trade on the York River in Virginia, assisting a strong reconnaissance in force launched by the land forces to test the defenses surrounding Richmond in the vicinity of White House, where the York River meets the Pamunkey. The naval flotilla was under command of Captain Pierce Crosby, and consisted of the *Barney, Commodore Morris, Western World*, and *Morse*.[7] The probe was executed flawlessly, and proved enormously successful. The defenses in the area were determined to be weak, and quite a few Rebel prisoners captured as a result, the most famous being William H.F. Lee, son of the Commanding General of the Army of Northern Virginia.

But the probe up the York River was at the time an operation of minor interest for the rest of the county, for the Rebel army under General Lee had in late June been reported crossing the Potomac River, and moving across Maryland toward Pennsylvania. Fear gripped the land. The *Commodore Barney* returned to Washington on June 29 to find the city in turmoil, and the north in a state of near panic. The northern states were trembling in anticipation of the Rebel's next move, Northern governors screaming for assistance from the Federal government, and Mr. Lincoln in Washington unsure of his next move.

In fact the Confederate Army had begun its movement north in relative secrecy in early June, heading west toward the Shenandoah Valley, then north through the valley using the majestic green ridges of Massanutten Mountain and later South Mountain to screen its advance. "Lafayette McLaws's division of Longstreet's corps was first to move, from its position behind Fredericksburg. In the event, McLaws's troops setting the pace on the bright morning of Wednesday, June 3, 1863, formally marked the start of the Pennsylvania campaign. Precisely one month later the campaign would reach its climax."[8]

"The capital was full of strange rumors. It was very hot, and everyone was suffering from prickly heat. A spy in the streets of Chambersburg, someone said, had counted Lee's troops — more than ninety thousand men. Out on the fringe of Lee's advance the Pennsylvania roads were choked with refugees. Fourteen thousand citizens turned out to dig trenches at Pittsburgh (no one knew where Lee was heading); in Harrisburg the militia drilled in the streets with fowling pieces and scythes because there were no muskets. Business stopped in Philadelphia, and veterans of the War of 1812 offered to form a regiment."[9]

Lt. W.B. Cushing in 1864 (U.S. Naval History and Heritage Command).

Initially Joe Hooker could only guess at Lee's intentions, but at Brandy Station, Virginia, Federal cavalry had broken through the Confederate cavalry screen in a surprise attack, and discovered Rebel infantry in the vicinity of Culpepper, Virginia. That discovery seemed to indicate only one thing — the Confederate Army had shifted away from the old Fredericksburg line, and Lee was moving north in strength. The Union army would do the same. "General Hooker, for his part, would be following what Mr. Lincoln termed the inside track, marching due north from Falmouth, keeping his army always between the Rebels and Washington."[10]

That march began in mid–June. The weather turned hot and dry, the roads heading north churned into a powdery dust under the pounding feet of thousands upon thousands of Union troops, and good water was everywhere at a premium. Alonzo Cushing's Battery A of the 4th U.S. Artillery was attached to the Federal II Corps now commanded by General Winfield Hancock, and they were shadowing the Confederate advance on the inside track, up the narrow Maryland roads toward the Pennsylvania line. Despite the difficult conditions, the army was marching rapidly. One Midwestern officer wrote home saying, "We marched Sunday morning and all day Sunday and all night, and until the middle of the afternoon to-day, when we reached this point, tired, sore, sleepy, hungry, dusty and dirty as pigs.... Our army is in a great hurry for something."[11]

For President Lincoln the Federal Army's march north brought with it new and trying difficulties. Unable to work within the tactical constraints imposed by the administration, on June 27 General Hooker offered his resignation, and — despite the immediate presence of the enemy — Lincoln, no doubt concerned about the lack of confidence displayed by Joe Hooker's subordinates, at once accepted. "Nor did Lincoln hesitate about naming a successor. The Potomac army's chief officers had left no doubt they wanted George Meade for the post, and in any event four other eligible generals had already turned it down. That evening General Orders No. 194 was drawn up, relieving General Hooker as commander of the Army of the Potomac and appointing General Meade in his place."[12] Events seemed to be careening toward some climatic event, but just what that might be, and where that event might take place, remained a mystery. In Northern cities tension was in the air, and newspapers were hot with all sorts of speculation. What was Lee up to? Where was he headed?

On June 29, the day Will Cushing arrived at Washington aboard the *Commodore Barney*, his brother Alonzo was marching with his battery toward Taneytown, Maryland,[13] a small village where much of the II Corps would spend the following day in camp, eagerly awaiting news of the enemy, and fresh orders for the march. Yet the Confederate Army was thought to be north and west of Taneytown, and all the roads from the surrounding villages, like the spokes of a great wheel, led to a small town just across the Pennsylvania border, not fifteen miles from where the 4th U.S. Artillery had gone into bivouac. The name of that town was Gettysburg.

CHAPTER 10

Magnificent, Grim, Irresistible

" HERE THEY COME! Here comes the infantry!"[1] A thousand heads turned to gaze out across the open plain toward a low ridge and line of trees about a mile distant. It was approximately 3:00 P.M., July 3, 1863, and from the trees and over a small swale the enemy was spotted in long lines of battle. The scene was breathtaking.

"Three gray lines came out of the woods, with skirmishers fanned out ahead. Pickett's Division on the right and to its left Pettigrew's, not abreast but somewhat behind. Fifteen thousand men. Ranks dressed and intervals so beautifully kept that the assault waves seemed to merge into an unbroken sea flooding the valley. Sun glinted on the slanted rifle barrels and on the drawn swords of a few mounted officers, looming above its broad expanse."[2]

Along the battle lines the cannon had just recently ceased smoking, momentarily silent like exhausted beasts drawing breath after a titanic struggle. For over an hour Federal and Confederate artillery had blasted away at one another across the small valley, 172 Rebel pieces blazing away as 220 answered from the Union side.[3] Alonzo Cushing had been in the center of the storm, working his guns from a ridge named Cemetery, his men and pieces shot almost to splinters in the effort. No one had ever seen or experienced anything like it. It was as if hell had come to earth.

Colonel Frank Haskell, an officer on Hancock's staff, sat his horse not far from Alonzo Cushing's guns, and later tried to capture in words the extraordinary experience. "The shells swoop down among the battery horses standing there apart. A half dozen horses start, they stumble, their legs stiffen, their vitals and blood smear the ground.... Only a few yards off a shell exploded over an open limber box in Cushing's battery, and at the same instant, another shell over a neighboring box. In both boxes the ammunition blew up with an explosion that shook the ground, throwing fire and splinters and shells far into the air and all around, and destroying several men."[4]

The air was alive with shrieking shells, smoke filled the valley, and the ground reverberated as salvo upon salvo crashed to earth. It was hellish, maddening, mind-numbing. Haskell, like Alonzo Cushing working his guns nearby, having somehow survived at the very center of the tempest, described the carnage with compelling flourish. "We watched the shells bursting in the air, as they came hissing in all directions. Their flash was a bright gleam of lightening radiating from a point, giving place in the thousandth part of a second to a small, white puffy cloud, like a fleece of the lightest, whitest wool. These clouds were very numerous. We could not often see the shell before it burst; but sometimes, as we faced toward the enemy, and looked above our heads, the approach would be heralded by a prolonged hiss, which always seemed to me to be a line of something tangible, terminating in a black globe, distinct to the eye, as the sound had been to the ear. The shell would seem to stop, and hang suspended in the air an instant, and then vanish in fire and smoke and noise."[5]

This maddening, deafening exchange went on for well over an hour. Finally General Henry Hunt, commander of the Federal artillery, sent word to his batteries to cease fire in order to conserve ammunition, and hopefully as well to lure the anticipated Confederate infantry assault into the teeth of his guns while their ordinance remained plentiful. Hunt would later clarify his thinking: "I knew the severity of the trial to which I was subjecting all the troops," he readily admitted. "I knew, also, that while the batteries would be the direct object of the enemy's fire, their men must stand idle at the guns and bear its full fury, while the infantry lying on the reverse slope of the ridge and out of the enemy's sight would be partly sheltered from it. Yet I felt no doubt as to the fortitude of my cannoneers."[6]

One of those cannoneers who had already displayed uncommon valor was Alonzo Cushing. Fighting his pieces as calmly and professionally as though he were at drill, Allie had already been wounded twice, once in the shoulder and again in the groin. But nothing was going to stop him from performing his duty that day. As the historian Stephen Sears notes, "Probably the most often hit of the Second Corps batteries was Lieutenant Alonzo Cushing's Battery A, 4th U.S. Young Cushing, graduated early from West Point in 1861 to meet the need for educated soldiers, kept his guns firing steadily despite grievous losses among the crews. 'He was as cool and calm as I ever saw him,' recalled one of his men, 'talking to the boys between shots with the glass constantly to his eyes, watching the effect of our shots.' But so many gunners were down that Cushing too had to call on infantrymen to help man the guns. John

Gibbon saw three of Cushing's limber chests blow up at once, sending up a huge column of smoke and fire and triggering 'triumphant yells of the enemy.'"[7]

Men had been torn to pieces, smoke poured from what remained of several wrecked limbers, horses screamed and died in harness, the ground trembled beneath the crew's feet, smoke was so thick and swirling that visibility was reduced to almost nothing — the gun crews could only fire at the red flashes of Confederate artillery on the ridge opposite, and hope for success. Surely it seemed a scene from the inferno. Two of Cushing's pieces had been struck and disabled from Rebel counter battery fire, the wheels of other guns knocked off or mangled. Battery A had been reduced to a shambles. Arsenal H. Griffin, a private in the battery had been wounded so severely that he simply pulled out a pistol, painfully adjusted it to the side of his head, said, "Good-by boys,"[8] and shot himself dead. Alonzo, wounded badly, could hardly stand.

Then, suddenly, the Confederate infantry was on its way. Frank Haskell, watching the scene unfold from near Cushing's wrecked battery, realized at once that the climax of the monstrous, three-day battle was finally at hand. "None on that crest now need be told *that the enemy is advancing.* Every eye could see his legions, an overwhelming resistless tide of an ocean of armed men sweeping upon us! Regiment after regiment, and brigade after brigade, move from the woods and rapidly take their places in the lines forming for the assault."[9] Soon the issue would be decided.

For Allie Cushing the road to this climatic moment at Gettysburg had been one of high valor and rapid advance. In May, when the Potomac army had crossed the Rappahannock River under orders from Joe Hooker, Alonzo's battery wound up in the thick of the fighting at the crossroads called Chancellorsville. On May 1, while the army was moving out of the Wilderness toward open ground south of the crossroads, the division was attacked on the road, and heavy fighting ensued. "They were soon hotly engaged and were confident of success, but Hooker, losing his nerve, ordered them all back; he would setup a line of entrenchments and let the Confederates batter themselves to pieces against it."[10] Having witnessed first hand the terrible carnage involved in assaulting well fortified positions at Fredericksburg, Hooker had in all probability determined to fight on the defensive and let the Rebels deal with the bloody consequences. The army was thus pulled back and placed in a defensive posture, and that would have done well enough except that Lee had sent Stonewall Jackson with much of his army through the tangled undergrowth of the Wilderness only to emerge on the Potomac army's exposed right flank. Jackson's assault swarmed out of the woods into the unsuspecting 11th Corps, and chaos ensued. Cushing was promoted to brevet major on the field for his gallant actions in resisting the assault,[11] and later his battery assisted in the rear guard action when the army finally managed its retreat back across the Rappahannock. But in the end the battle at Chancellorsville had been little more than another sad Federal defeat, and a defeat that had cost the Potomac army many fine officers and men.

For the remainder of May and the early portion of June, Alonzo had been busily engaged training new officers and men for his battery. With word of Lee's movement north up the Shenandoah, however, the Potomac army began the long march on the "inside track" dogging the Confederate advance as best they could. Finally Lee, with word that the Federal Army was near and rapidly approaching, ordered the concentration of his scattered divisions. Since most roads in that portion of Pennsylvania radiated out from Gettysburg, that location was sensibly chosen for the concentration.

Neither army commander had picked the small Pennsylvania hamlet as a preferred site for battle, but fighting erupted by means of a chance encounter of the advanced elements, and expanded almost uncontrollably from there. As divisions arrived, they were fed into the spiraling violence. Fighting on the ridges west of town, the I Corps of the Potomac army held its ground admirably during the morning hours that first day; but as more and more Confederate divisions arrived on the field in accordance with Lee's orders to concentrate, the now outnumbered Union forces eventually gave way, then collapsed entirely, retreating back through the town, often in disorder.

Earlier in the day, General John Reynolds, then in command of the left wing of the Federal forces, had been shot and killed, and when General Meade received word of Reynolds' death, he immediately turned to Winfield Hancock to leave at once for Gettysburg and assume command of the field. Hancock "gathered the reserve artillery and some cavalry and went off at a trot, claiming priority over infantry on the road because he could move faster."[12] But Hancock knew he would need all the help he could muster and, spotting Alonzo Cushing standing near his guns he called out, "Cushing! Leave your battery — we haven't time to take it — we'll get guns."[13]

Alonzo jumped on his horse, and galloped along with the small detachment north, and arrived upon Cemetery Hill with General Hancock just as the Federal position to the west was crumbling. Below they spotted the beleaguered Federal soldiers streaming back through town, and it became their task to patch a suitable defense together from what remained before the Confederates could strike again. Hancock, once referred to as "The Magnificent" by George McClellan, set at once to work, and slowly order was restored from disorder. "When the beaten troops saw the new general ride along the line their hearts lifted; they gave a yell and tightened their hold."[14] Hancock selected a strong position, and soon fresh Federal divisions began to arrive up the dusty roads from Maryland, strengthening the line against a possible Rebel stroke.

Throughout that long afternoon and evening, Alonzo Cushing rode hither and yon, delivering Hancock's orders, often through a torrent of shot and shell, all acts of such unflinching courage that Hancock — not one to engage in empty rhetoric — exclaimed, "He is the bravest man I ever saw."[15] Indeed, so impressed had been Hancock that he presented the young major to General Meade upon that officer's arrival, and Meade promoted him on the spot to lieutenant colonel.[16] While the first day at Gettysburg had eventually proved discouraging for the Federal cause, it had not, through the efforts of thousands of Federal soldiers, and most certainly General Hancock and his impromptu staff, proved disastrous.

The two competing armies had taken positions on opposing ridges, and the second day's fighting had swayed back and forth, Lee attacking both Union flanks. The contest that day had been furious, and while gaining some ground, the Rebels had not been able to break the Union line significantly at either extreme, thus forcing yet a third day of combat.

That fighting had begun in the early morning hours of July 3 far off on the Federal right, but had fizzled by noon. But the long line of artillery the Confederates had assembled just across the way did not fool anyone, and soon it became apparent that the Rebels would attack in force somewhere along the Union center. Private Augustus Buell, a Federal cannoneer watching with some interest as the line of batteries took shape recalled that he "could see over across the valley a line of Rebel guns reaching from near the Seminary on the north clear down to a point nearly opposite the Peach Orchard on the south, lining that ridge for over a mile in length with what was almost one unbroken battery, over 100 guns strong!"[17] What did it mean? In all probability it meant a thunderous artillery bombardment followed by a massive infantry assault, all directed at the Union center. And Alonzo Cushing's battery A had been placed very near the center of the Union line.

At approximately 1:00 P.M. Longstreet sent word to commence the cannonade, and a signal gun was fired. Edward Porter Alexander, then in charge of Longstreet's artillery, recalled clearly that "it was just 1 P.M. when the signal guns were fired and the cannonade opened."[18] Then the Confederate artillery cut loose with a vengeance. T.W. Haight writes that "the thunder of artillery was like a continuous roar that filled the atmosphere. The fire of most of the one hundred and fifteen Confederate cannon then in action seemed directed by a kind of instinct towards the point in our line where the batteries of Cushing, Woodruff, and Rorty were belching destruction in the faces of their assailants, a mile and a half away."[19] In fact, Lee had directed Longstreet to take full command of the infantry assault, and the point of concentration was to be a small copse of trees located directly to Alonzo Cushing's left, no more than forty yards away from Battery A. In a sense, the entire assault had been

Alonzo Cushing (second from right) and Burnside's staff (Library of Congress).

aimed directly at what was left of Cushing's shattered battery, and it would be a massive attempt to punch through the center of the Federal line and, if successful, perhaps end the war that very afternoon.

Then for what seemed like an eternity, the guns had boomed and the shells had shrieked overhead in a bombardment far beyond anything anyone had ever before witnessed, but eventually the artillery fire from both sides ebbed, and across the small valley the Confederate infantry was seen to make ready their advance. Thus had Alonzo Cushing been delivered to that dreadful place soon to become the very vortex of what would be known forevermore as Pickett's Charge.

Cushing, already severely wounded, and barely capable of standing, refused to leave the contest. "A primary concern for Webb [whose infantry brigade held the center near Cushing's guns] was his artillery support, and he spoke of this to Lieutenant Alonzo Cushing, whose Battery A, 4th U.S., was posted behind the Angle. Only two of Cushing's 3-inch Ordnance rifles were still operable after the bombardment, and Cushing himself was grievously wounded and could barely stand. When Webb said he expected the enemy would come straight at them, Cushing replied, 'I had better run my guns right up to the stone fence and bring all my canister alongside of each piece.' 'All right,' said Webb, 'do so.'"[20] Cushing then had the guns pushed up to the very face of the small stone wall in front, and there awaited the assault. It was not long in coming.

Again, Frank Haskell breathes life into the scene from his perch near Cushing's guns, as the Confederate assault forms for the great test then lurches forward like a mighty wave. "The first line at short interval is followed by a second, and that a third succeeds; and columns between support the lines. More than half a mile their front extends; more than a thousand yards the dull gray masses deploy, man touching man, rank pressing rank, and line supporting line. The red flags wave, their horsemen gallop up and down; the arms of eighteen thousand men, barrel and bayonet, gleam in the sun, a sloping forest of flashing steel. Right on they move, as with one soul, in perfect order, without impediment of ditch, or wall or stream, over ridge and slope, through orchard and meadow, and cornfield, magnificent, grim, irresistible."[21]

The great charge advanced hundreds of yards while the Federal artillerymen, as if mesmerized by grand spectacle, simply looked on in wonder. Not a shot was fired, although the Rebel infantry was within range of most of the Yankee's rifled pieces. "It was as if the Union gunners were caught in a trance, fascinated by that splendid display of martial pageantry — the last great charge in the old tradition. Men would not look upon its likes again."[22] For Alonzo Cushing the delay in firing was not a matter of choice, however. Under orders from General Hancock to respond to the Confederate guns during the bombardment, the batteries in the II Corps manning the center of the Federal line had used up most of their long range ordinance during the exchange, and were at the moment incapable of further long range response. What remained for them was canister alone, anti-personnel cans of metal balls that could be lethal at short range, but useless at long. Thus Alonzo had little choice but to look on and count the range of the Confederate wave as it closed on his position.

While the great charge appeared both "grim and irresistible" it was also without question a desperate venture, born of both hope and the reality of diminishing possibilities. "The 13,000 or so men of Pickett's charge needed to cross three-quarters of a mile of open ground to reach their aiming points on Cemetery Ridge. To be sure, there were several shallow swales in that ground that might offer brief shelter, yet for most of the distance, especially when they reached the Emmitsburg Road, they would be completely exposed to a concerted fire by the Yankee defenders. Marching at 'common time,' with perhaps a pause or two for realignment on the way, would require some twenty minutes to half an hour to cover the distance."[23]

While many of the artillery pieces deployed by the Federal II Corps could not immediately respond, many others, those that had obeyed Hunt's order for a premature cease fire, could and did with sudden fury. The Union line exploded with the flame and smoke of heavy artillery fire. Lieutenant Rittenhouse's battery of guns atop Little Round Top at the far left of the Federal position, watched from on high as the spectacle unfolded, and Rittenhouse ordered a prompt and deadly response. "I watched Pickett's men advance," he later recalled, "and opened on them with an oblique fire, and ended with terrible enfilading fire."[24] That battery, consisting of six rifled guns, had the ability to reach almost all of the marching assault lines, and using exploding shells, did deadly service. "Many times," the lieutenant remembered, "a single percussion shell would cut out several files, and then explode in their ranks; several times almost a company would disappear, as the shell would rip from the right to the left among them."[25]

Almost immediately the red battle flags of the Confederacy began to dip and fall. Whole ranks of men simply disappeared in the sudden storm of metal. "Parrott and 3-inch ordnance rifle, Rodman and James and Napoleon. They flamed and thundered — leaped back in recoil — were rolled back into battery — loaded, sighted, and fired again and again.... Here was retaliation for the punishment they had suffered from the enemy's cannonade. They saw their shells rip rents in the oncoming ranks and the flags reeling and going down."[26] Yet despite the murderous pounding, the great assault pressed on, men quickly filling the spots of those who had fallen, the huge formations of troops pressing ever forward, steadily aiming for the small clump of trees near where Alonzo Cushing waited.

The panorama of battle was unforgettable. One artillerist on the Confederate line behind the advance recalled seeing "a vast bank of thick battle smoke, with thousands of shells exploding above the surface of a white, smoking sea. The sight was grand beyond description and awe-inspiring in extreme. Our line looked to me from our point of observation to be about three miles long and enveloped in thick smoke, from which came a fearful roar and clash of musketry accompanied with a deep, continuous roll of booming artillery, such as an American soldier never heard before on this continent."[27]

No matter. Through this deluge of smoke and screaming shells the assault continued, declining in numbers, of course, but never faltering as it swept forward. The legions marched ever forward until the advanced lines struck the wood fencing that ran the length of the Emmitsburg Road, where the Confederate infantry, stalling now to start and climb, became sitting targets. "Cushing and his neighbors open upon them with canister and case, every discharge sending a shower of small metal into the approaching ranks. However, the survivors press onward, firing as they come, and the batteries behind them send their shell among our cannon, killing horses and men."[28]

As the Rebels clambered over the fence, the Yankee infantry opened a murderous fire, and as well the silent tubes of the II Corps artillery, now shotted with canister, continued belching hot, hissing metal. With the Rebels now in range, Alonzo Cushing went to work. "Cushing had brought his guns down to the fence on this side of the road; he was firing now, double charges of canister, at four hundred, three hundred, two hundred yards range."[29] Double charges of canister quickly gave way to triple charges, and still the Confederates came on, but no longer in neat ranks, now massed instead like a great fist of determined men aimed at Cushing's stone wall. Behind the ranks of Rebel infantry the ground was littered with wounded and dead for a half mile, the pounding throb of combat still shaking the ground, the trees, it seemed, the very sky above.

A ball struck Alonzo suddenly in the shoulder, then another in the stomach. He was suffering a great deal, but refused to leave his last working gun. "You must go to the rear," Sergeant Fuger insisted. "There's no time, Fuger," Alonzo cried, "I stay right here and fight it out, or die in the attempt."[30]

The Rebel tide was now no more than one hundred yards away, closing fast. The bloodied fist of men now had a leader, however, a general with a hat topping his sword, gallantly leading what remained of the great assault up the small ridge straight toward Alonzo Cushing's last remaining gun at the wall. General Webb was standing nearby with his troops, ready to meet the charge head on. "I'll give them one more shot, Webb," Alonzo cried, his voice rising almost to a scream. He steadied himself as best he could, and cried to Webb, "Good-by!" A bullet struck him in the head, and he fell into Fuger's arms.[31]

The gallant Confederate general jumped to the top of the stone fence where Alonzo had been standing, screaming for his men to follow and turn the guns on the enemy, but then he too was cut down in a hail of musketry, and fell into the grass near where Alonzo lay. Now it was man against man — pistol and saber and fist. It was as if the great sweep of an emerging future had at this instant collided head first with the grim determination of a defiant past, and the horrific sound of this catastrophic collision was recalled by one survivor as "strange and terrible, a sound that came from thousands of human throats, yet was not a commingling of shouts and yells but rather like a vast mournful roar."[32] Perhaps a few hundred Rebels followed their general over the wall, but there was no support behind them, and in minutes only they were beaten and shot and clubbed into submission.

The great assault had been repulsed. On the floor of the small valley thousands upon thousands of men lay dead, dying, or wounded, many still writhing in excruciating pain. In human terms, the price of both victory and defeat had been almost incalculable. The beaten remnants of the great charge streamed back across the smoky, blasted terrain, leaving behind only fleeting memories of glory. In the grass by his broken guns, Alonzo Hersford Cushing lay dead.

CHAPTER 11

The Good Ship Albemarle

GENERAL ROBERT E. LEE'S fateful decision to hurl the cream of his army at the center of the Federal line that July 3 at Gettysburg only to see it shot to pieces in the process had, like shock waves emanating from an earthquake, a demoralizing effect all across the South. While some few still clung to the delusion of victory — Alexander Stephens, for instance, would declare in a speech that "General Lee's army had whipped the enemy on their own soil"[1] — most judgments were far more somber. "We came here with the best army the Confederacy ever carried into the field but thousands of our brave boys are left upon the enemy's soil and in my opinion our Army will never be made up of such material again,"[2] one soldier offered in grim summation. Yet his feelings were hardly unique. Another Virginian wrote, "I am glad it is over. I never expected to wage invasive warfare and I had enough of Maryland last year to satisfy me that we could never fight successfully upon that soil."[3] The *Charleston Mercury*, marshaling to the task its editorial angst, counseled its readers that "it is impossible for an invasion to have been more foolish or disastrous."[4] Writing in North Carolina on July 11, eight days after the Confederate defeat, but still hopeful that the bad news she had heard was in fact the wrong news, Catherine Edmondston noted in her journal, "I do not tell all the Yankees say of our pretended defeat. I shall have the truth soon from our own side. We are sad enough today without their lies to madden us in addition."[5]

For Robert E. Lee and the Confederacy, the future of the war had changed from one of hopeful victory by means of offensive improvisation, to one of defense and obstruction. The very means to a stunning triumph through aggressive maneuver had been consumed in the disastrous mistakes of the

Pennsylvania campaign, and the South had not the capacity to make good the losses. Now the Confederacy had to look to other, less flamboyant means for success. "Lee had staked everything — his splendid army, the fate of Richmond, and perhaps even the Confederacy itself — on a campaign aimed at destroying the Federal army. He had lost the bet, and now the prospect of an endlessly lingering war stretched before him like a dimly lit corridor lined with mirrors."[6]

After the debacle at Gettysburg, Lee's army fell back upon the Potomac River at Williamsport in Maryland, but the river had risen, and for a few days it appeared the Army of Northern Virginia might be pinned against the Potomac and destroyed by the pursuing Federals. But Meade, who had lost many of his senior officers to death and wounds at Gettysburg, was both slow and late in his pursuit, and Lee was allowed to escape across the river to Virginia, where the Rebels would naturally return to the defensive. In Washington, Abraham Lincoln became despondent, seeing this best of all opportunities to end the war slip through his fingers. Yes, the war might be changed in style and strategy, but once Lee had slipped across the Potomac, it became evident that the war would still labor on.

In the North the victory at Gettysburg was naturally greeted as a great triumph, but for William Cushing, sitting near the telegraph in Washington as the contest reached its bloody crescendo, the battle proved the manifestation of his very worst fears. When word was received of his brother's death, William left immediately for the front intent somehow on taking over Alonzo's battery and fighting it in his stead. It was a noble, if unrealistic sentiment. What he discovered upon arriving at Gettysburg — even days after the conflict — was a scene far beyond his prior reckoning. "The field, when I reached it was a sickening sight," he later wrote. "Thirty thousand wounded men, and thousands of unburied dead lay on the earth — in road, field, wood and orchard and under the scorching sun on the bare hillside amidst all the wreck of a great battle. Dismounted cannon, dead horses, exploded caissons and broken muskets were everywhere — and the artillery position on Cemetery Hill was almost paved with the rebel iron that had been hurled by the hundred and fifty guns massed against it previous to the final charge."[7] William then sought to remove his brother's body to Fredonia for burial, but that too would be denied him. Alonzo's body, it was explained, had already been shipped off to West Point where he would be buried with full honors. "My brother's battery was destroyed.... Our army had moved on in pursuit of the foe, and there was nothing left for me to do, but to return to naval duty."[8] The pain of Alonzo's death would haunt him for months. He wrote his mother: "The wounds were not alone for those who fell upon the field. There is suffering greater than the dying know, the prolonged anguish of those left behind to mourn them."[9]

Across the South the shock of defeat and the assimilation of its meaning proved painful tonics to swallow. Gone were the high talk and windy speeches of the early days of the rebellion, replaced now with more moderate goals and more temperate language. A new strategy was called for, and over time Robert E. Lee settled upon a Fabian strategy of delay. "If a decisive victory, the battle of annihilation, could not be realized, what else could Lee do to satisfy his exacting personal sense of duty and honor? In time, he would fashion a new mission for himself. No longer would he and his army be the means to ultimate victory; instead they would be a thorn in the enemy's side, delaying and embarrassing Lincoln's general designs. In this way, Lee and his men might just buy Jefferson Davis enough time to work out a political settlement that would preserve the Confederacy."[10]

In North Carolina, as across the remainder of the South, the implosion of Confederate offensive capabilities in Virginia meant a redoubling of defensive efforts elsewhere. If victory could not be gained through winning, it might still be gained by not *losing*; and in North Carolina the accomplishment of this goal would require, now more than ever, watercraft suitable to the task. For Gilbert Elliott and Commander Cooke, work continued slowly but steadily upon the ironclad in the cornfield at Edwards Ferry; and as the ram gradually took shape, their efforts naturally came to the attention of the Federal Navy. Indeed, in mid–August Admiral Lee sent a report to Gideon Welles informing him of the looming danger the ram seemed to represent. "The ironclad on the Roanoke at Edwards Ferry," he wrote, "40 miles above Rainbow Bluff, heretofore reported to the Department, is considered by Lt. Commander Flusser as a formidable affair, though of light draft. The fortifications at Rainbow Bluff, and the low stage of water in the river, make it impracticable for the navy to destroy her before completion, which is reported near."[11] On the Federal side there was talk of a land expedition to take out the ironclad, and the possibility of bringing their own ironclads into the sounds, but the infantry could not be marshaled to the task, and the monitors all drew too much water to enter the sounds. So for the time being, at least, the construction at Edward's Ferry appeared safe.

For Gilbert Elliott the critical piece finally fell into place with the long anticipated cooperation of the North Carolina government in the procurement of iron. The iron at Besse's Station and a second load at Laurinburg had been approved for removal. Indeed, so consistent and far-flung had been Commander Cooke's efforts to procure iron from every conceivable source in the state — rakes, wheels, shovels, etc.— that he had inherited the somewhat dubious nickname of the Ironmonger Captain.[12] "Cooke had gathered men, mules and wagons for the Herculean task of loading and carting 450 tons of rail road iron stored at Besse's Station. Whoever he had selected as supervisor performed his task expeditiously.... The important fact was that procurement of railroad iron had proven successful. It can be assumed the rails were shipped to Tredegar in Richmond, since they had stated '30 tons of plates could be rolled daily.'"[13]

With framing complete, and iron now on hand, it was determined to remove the vessel from the stocks and "launch" her upon the Roanoke. This command came from Flag Officer Lynch, who was becoming increasingly concerned by reports of a potential Federal assault on the vessel. The launch was considered by Elliott as premature, but was accomplished nevertheless on October 6, 1863, to both the joy and amazement of the local population. "There were animals heaving on taught lines with teamsters encouraging them on with shouts and with cracking of whips. Other workers were seen using long poles with swabs attached, with which they applied more grease to the ways. Elliott was observed by all, as he hurried from one area to another offering encouragement to some, and words of caution to others."[14] Elliott himself later recalled, "Seizing an opportunity offered by comparatively high water, the boat was launched, though not without misgivings as to the result, for the yard being on a bluff she had to take a jump, and as a matter of fact was 'hogged' in the attempt, but to our great gratification did not thereby spring a leak."[15]

Catherine Edmondston, along with most of her friends and neighbors, had traveled from her plantation home down to the river's edge to take in the event, but due to the hour, had left before the grand finale. "On Monday, sue & I escorted by him [James, her brother-in-law] went down to see the gunboat launched, but like most of her sex she was uncertain & disappointing & beyond seeing all our neighbors assembled, we had our ride for nothing. She, however, took her future element without accident we heard at three o'clock the next morning, her builders being forced to wait for the moon to rise ere they could persuade the coy maiden to venture upon the slippery '*ways*' that lead to the water."[16]

With the boat finally in the water, work on the iron casement could begin in earnest; but this, like all construction without proper tools, proved cumbersome, time-consuming, and virtually futile. Elliott describes the difficulties encountered. "The work of putting on the armor was prosecuted for some time under the most disheartening circumstances, on account of the difficulty of drilling holes in the iron intended for her armor. But one small engine and drill could be had, and it required, at the best, twenty minutes to drill an inch and a quarter hole through the plates, and it looked as if we would never accomplish the task." At that extraordinarily slow rate, the application of the iron casemate would take a year, and the war might well be over by the time the ironclad was finally finished, if ever. "But 'necessity is the

11. The Good Ship Albemarle

The CSS *Albemarle* on the Roanoke River (U.S. Naval History and Heritage Command).

mother of invention,'" Elliott reaffirmed, "and one of my associates in the enterprise, Peter E. Smith, of Scotland Neck, North Carolina, invented and made a twist-drill with which the work of drilling a hole could be done in four minutes, the drill cutting out the iron in shavings instead of fine powder."[17]

With the proper drill in hand, work on laying the iron plating could proceed with dispatch. But this was no easy job, as the casemate was designed for thickness in order to withstand virtually point-blank shots from rifled naval guns. Once again, Gilbert Elliott explains the system that was utilized. "The iron plating consisted of two courses, 7 inches wide and 2 inches thick, mostly rolled at the Tredgar Iron Works, Richmond. The first course was laid lengthwise, over a wooden backing, 16 inches in thickness, a 2-inch space, filled in with wood, being left between each two layers to afford space for bolting the outer course through the whole shield, and the outer course was laid flush, forming a smooth surface, similar to that of the *Virginia*. The inner part of the shield was covered in a thin course of planking, nicely dressed, mainly with a view to protection from splinters. Oak knees were bolted in, to act as braces and supports for the shield."[18]

With workmen aplenty, tools now crafted especially for the job, and the necessary iron finally at hand, it surely seemed that time alone was the only obstacle now standing in the way of the ironclad's completion. This was not to be, but at least the boat was in the water, and at long last she had a name. A Confederate officer recalled the ram's christening. "The building of the iron-clad, under all the disadvantages of place and circumstances, was viewed by the community as a chimerical absurdity. Great was the general astonishment when it became known that the indomitable commander had conquered all obstacles and was about to launch his bantling. On the appointed day 'Cooke & Company' committed their 'nonesuch' to the turbid waters of the Roanoke, christening her, as she glided from the launching ways, 'the good ship *Albemarle.*'"[19]

Thus had the *Albemarle* at long last tasted water. Soon she would have to be reckoned with.

CHAPTER 12

Shokokon to Monticello

FOR THE MONTH FOLLOWING his brother's death, William Barker Cushing brooded through weeks of inactivity.[1] The *Commodore Barney*, too shot up to be made seaworthy again, had been withdrawn from service, and Will had yet to receive another assignment.[2] That assignment would finally arrive in August, and Will was soon back at sea on blockade duty.

His new boat was the USS *Shokokon*, a weathered ferryboat that, due to its light draft, was considered capable by some of slipping over the bar into the inland areas of Wilmington Harbor and once there causing trouble for Confederate commerce.[3] Such a notion appealed not only to Naval Command's desire to close the port of Wilmington, but William Cushing's basic aggressive instincts as well, and thus this new vessel embodied these twin aspirations. The *Shokokon* was a fast ferryboat, but whose seaworthiness was in serious question. But seaworthy or not, the vessel represented a new command and a new adventure, and soon Cushing was back on the high seas, joining the blockade just off of New Inlet.

Placed at the southern extreme of the blockading line, Cushing's task was to closely observe the comings and goings on Smith Island and the surrounding waters, a traditional hot spot for blockade runners. The Confederates proved accommodating, however, and the wait for action a short one. In August, and in the waters just a few miles off Fort Fisher, the blockader *Niphon* ran across the Confederate runner *Hebe* attempting to dash through the blockade into Wilmington through New Inlet Channel. The *Hebe*, "carrying a cargo of drugs, clothing, coffee, and provisions,"[4] was promptly run aground at Federal Point.[5] While the crew of the stranded raider fled up the beach, the *Niphon* and the *Shokokon* closed on the stranded raider. Landing parties were sent in to try and retrieve the vessel, and it was presumed the prize would be easily taken or, if not captured, at least scuttled.

But the surf was rough, and the landing parties became stranded. To make matters far worse, Confederate forces soon returned to the beach, well armed and looking for a fight. More boats with sailors were sent in to try and rescue the stranded men, but while one got through and some minimal rescue was accomplished, other boats foundered or were driven onto the beach and into the hands of the waiting Rebels. Unable to save his own men, Cushing waited until his stranded sailors had made their way safely off the beached vessel and surrendered, and then closed to within almost one hundred yards and tore away at the stranded *Hebe*, chewing the vessel to pieces and ultimately setting her on fire. The Confederates answered with artillery and small arms fire of their own; but this did no damage, and failed entirely in saving either the structure or cargo of the stranded blockade runner. But for Will Cushing, the destruction of the Rebel vessel could not make up for the loss of crew and boats; and he fumed over the incident for days, and was determined to even the score.

That opportunity would not be long in coming. Reconnaissance had determined that a sizeable schooner was tied up in New Topsail Inlet, some six miles up the channel. Will promptly proposed an operation to cut the schooner out by means of sending men in on a dinghy from below the Confederate defenses; but the local commanders thought the idea far too dangerous and vetoed the proposal. Perhaps still smarting from the loss of men and boats, or perhaps still hurting from the loss of his brother, Will Cushing made the unusual decision to ignore orders and attempt to cut the schooner out anyway. It was a rash decision, but not a rash plan. "Instead of going in at the mouth of the inlet; I took ashore, four miles above it," Cushing explained, "two boat's crews, made them shoulder the dingy (a very small boat) and carry it across the neck of land; launching it in the reeds, two miles from the blockade runner and in a position entirely outflanking the main battery."[6, 7]

At a distance the *Shokokon* had been spotted by the Rebels, and all the local defenses put on alert as to her presence. The landing party consisted of only seven men, and they silently paddled the dingy down to the where the schooner was moored, performed a quick reconnaissance, and although substantially outnumbered, decided to make a direct and immediate assault. Screaming at the top of their lungs, they stormed into the Confederate camp and quickly overwhelmed the startled defenders and crew. As T.W. Haight notes, Cushing "took ten prisoners, burned the vessel and some valuable salt works, threw the shore armament in the water,"[8] and all without losing a single man. For a party of only seven men, the lighting assault had been a remarkable achievement.

But the Federal sailors were not yet out of the woods. Night was falling, and it was determined that they could not make their way back to the *Shokokon* until morning. Gaming their prisoners with constant shouts to nonexistent boats and pretend Union commands throughout the night, they were able to keep up the ruse that the small landing party was in fact an active part of a much larger Federal operation soon to come ashore. "A great show of orders was therefore made," Cushing explained, "to imaginary boats off upon the water, and ordering three of the prisoners into the dingy, to be there to receive them."[9] The beleaguered Rebel prisoners, sure they were surrounded by a large combined contingent of Union land and naval resources, offered no resistance, although they did in fact outnumber their captors almost two to one.

Come morning several prisoners — thought to be the officers — were herded back to the *Shokokon,* while yet another trick was played on the remainder. "The rest [of the prisoners] were instructed to go a quarter of a mile up the bank and report to a 'Lt. Jones' who was supposed to be there to receive them. They were cautioned not to go too far out, or our pickets might shoot them, and went off without an idea of the smallness of our force, or our inability to take them with us."[10] As the nine Confederates started off to dutifully report to the nonexistent officer, the remainder of the landing party recrossed that narrow portion of the outer bank that led to the sea, and eventually the safety of the *Shokokon.* It had been a small success for sure, but nevertheless an ingenious one, cleverly executed, all done without the loss of a single man. The result hardly hurt William Cushing's growing reputation for both daring and stunning success.

Unfortunately, just days after completion of the successful raid at New Topsail Inlet, a serious storm rolled in, and the *Shokokon,* hardly seaworthy to begin with, took a terrible beating. Cushing had run her in and anchored on the lee side of Smith Island to try and ride out the storm, but even so the winds were terrific, the seas high, and the *Shokokon* took a pounding in the waves. "Sponsons torn off or crushed," Will reported afterward, "forward decks started and seams opened, forward ports carried away, and sternpost split ... wood ends opened about a half inch."[11] The poor *Shokokon* came virtually apart at the seams and began taking on a large volume of water. That Will Cushing was able to keep her afloat proved almost a miracle, but once the skies cleared, and the extent of her damages computed, it was determined to send the reeling vessel back to Hampton Roads for repairs.

The battered *Shokokon* limped back into port for extensive repairs where, due to his most recent exploits, new and bigger things awaited William Cushing. The Naval Department — in particular Gideon Welles — had become so impressed with Cushing's record of daring success, it had determined to allow him to captain one of the finest warships in the fleet—a far cry from the humble *Shokokon*! Assistant Secretary Gus Fox met with Will and assigned him to the command of the fleet *Monticello,* advising Will, "You are ordered to this command for distinguished services rendered."[12]

William Cushing, still only twenty years of age, had been given command of one of the most exceptional ships the Federal Navy could offer, and the young lieutenant rushed off for Philadelphia where the *Monticello* was then undergoing extensive repairs. No doubt bursting with pride as he first laid eyes upon her, he found a ship immensely different from anything he had commanded before. She was well armed and fast, a beautiful vessel by any standard. Lean, sleek, and low in the water, the *Monticello* was painted a dazzling black with her name printed in gold letters along the bow. No doubt it was love at first sight, and Cushing probably had his breath taken away when he first laid eyes upon her, for Will thought without question that the *Monticello* was "the most beautiful ship in the navy."[13]

But work on the *Monticello* proved slow, and Cushing once again felt the listless itch of inactivity. He briefly visited home, but found that he could no longer abide the relaxed pace of rural Fredonia nor his mother's unspoken grief. He fretted, became irritable, and found excuses to leave.[14] He took a train back down to Philadelphia, but the work on the ship continued to drag, and he became despondent over ever getting back out to sea.

On the 19th of November, Will Cushing took the train up to Gettysburg in order to be present at the dedication of the new National Cemetery. It was a significant event, and attracted notables from all across the North. Indeed, so intense was the crowd and limited the traveling facilities, that many of the dignitaries scheduled to be present got caught up en route, and failed to make a timely appearance. Over 20,000 visitors crammed the small Pennsylvania town of only 2,500, and Cushing was lucky to have gotten through on the train. Perhaps upon arrival he took the walk from the train station on the west side of town down Baltimore Street, then out the Emmitsburg Road to the stone wall where Alonzo had perished for a quiet moment of reflection.

President Lincoln had been invited to provide a few words at the ceremony, but Edward Everett, not Lincoln, was the keynote speaker of the day. "Everett was that rare thing, a scholar and Ivy-League diplomat who could hold mass audiences in thrall. His voice, diction, and gestures were successfully dramatic, and he always performed his carefully written text, no matter how long, from memory. Everett was the inevitable choice for Wills [the event's organizer], the indispensable component in his scheme for the cemetery's consecration."[15]

President Lincoln was not an afterthought at the event, but neither was he expected to speak at length or offer anything of great substance. In the early morning hours the President and the Secretary of War had taken a brief tour of the battlefield, and by 11:00 A.M. were ready for the ride up to the cemetery. "Lincoln sat his horse gracefully (to the surprise of some), and looked meditative during the long wait while marshals tried to coax into line important people more concerned with their dignity than the President was with his. Lincoln was wearing a mourning band on his hat for his dead son. He also wore white gauntlets, which made his large hands on the reins dramatic by contrast with his otherwise black attire."[16]

Everett was first to speak, and he arose and spoke for over two hours, detailing, not only the facts of the great battle, but placing those facts within a larger framework of war and sacrifice. By all accounts, his speech was well delivered and well received. "The setting of the battle in a larger logic of campaigns had an immediacy for those on the scene that we cannot recover. Everett's familiarity with the details was flattering to the local audience, which nonetheless had things to learn from this shapely presentation of the whole three days' action."[17]

When Everett finally took his seat, Lincoln rose. He spoke all of 272 words, and was said to be done in only three minutes. Will Cushing, far to the rear in the audience, strained to hear the President's message, but could not pick up a word. He left Gettysburg frustrated. "Will returned to Washington, disappointed, and read the President's speech the next day."[18] This is what Will Cushing read:

> Four score and seven years ago our fathers brought forth on this continent, a new nation, conceived in Liberty, and dedicated to the proposition that all men are created equal. Now we are engaged in a great civil war, testing whether that nation, or any nation so conceived and so dedicated, can long endure. We are met on a great battle-field of that war. We have come to dedicate a portion of that field, as a final resting place for those who here gave their lives that that nation might live. It is altogether fitting and proper that we should do this. But, in a larger sense, we can not dedicate — we can not consecrate — we can not hallow — this ground. The brave men, living and dead, who struggled here, have consecrated it, far above our poor power to add or detract. The world will little note, nor long remember what we say here, but it can never forget what they did here. It is for us the living, rather, to be dedicated here to the unfinished work which they who fought here have thus far so nobly advanced. It is rather for us to be here dedicated to the great task remaining before us — that from these honored dead we take increased devotion to that cause for which they gave the last full measure of devotion — that we here highly resolve that these dead shall not have died in vain — that this nation, under God, shall have a new birth of freedom — and that government of the people, by the people, for the people, shall not perish from the earth.[19]

Perhaps after reading President Lincoln's short speech William Cushing had a greater sense of the war, and of his own brother's death — that his brother had died, as Lincoln had phrased it, so that the nation might live. Or perhaps it made no significant impression upon him at all, and he was left with only the gnawing sense of loss that had dogged his days since that fateful July 3. That Lincoln's speech came to signify over time the very meaning of the war, and in a sense the metamorphosis of a nation, does not mean that it moved a troubled young man, lost in mourning. No one will ever know.

Chapter 13

Winter Offensive

WITH THE COMING OF WINTER and the arrival of yet another year of war, in Richmond plans were afoot for a new wrinkle that might simultaneously reduce the Federal control of eastern North Carolina, while providing the government in Richmond some much needed room to breathe. On January 2, 1864, Robert E. Lee wrote to Jefferson Davis and suggested a combined land sea offensive to retake New Berne, North Carolina.[1] The point was to open the sounds again to commerce and restore much of the fertile, food producing regions of Carolina to Confederate control. With both the Army of Northern Virginia, and their adversary, the Army of the Potomac, in winter quarters, Lee pointed out that he could spare the requisite troops for such an operation, but only if completed before spring, when he would once again be confronted by an aggressive opponent on the move. It was Lee's conception that two brigades of infantry, supported by the ironclads then under construction in North Carolina on the Neuse and Roanoke Rivers, would constitute an ample force for the task. Unfortunately, due to the endless setbacks regarding iron, neither vessel was immediately available, and on January 4 Jefferson Davis replied to Lee's inquiry. "The progress on the boats," Davis advised his general, "on the Neuse and Roanoke is slow and too uncertain to fix a date for completion, your suggestion is approved."[2]

Despite the lack of naval support, the mission was deemed so important it was decided that an attempt should be made at any rate, thus planning went ahead and an expedition launched later that month. "Late in January, under orders from Lee's headquarters, Maj. Gen. George E. Pickett undertook to capture the town of New Berne. He was allotted infantry who seemed entirely adequate for the purpose and, in addition, he was to enjoy the co-operation of a force of naval commandos, under Col. J. Taylor Wood, one of the most daring of Confederate leaders. Through poor planning and probably because of defective intelligence service and the slowness of Brig. Gen Seth M. Barton, the expedition failed."[3]

When that expedition met with failure, a new plan, devised by General Braxton Bragg — now in Richmond as President Davis' advisor — was developed. This plan initially called for a movement once more against New Berne, but in addition added an additional assault against Plymouth, a town below Halifax on the Roanoke River. General Robert Hoke, who had been with Pickett during the original New Berne fiasco, remained in the area under orders to try and coordinate the attacks, but ultimately Bragg turned his attention solely toward Plymouth. "Hoke was to take the lead. With him were to work the crew of the Confederate ram *Albemarle* which was then nearing completion farther up the Roanoke River. Tactfully Bragg disposed of Pickett by explaining that the expedition had been entrusted to General Hoke 'so as not to withdraw you from a supervision of your whole department at this critical time.'"[4]

Suddenly the completion of the *Albemarle* had taken on a whole new meaning and sense of importance. If the vessel could be completed soon, it might well be the centerpiece of a Confederate offensive in North Carolina that might not only open those areas under firm federal authority again to Confederate control, but ultimately provide a much needed pipeline of food and material to Richmond — and ultimately Lee's army — without which the Confederate war effort might wither.

That was all well and good, but a new problem quickly reared its head. The construction time line on the *Albemarle* might have been far more respectable had not Flag Officer Lynch suddenly become involved in an oblique and questionable way. Either out of genuine concern for the project's integrity, or a desire for authority and credit undue him, Lynch interceded directly in the project, and initiated a number of vexing problems for Elliott and Cooke. "The *Albemarle*'s premature launch, as directed by Flag Officer Lynch, was the beginning of a series of written accusations, rebuttals, and complaints, each of a recriminatory nature. Principals in the unfolding tableau were Flag Officer Lynch, Commander Cooke, Gilbert Elliott, Governor Vance, and Secretary Mallory. Difficulties included a jurisdictional dispute over how and when the vessel would be completed, and who would be responsible for the work."[5]

After forcing the ram to be launched prematurely, when the structure was not yet sufficient, and the water in the river still too low — an order that caused the craft to be 'hogged" or twisted unnecessarily — Lynch insisted that the entire project be moved back to the Halifax Yard for completion, the first step in what appeared to be an effort to gain control. Lynch then began a campaign of intrigue and accusation to have Elliott removed from his contract, and the ironclad placed under his own jurisdiction. Cooke and Elliott, dismayed by Lynch's shenanigans, had dinner with Catherine Edmondston one evening, and could barely conceal their dismay. After hearing them out, she later sharpened her most venomous pen and wrote, "Commander Lynch, that little great man, is ordered to Wilmington & has interest enough to get the iron intended for the *Albamarle* transferred with him to that point to be put on a gunboat in process of construction there. It was originally brought from Wilmington so that the freight on it going & coming & expenses incident to so many handlings will make it mount up to $5 per lb, before it is finally fixed in its place. But what can we expect of a pudding headed bag of wind like Secy Mallory & a man who has weakened the little judgment he originally possessed by opium eating, as Comm Lynch has done, when they meet in conjunction."[6]

For two months letters and accusations flew every which way, and work on the ironclad was unnecessarily delayed by Lynch's detouring iron bound for the *Albemarle* to Atlanta. Both the *Albemarle* and the *Neuse* had been, at Lynch's insistence, launched early without their engines installed, and those premature launchings had caused a variety of serious construction problems and additional delays. But what goes around soon comes around, as is said, and Lynch's conniving and poor decision making finally backfired. Rather than providing him the praise and authority he had been courting, his scheming became commonly known and eventually blew-up in his face. Fuming over the rank mismanagement of the ironclad projects, Governor Vance wrote directly to Secretary Mallory regarding the situation, complaining of Lynch's involvement in no uncertain terms. "I beg to call your attention to the enclosed letter from Lt. G. Elliott in regards to the gun boat *Albemarle*," he wrote. "I endorse the statement fully in regards to the delay and blunders of Flag Officer Lynch. I am satisfied of his total and utter incapacity for the duties of his position," he went on, "which has for some time been evident to the whole State.

"The iron furnished by the State under express promises of both himself and you has been applied to other purposes and our rivers are yet at the mercy of the most contemptible boat of the Yankee Navy," the governor pointed out angrily.

"The '*Neuse*' has been launched and her iron plates put on without her machinery and in the face of the known fact that it will all have to come off before the machinery does go in. Many other ridiculous things have been done merely to keep the hands employed and deceive the public for it cannot deceive the enemy.

"In short Sir," the governor began his heated conclusion, "I am so out of heart in the matter that if the water defenses of NC are to continue in the hands of Commander Lynch, I feel it useless and will decline to furnish any more iron or other assistance whatsoever. It would be labor and machinery thrown away. I desire of course that Lt. Elliott should be allowed to finish the boat."[7]

With that, and with General Lee's original suggestion of a winter offensive in North Carolina, Commander Lynch's meddling desisted, and control of the construction of the *Albemarle* was sensibly returned to Cooke and Elliott. In the words of Gilbert Elliott, "For many reasons it was thought judicious to remove the boat to the town of Halifax, about twenty miles up the river, and the work of completion, putting in her machinery, armament, etc., was done at that point, although the actual finishing touches were not given until a few days before going into action at Plymouth."[8] At the Halifax yards, then, work picked up considerably. The engines and naval guns were installed, and the ironclad began to take on the appearance of a fearsome ship of war. Gilbert Elliott again provides the details: "The armament consisted of two rifled 'Brooke' guns mounted on pivot-carriages, each gun working through three port-holes, as occasion required, there being one port-hole at each end of the shield and two on each side. These were protected by iron covers lowered and raised by a contrivance worked on the gun-deck. She had two propellers driven by two engines of 200-horse power each, with 20-inch cylinders, steam being supplied by two flue boilers, and the shafting was geared together."[9]

With Pickett's failure to secure New Berne in early January, immediate steps were taken to prepare for another attempt. First, James Cooke received orders placing him in command of the *Albemarle* and requesting that he do everything possible to expedite the completion of the project. Then, anxious to move the prospects of a successful offensive along, Lee again wrote to Jefferson Davis in late January: "I regret very much that the boats on the Neuse and Roanoke are not completed," he stated. "With their aid I think success would be certain. Without them, though the place may be captured, the fruits of the expedition will be lessened and our maintenance of the command of the waters in North Carolina uncertain. I think every effort should be made now to get them into service as soon as possible."[10]

In the Southern Confederacy, Robert E. Lee's wishes were not taken lightly, and in February Governor Vance sent an independent observer to the Halifax yard to provide a report regarding the conditions and progress of the ironclad. Colonel James Hinton, commanding a regiment of infantry in nearby North Carolina, was charged with the mission, and soon after offered his positive report. "I arrived at this place late yesterday evening," he wrote. "Captain

Cooke has arrived here and the work on the gunboat is progressing finely. He is not trammeled at all by Lynch's old fogyism. We have no two-inch iron here, the difficulty being to get transportation for it on the Wilmington Road. I have just dispatched Elliot to Wilmington with an urgent appeal to the master of transportation to let the iron come up at once. If the boat is not delayed for want of iron, she will be completed in thirty days."[11]

In mid–February Catherine Edmondston traveled upriver from Scotland Neck and paid a visit on the gunboat at the Halifax yard. She, like Hinton before her, was impressed with the remarkable progress, and was convinced the boat would be ready to head downriver and take on the Yankee flotilla in a matter of weeks only. She wrote: "Went to see the Navy Yard and the gunboat *Albemarle*, our old acquaintance upon whom we waited until dark last summer at Edwards Ferry to see her take her proper element. She is now nearly completed, engines & propeller in & will, if the Department at Richmond send on the iron to complete her armour, steam down the river next month. Captain Cooke is in command of the station & his energy & decision in getting so much accomplished in so short a time is surprising. Saw some of the famous Brooke Guns, much smaller in the bore than I had supposed."[12]

Thus had the suggestion of a winter offensive from on high brought about sudden and rapid changes in the completion of the *Albemarle*. Both Catherine Edmondston's and Colonel Hinton's assessments would prove reasonably accurate, and the ironclad, years now in the planning and construction stages, would soon be ready to make her maiden voyage down the Roanoke to test, not only her own seaworthiness and power, but the strength of the Federal flotilla that had been accumulated for her reception. One or the other would have to give.

CHAPTER 14

The Essence of Impudence

So far, all had gone as planned. It was February 29, 1864.[1] The gig and small cutter loaded with Yankee sailors slipped through the darkness in detail, then started up the Cape Fear River toward the small town of Smithville, North Carolina, slicing across the water almost silently on muffled oars.[2] All day Will Cushing, aboard the *Monticello*, had lurked at the mouth of the river, waiting for darkness to fall, anxious to initiate a bold new plan. Now the plan was in full action, and if his scheme worked as designed, he would put a crimp in Confederate commerce on the Cape Fear River near Wilmington.

The city of Wilmington, North Carolina, sits some thirty miles up the Cape Fear River from the ocean. Near the river's mouth, the Cape Fear has two separate channels leading out to the Atlantic, one that runs eastward called New Inlet, and the other to the south named the Western Bar Channel. Smithville, somewhat in the center of the two channels, was used by most blockade runners as the jumping off point for their dashes out past the Federal blockade. At Smithville they would hover until it was determined which channel might be more advantageous on any given occasion, then dart out and make a run for it past the blockading fleet. Two Confederate forts guarded the channels: Fort Fisher just north of New Inlet, and Fort Caswell at the river's mouth on the Western Bar Channel. The blockade runners that were returning with cargo would wait off shore until dark, then race through the fleet until they were under the guns of one fort or the other, there safe at last from further Yankee pursuit. Thus either coming or going, the area had developed into a critical problem for the Federal blockade, and a problem that had eventually to be resolved.

Cushing had arrived off the Cape Fear River on February 17 after having finally taken command of the rakish *Monticello* in late January. "She was beautiful, her captain thought: sleek and long and shiny black, with her guns oiled and ready for carnage, her engines in perfect order, her sails new and clean."[3] The Navy had allowed him to pick his own crew, and he chose the very best men he could find. Naturally, Will Cushing chose them not simply for their nautical skills, but for their audacity, their personalities, and how well they could handle a carbine and cutlass. Among them were Acting Master's Mate William Howorth and Acting Ensign J.E. Jones, two officers with whom he would come to share many an adventure.

Since arriving off the mouth of the Cape Fear, Cushing had taken a cutter in past the forts late at night on more than one occasion, and while driven off, he'd become convinced that he could sneak unnoticed onto Smith Island.[4] His first plan had been to go ashore with two hundred sailors and hold the island until the army could arrive in force. That would have been a touchy chore, sure to be aggressively resisted by the Rebels who had the island garrisoned with something over a thousand men; but success would have closed one channel to the runners, and allowed the blockading fleet to concentrate on the other. No matter, his plan had been rejected by his senior officer, but Will remained determined to accomplish something significant nevertheless. "I could have affected this result with two hundred men," he insisted, "but as usual met the reply to my proposal — 'Can't take the responsibility.' This, I confess provoked me — and I told the Senior Officer that I could not only do that; but if he wanted the Confederate General off to breakfast I would bring him. I then left and went to my ship."[5]

That night they had shoved off from the *Monticello* around 8:30 P.M., some twenty sailors in a gig and cutter, both craft with carefully muffled oars.[6] Cushing did not have approval for the venture, but he did have his roving commission, and for William Cushing that seemed orders enough. After shoving off from the *Monticello* the party slipped past Fort Caswell in the darkness, "pulled by the forts and straight up the river to the town of Smithville, the rebel headquarters. I knew nothing of it," Cushing admitted, "excepting that fact, and its position on the chart; but my plan was too bold to fail."[7]

As they approached the town, a lone sentinel was observed on the wharf. The small expedition rowed quietly beyond the sentry and found a suitable spot to pull onto the shore unobserved about 50 yards from the Confederate guard.[8] "I succeeded in landing right in front of the hotel not thirty yards from the angle of the fort, in the centre of the town, and hid my men under the bluff," Cushing explained.[9] After positioning his men along the small bluff overhanging the river, Cushing slipped down to a salt works near the point and captured two black men who were still hard at work. The two proved cooperative, and quickly provided Cushing the rough layout of the town and the information he required. "My object," Will later explained, "was to take the Commanding General from his bed, in the middle of his men and to take him out of the harbor in one of his own steamers. But alas! no steamer was there."[10] While the steamer would have provided a quick and simple exit — not to mention a nice flourish — it was not a prerequisite for success. While it would certainly be more difficult, dangerous, and time-consuming, the Commanding General could still be snatched and rowed out to the *Monticello*. Thus the effort would go on as planned.

Cushing started up the main street with Acting Ensign J.E Jones and Acting Master's Mate W.L. Howorth along with one additional seaman close behind. Will also had one of the two black men lead the way toward the general's house.[11] The journey proved a short one. Cushing recalls: "Leaving most of the sailors in ambush I crept up the street with the negro guide and two of my officers, soon reaching a large house with the southern veranda — the general's residence."[12]

Just ahead, the black man pointed through the darkness, the Confederate barracks was located where, Cushing knew, a garrison of perhaps a thousand Rebels lay sound asleep. The distance from the house to the barracks was no more than fifty feet, and Will knew at once that with the enemy quartered so nearby there would be no margin for error. The slightest slip up might have a thousand Rebels on top of them before they could blink.

Cushing sent the black man back down to rejoin his companion, then split his small party, placing each remaining man on a different exterior wall of the general's residence to assure no premature escape. That accomplished, he slipped gently onto the front porch and felt his way along toward the door. "The windows were dark, but one was open, and the curtains blew in the wind. The door was open, and Cushing entered softly and closed the door behind him."[13] It is easy to imagine Will Cushing's emotions at the moment, his heart pounding lightly in his chest, the uncertainty brought on by total darkness, the confusion of an unknown household. He was in the center hall of a large home. Straight ahead he could just make out the contours of a long hallway, above that a very high ceiling, arching up toward the top of the house. Just off to his right there was a large room with a table, chairs, and silver — no doubt the dining room — while on his left above a ticking clock loomed a set of stairs leading up toward the second floor.[14] He did not hesitate, but started up the steps immediately, pistol in hand. He took each step carefully, and arrived on the second floor, still undetected.

Here on the upstairs landing it was too dark to see, so Cushing pulled a match from his pant's pocket and struck it.[15] The light flared like a beacon all around him, momentarily flooding the landing with a radiant, orange flash.

He looked about quickly, saw several doors along a long hallway, decided to open one when the match burned out. He had just grabbed the door knob when a commotion came up to him from downstairs.

"Captain! Captain!"[16] It was Howorth. What did it mean? Trouble?

Cushing bounded back down the stairs then raced through a hallway toward where he thought the sound had come. He shoved open a door, leaped into another black space, could see nothing, immediately grabbed for, found, and struck another match. Dead ahead stood a man in a night gown holding a chair above his head, apparently determined to crush the first intruder that neared him. Without so much as a thought Cushing rushed the man, tackling him to the floor. "Dashing in at once," Will later explained, "I had him on his back in an instant with the muzzle of a revolver at his temple and my hand on his throat."[17] Will struck another match, then lit a nearby candle, only to discover that he had not captured General Hébert after all, but rather a Captain Kelly who turned out to be the chief engineer for defense of the entire port. Kelly's capture was no doubt a small intelligence coup, as he could provide sophisticated information on the port's interior defenses, and Will quickly had him put on a pair of pants, and prepared to leave with the raiding party. General Hébert, Kelly explained, had gone off for the night to Wilmington, and was not expected back until the morning. That was a pity, but there was no time to lose.

Just then Howorth burst into the room in a panic, hissing that he had seen a man run from the house up toward the Confederate barracks nearby. No doubt, Howorth presumed, the man would spread the alarm. "It seems," Cushing later discovered, "that his bed was close to the window and hearing a noise, he arose and looked out. The first sight that met his eye was the muzzle of a navy revolver about two inches from his nose. Down went the window with a crash and the fearfully demoralized officer wrenching his arm through — dashed out the back door — in garments hardly fitted for display. It was a good joke but not exactly the time for me to laugh at it, as I knew that soldiers would swarm out like angry bees in a minute."[18] There was little question that this spelled trouble for Will and his small party. One thousand to twenty were hardly good odds. Cushing and Howorth quickly grabbed whatever papers were lying around loosely just in case they might be of importance, took hold of Captain Kelly, and headed back outside toward the boats.

But out on the street things had changed radically. The quiet town they had just come through on the way up to the general's house had already been turned upside down. "The alarm had been given by this time and the streets were full of running men,"[19] but the Rebels, apparently in a panic now themselves, hardly knew what they were looking for, or just where, for that matter, to look. They knew only that a vague report of Yankees had been received, and just what it meant was unknown. As a result they were "looking everywhere but in the right place," as Will later wrote, "like the old gent with the spectacles on his forehead."[20] The Confederates, presuming in all probability that whatever Yankees had landed on the island would be hiding in the most discreet and concealed locations, were off looking everywhere but where Cushing and his small party were actually located — which happened to be right on the town's main street.

Responding coolly to the situation, Will Cushing took his three men along with Captain Kelly (with Will's pistol planted firmly in the Rebel captain's side) straight back down the main street of town — as Confederate search parties ran every which way around them — walking nonchalantly toward the water just the way they had come up. "Nobody paid any attention to them, though once a party of searchers almost knocked them down when they ran around a corner."[21] As they walked back down to the river, Cushing picked up the men he had detailed along the way, and the two black men from the salt works who preferred to leave for freedom. All falling in line, the Yankees marched unhurriedly through a Confederate storm of confusion back to their boats; never once being spotted, never once being challenged.

The entire landing party, safe and sound, including the two black men and Captain Kelly, were then piled into the gig and cutter, and quickly the boats were turned out into the river. Soon a few rifle shots were heard along the riverbank, and balls began to splash in the water, but few nearby and no one was injured. The men rowed hard, mindful that the *Monticello* was still far off, and that there were Confederate stations along the riverbanks for miles that could still create problems. Cushing would later write in his official report of the mission: "My boat was about 50 yards from the Smithville fort, and not so far from the sentinel on the wharf, but I succeeded in bringing my prisoner off so quietly that they did not discover me. The signal lights were made so tardily that I was abreast of Fort Caswell before they knew that boats were in the harbor, and they did not get a shot at us."[22]

It had proven a spectacular operation, well planned, coolly executed, and properly rewarded. By 3:25 A.M.[23] they were back aboard the *Monticello* where Cushing provided Captain Kelly some comfortable clothes, a glass of sherry, and a bunk for what remained of the night. Bright and early Cushing then had Kelly rowed over to the commanding officer's table for breakfast, just as he had boasted he would. It can only be imagined what sort of scene that introduction might have caused.

Late that afternoon Lieutenant Cushing had Ensign Jones rowed back to Fort Caswell under a flag of truce. His mission was to secure Captain Kelly's personal belongings, and Jones was at once properly conducted to the Colonel who commanded the fort, who met him along the beach. The Colonel was at first cool toward the Federal ensign and, considering the circumstances, it can be understood why — the Confederates had been made to look amateurish by the lightning success of Cushing's raid. "They walked up and down the beach in silence and passed each other several times, when the rebel wheeled sharply and suddenly round and exclaimed 'That was a d — d splendid affair, Sir.' This broke the ice, and a chat ensued; soon joined in by the Adjutant General [who had been injured escaping the general's residence the night before], with arm in sling, and limping from the effects of his impromptu promenade of the night before."[24] Adjutant General Hardeman proved to be in no mood for pleasantries.[25]

Ensign Jones then produced a note written by Will Cushing and meant for General Hébert, but in that the general was still off to Wilmington on his visit, Jones turned it over to the good Colonel instead. It read:

My Dear General:
I deeply regret that you were not at home when I called.
Very respectfully,
W.B. Cushing.[26]

Neither the Colonel nor his adjutant were particularly pleased by the note, indeed declared it the absolute "essence of impudence,"[27] but accepted it nevertheless. Then the Confederate colonel, who apparently had a keen appreciation for excellence no matter what uniform it wore, provided Ensign Jones with copies of the local newspaper, "which contained a story of the affair highly complimentary to Cushing."[28] The colonel then suggested to Jones that he would enjoy a meeting with the daring Federal lieutenant if properly arranged sometime in the future, but also warned Jones that he would see to it that Cushing's raid could never again be duplicated. Ensign Jones was then escorted back to the gig, and the Confederate colonel immediately set about strengthening his defenses so that a raid such as Cushing's might never happen again on his watch.[29] Or so, at least, he hoped.

Within weeks the story of Cushing's raid on Smithville, North Carolina, ran in numerous newspapers across the North, and thousands of readers thrilled to his exploits.[30] It seemed that William Barker Cushing was beginning to make a name for himself.

CHAPTER 15

All Ahead, Full

ON SUNDAY, APRIL 17, 1864, the *Albemarle's* lines were cast off, and she began her maiden voyage down the Roanoke River toward Plymouth. A great deal of work still had to be attended to, but Commander Cooke had given his word that the ironclad would be put in motion by the 17th no matter what her state of completion, and he was not about to break that promise. Much now depended upon the ironclad. Confederate infantry was gathering for the land assault on Plymouth, and the presence of the *Albemarle* was required to subdue the Federal flotilla and diminish the shore batteries, a requirement only she could fulfill, and a necessity for the land assault to be successful. As the great mass of iron slipped away from shore, Cooke made this note of the occasion, no doubt with considerable pride. "The C.S. Steamer *Albemarle* was placed in Commission this day at 2 o'clock P.M.," he wrote. "The officers ordered to her hitherto awaiting her completion will be entered on your Books on duty afloat from this date inclusive. I am very respectfully, J.W. Cooke, Commanding C.S.N."[1] No doubt it was a thrilling moment for both Commander Cooke and Gilbert Elliott.

The month of March and the beginning of April had proved hectic indeed for the completion of the Confederate ram. "During the first seventeen days of April, observers could see accelerated activity aboard the *Albemarle*. There were iron plates to be fastened. Interior wood work was being finished with special attention paid to surface smoothness. Ships stores had to be assembled and loaded on board. Even the engineers were busy adjusting machinery, firing the boilers, and raising steam to test both engines."[2]

In early April Cooke and Elliott had agreed to move the ironclad down river from Halifax to Hamilton due to the fact that, as the *Albemarle* took on more and more iron, she began to sink deeper into the river as a result, and the river further south was far more accommodating for a vessel of deeper draft. There in early April Cooke was visited by General Robert Hoke who informed him of his orders to move on Plymouth with the infantry on April 18. Hoke made it abundantly clear at that meeting that the ground assault was utterly dependent upon the *Albemarle*'s ability to neutralize any Federal gunboats in the area, and hopefully subdue the Yankee land batteries in and around the town. If the *Albemarle* failed to appear, no doubt Hoke made clear, and the Confederate infantry were to go ahead and assault in the face of the Federal naval guns, there was little question they would be overmatched and probably cut to pieces. For his promise to arrive on time, Hoke agreed to provide Commander Cooke with whatever assistance he could render in the way of additional skilled manpower for the ironclad's completion along with much needed supplies. Hoke also promised Cooke a number of true Confederate seamen to fill out his crew, and for Cooke that promise was worth its weight in gold. For Cooke's crew at the time consisted of few other than North Carolina infantrymen, brave fellows to say the least, but hardly a one of them who knew stem from stern.

The ironclad began its journey downriver stern first, surely an odd picture for all who happened to catch a glimpse, but a necessity nevertheless. Due to the river's multiple turns and narrow bends, Cooke deemed it essential to proceed in that manner. In his official report he explained, "On account of the numerous bends and difficult navigation of the river I was compelled to move the boat down sternforemost nearly all the way."[3] On the decks workmen had stacked iron plates, yet to be installed, and portable forges were set up on the flush deck with still others towed behind. At about 3:00 P.M., the orders were finally given by Cooke to "cast off all lines!"[4] and the ironclad gradually pulled away from the riverbank and into the rushing current. The ram at that point was quite literally a work in progress. Gilbert Elliott, eagerly along for his vessel's maiden run, recalled years later, "Forges were erected on her decks, and black-smiths and carpenters were kept hard at work as she floated down the river to her destination."[5] There remained a hundred jobs to be done, orders to be issued, and a crew to train. It was an exhausting, taxing job, as men scrambled all over the drifting ironclad. "Towing a portable forge, Cooke literally finished the vessel on her maiden voyage. Standing atop the pilot house, bellowing through a trumpet, he simultaneously drilled the crew at the guns while giving orders for bolting the final plates to the casemate: 'Drive in spike No. 10! On nut below and screw up! In vent and sponge! Load with cartridge!' A farmer standing on the riverbank watched her pass down, and later wrote, 'I never conceived of anything more perfectly ridiculous than the appearance of the critter as she slowly passed by my landing.'"[6]

Just a few miles south of Hamilton, the *Albemarle* encountered the small steamer *Cora*. She was carrying the twenty or more sailors Hoke had promised, and the exchange was made in the center of the river, much to Cooke's delight. Now he had men who knew port from starboard, and could load and fire a naval gun without exhaustive training and drill.[7] After the brief exchange, the ironclad was off again, heading south toward the town of Williamston, where a throng of visitors had gathered in anticipation of the ironclad's arrival. For the people living along the river, the arrival of the *Albemarle* had become a festival of sorts.

"The folks at Williamston were waiting for the *Albemarle*'s arrival. In fact, for two days inhabitants of the countryside had been gathering for the event. Visitors arrived by carriage, canoes, pirogues, on horseback, and afoot. All available rooms in the community were taken, and the Yellowley Hotel was 'filled to triple its capacity. Folks slept in carts or wagons and ate where they could.'"[8] As the great moment approached, bands played, soldiers were on hand, and local dignitaries waited impatiently to make their speeches. "It was a historic day for the people of Williamston. For months the town had seen Union troops marching in her streets, as they fanned out across the countryside to raid and attack other places in North Carolina. For the moment it was glorious to be free."[9]

The *Albemarle*, no doubt to the delight of the assembled crowd, put in to Williamston around 5:00 P.M., but only briefly, and only to put ashore men and equipment that was no longer needed. Cooke knew he had serous business ahead at Plymouth, and precious little time to lose along the way. That accomplished, the lines were once again cast off promptly, and the ironclad headed downriver again, turning the near bend as Cooke continued to drill his gun crews and instruct his workmen from atop his perch on the gun deck.

Things went smoothly enough, but later in the evening the ram's machinery malfunctioned. "At 10 o'clock on the night following a portion of the machinery broke down," Cooke later reported. "The damage consisted in the wrenching up the bolts which fastened the main coupling of the center shaft. Having taken the precaution to carry a portable forge down with me in a flat, we were enabled to repair damages and get underway after about six hours' delay. Having proceeded some distance down the river the rudder-head broke off, and another delay of four hours was sustained."[10] Despite all the mechanical failures and ensuing delays, Cooke still managed to drop anchor some three miles above Plymouth that night. Gilbert Elliott explains what then transpired. "She came to anchor about three miles above Plymouth, and a mile or so above the battery on the bluff at Warren's Neck, near Thoroughfare Gap, where torpedoes, sunken vessels, piles, and other obstructions had been placed. An exploring expedition was sent out, under command of one of the lieutenants, which returned in about two hours, with the report that it was considered impossible to pass the obstructions. Thereupon the fires were banked, and the officers and crew not on duty retired to rest."[11] The *Albemarle* anchored for the time being, and was joined by the smaller *Cotton Plant*, carrying troops and sporting a few guns. That vessel also dropped anchor above the obstructions.

This delay represented a disaster for the ram and for the Confederate assault, which was then already in motion. Fortunately for Confederate aspirations, Gilbert Elliott did not believe for a moment that the ram could not successfully pass over whatever obstructions the Yankees had placed in the river, due principally to the fact that the river was then experiencing a considerable freshet. With the high water and the ram's shallow draft, he deemed it well nigh impossible for the ironclad to get caught on any obstruction no matter how elaborate, and asked for permission to perform another reconnaissance. Gilbert Elliott explains: "Having accompanied Captain Cooke as a volunteer aide, and feeling intensely dissatisfied with the apparent intention of lying at anchor all that night, and believing that it was 'then or never' with the ram if she was to accomplish anything, and that it would be foolhardy to attempt the passage of the obstructions and batteries in the day-time, I requested permission to make a personal investigation."[12]

Commander Cooke promptly agreed, and provided Elliott with the necessary personnel to successfully accomplish the task. Elliott took a small group of men down the river. They floated over the line of obstructions, and took a new, careful set of soundings. "To our great joy it was ascertained that there was ten feet of water over and above the obstructions. This was due to the remarkable freshet then prevailing; the proverbial 'oldest inhabitant' said, afterwards, that such high water had never before been seen in Roanoke River."[13] But the Yankees were everywhere around, and Elliott still had to get back to the ram and report his findings to Cooke. "Pushing on down the stream to Plymouth and taking advantage of the shadow of the trees on the north side of the river," he later wrote, "opposite, the town, we watched the Federal transports taking on board the women and children who were being sent away for safety, on account of the approaching bombardment. With muffled oars, and almost afraid to breathe, we made our way back up the river, hugging close to the northern bank, and reached the ram about 1 o'clock, reporting to Captain Cooke that it was practicable to pass the obstructions provided the boat was kept in the middle of the stream."[14]

Upon hearing the report from Elliott, Cooke immediately had his crew awakened, ordered the boilers fired, and as soon as possible slipped away down stream. The *Albemarle* was in motion again. "Cooke probably stood beside the helmsman as both peered through small cupola ports into the misty darkness. He ordered 'all ahead, slow' as he quietly directed the helmsman to steer towards mid-stream. His intention was to ride the river's flow and float over the obstructions."[15] As Elliott had predicted, the *Albemarle* coasted over the obstructions without the slightest problem, and was then in open waters. But soon the ram came under the daunting guns of the nearby Federal battery at Warren's Neck, which promptly opened on the ironclad, scoring more than one direct hit. But the months of exacting labor proved well worthwhile, as the Federal artillery had little effect upon the metal casemate. The heavy artillery shells simply ricocheted off the top and sides of the ironclad, causing no damage and injuring no one inside. "Protected by the iron-clad shield, to those on board the noise made by the shot and shell as they struck the boat sounded no louder than pebbles thrown against an empty barrel,"[16] Elliott later recalled.

Another heavy battery was passed at Boyle's Mill just as easily as the first, and then the *Albemarle* was in the open waters just above Plymouth, now closing rapidly on the Federal flotilla. "Cooke had worked a year for the moment at hand. His ship was under steam, guns were loaded, he had faith in his crew, they were snug inside their iron cocoon, and his destined encounter with the enemy vessels was minutes ahead."[17]

Those Yankee vessels were commanded by none other than William Cushing's friend and mentor, Lieutenant Commander Charles Flusser; and Flusser, "skipper of the Federal double-ender *Miami*, had planned this moment for months."[18] The Federal flotilla under Flusser had been beating off Confederate infantry assaults all day around Plymouth, and his men were worn and near exhaustion. Flusser had already lost one of his boats, the *Bombshell*, to Rebel artillery fire, and had few left to contend with the *Albemarle*, which from reports he knew was rapidly approaching. He had come up with the novel, and somewhat desperate idea, of lashing two vessels together, then attempting to snare the approaching *Albemarle* between the two. If that might be accomplished, it was Flusser's hope to pummel the ram into submission with broadsides at point-blank range, and boarding parties from both sides. Alas, as the *Albemarle* drew near Flusser was down to so few vessels that he could either support the Federal infantry, or fight the ram, but he could not do both simultaneously. He decided, wisely, to take on the ram first, since any advantage gained on land would be quickly lost if the *Albemarle* were allowed to roam free near Plymouth.

"After turning back the latest rebel assault on Plymouth with his ships' guns, Flusser withdrew to rest and feed the crews. He knew the morning would see the Confederate ram, and he ordered the *Miami* and the former Staten Island ferry *Southfield* lashed together. In the predawn, the *Whitehead*, picket gunboat at the pile line, came tearing downriver with her steam whistle blasting and rebel shells falling in her wake."[19] The *Albemarle*, firing away with her forward Brooke rifle, was hot on the *Whitehead*'s tail. Catching the *Whitehead*'s frantic warning, Flusser reportedly ran up on the deck and quickly ordered both the *Miami* and the *Southfield*, now dutifully lashed together, to head straight for the intruder "as fast as possible and run the ram down."[20]

On board the *Albemarle* all was quiet but tense. It was clear that soon they would be intercepted by the Federal flotilla, but where and when exactly was not yet known. It was approximately 3:40 A.M. at the time, and all eyes were peeled for the enemy. "Lookouts were posted, one in the hatch topside the casemate, and another forward on the main deck. Easterly, the sky's color announced a hint of dawn as the *Albemarle* steamed slowly and quietly downriver. Her course, probably just north of center stream, allowed abundant room for maneuvering."[21] As the ram neared Plymouth, Cooke ordered the gun ports cranked open, and the rifles swiveled into place. The ram boasted two Brooke rifles, one forward, one aft, each on a swivel that allowed each gun to turn in a 180-degree arch, thus each capable of sweeping the river from side to side.

As the few flickering lights of Plymouth appeared off the *Albemarle*'s starboard bow in the darkness of early dawn, the running lights of two approaching vessels were spotted ahead. Gilbert Elliott recalled the moment clearly. "They proved to be the *Miami* and the *Southfield*. The two ships were lashed together with long spars, and with chains festooned between them. The plan of Captain Flusser, who commanded, was to run his vessels so as to get the *Albemarle* between the two, which would have placed the ram at a great disadvantage, if not altogether at his mercy."[22] In the darkness, however, Cooke did not immediately notice that the two Federal craft were linked together, only that they were fast approaching off his starboard bow. The Confederate captain then ran the *Albemarle* at full speed along the shore of the Roanoke, paralleling the course of the approaching Federals, then ordered a sharp turn toward the center of the channel, a course that would bring him straight in on the bows of the two approaching vessels. His intent became at once apparent. Cooke's plan was to run them both down, slicing the bow off the lead Federal vessel, then ramming the second at midship. It was a simple, bold, and brutally practical idea. Cooke yelled, "All ahead, full,"[23] and at full speed, the "376-ton *Albemarle* headed straight for the space between the bows of both approaching vessels."[24]

Chapter 16

Plymouth Is Ours

As the *Albemarle* closed on the two approaching vessels, the heavy Federal guns began a booming welcome, and the frantic shouts of their officers could be clearly heard even above the clanging thunder of artillery. The ram bore down on the twin Yankee gunboats like an iron behemoth, angling straight for the bow of the *Miami*— the closest of the two Federal vessels to the *Albemarle*, and just then off the ram's port bow — and dead on the *Southfield* at midship. The shells from the Yankee ships struck the ram at almost point-blank range, but simply bounced into the air like marbles off a barn roof, and did no damage to speak of. The two Federal vessels, lashed together as they were, could not possibly maneuver at such close quarters to avoid the collision, and the *Albemarle* struck at full speed and with full power. "The curved knuckle of the *Albemarle*'s port knuckle rammed the *Miami* at her port bow. For about ten feet along the hull at the waterline, two planks were nearly gouged through by the impact. At practically the same instant the *Albemarle*'s ram penetrated the *Southfield*'s starboard bow, crashed through her forward store room, and came to rest in the fire room ten feet inside the hull."[1]

It proved a massive penetration, and the *Southfield* immediately began to list to starboard, sinking rapidly. Gilbert Elliott recounts the collision as the *Albemarle*'s pilot took his orders from Captain Cooke, "And then suddenly turning toward the middle of the stream, and going with the current, the throttles, in obedience to his bell, being wide open, he dashed the prow of the *Albemarle* into the side of the *Southfield*, making an opening large enough to carry her to the bottom in much less time than it takes to tell the story. Part of her crew went down with her."[2] But all did not go as planned. The ram had penetrated the *Southfield* to such an extent, and the Federal ship turned and went down so quickly, that the ram's bow became entangled in the sinking vessel, and the *Albemarle* began to go under right along with the *Southfield*. "The chain-plates on the forward deck of the *Albemarle* became entangled in the frame of the sinking vessel, and her bow was carried down to such a depth that water poured into her port-holes in great volume."[3] The ram, going down rapidly, could neither maneuver or return fire. More than that, if the *Albemarle* could not quickly free herself, she would wind up on the bottom along with the *Southfield,* and victory would have, in the blink of an eye, been turned into defeat. Cooke ordered the engines reversed, but the ram did not budge. In seconds only the situation became one of utter desperation.

Aboard the Federal gunboat *Miami*, Commander Flusser was personally directing the artillery fire at the disabled ironclad, but the ram's casemate appeared virtually impervious to even the largest naval shells. "On the Federal side, Flusser, personally directing the fire, opened with every gun, pouring broadsides of solid shot at spitting range."[4] The Yankee fire was murderous, but virtually useless despite its intensity. The collision, however, had caused many of the lashings to break loose between the two Federal vessels, and the *Miami,* freed now somewhat from the sinking *Southfield,* swung around close to the sinking ship, and many of the crew, including her captain, Lieutenant Charles A. French, were able to leap to the comparative safety of the *Miami*.

Inside the sinking *Albemarle* Cooke ordered the engines reversed repeatedly, but this accomplished nothing as the ram simply remained lodged inside its swamped adversary. Cooke would later report, "I immediately commenced backing the *Albemarle*, but was unable to extricate her from the sinking vessel for some time. In the meantime the weight of the vessel so depressed the forward deck of the *Albemarle* as to cause the water to run into the forward port."[5] For seconds that no doubt felt like hours, the ram continued to sink, and for the moment appeared to be going down with all hands.

"The *Albemarle*'s broadside could not be swung round to hit the *Miami*, so Cooke ordered the crew on the top deck to engage the Union vessel with small-arms fire. At the same moment part of the crew of the *Miami* was gathering on their own top deck, preparatory to board; as many of them as could crowd into the small space available were keeping up a hot fire."[6] On the top deck of the ram, the Rebels answered, firing rifles as fast as they could manage, men down below who could not get off a shot, reloading and handing the rifles up to those in better position. In this manner, and for the time being at least, the Federal boarding party was held at bay.

Aboard the *Miami* the frantic Federal response continued unabated. The *Miami* carried six 9-inch guns, a 100-pounder Parrott rifle, and a 24-pounder howitzer[7] and all the guns were blazing away as fast as the tubes could be fed fresh ordinance, but all of it to no discernable effect. "Commander Flusser steered his ship as close as he could and then leaped to take personal command of one of his forward guns. On the third round of fire Flusser himself pulled the lanyard, sending a nine-inch shell with a ten-second fuse against the side of the ram, now at point-blank range. The shell rebounded and landed on the *Miami*'s deck near the place where her commander stood, the lanyard still in his hand, and exploded, tearing him almost to pieces and killing him instantly, and wounding several of his crew."[8]

The *Albemarle* continued to sink despite all efforts to reverse the engines and back her out of the death trap, but then suddenly the *Southfield* struck the river's bottom, and turned slightly as it did. This slight turn caused the sinking Federal ship to suddenly release its grip on the ironclad's bow, and the *Albemarle* almost immediately bobbed back up to even keel, much to the relief of her terrified crew. At once Cooke called for the gun crews to find the *Miami* and return fire. The engines were reversed, and the ram, like an angry, cornered beast, came about.

Those aboard the *Southfield* who could manage, scrambled for their lives. Many jumped into the water, others lowered boats into the river and tried to pick up their struggling shipmates. Men were screaming, some burned by boiling hot steam; the *Southfield*'s timbers twisting and groaning as she slid under water.

Cooke ordered, "All ahead, full,"[9] and the ironclad surged forward in search of the lone remaining Federal vessel, while aboard the *Miami* the ship's executive officer, William Welles, had similar ideas. The *Miami* reversed, to avoid a collision with the riverbank, then turned to fire when suddenly Welles decided that perhaps — in light of the *Albemarle*'s proven strength and firepower — discretion may have been the better part of valor, and gave orders to withdraw. Welles would later report, "During the time of straightening the steamer the ram had also straightened, and was making for us. From the fatal effects of her prow upon the *Southfield* and of our sustaining injury, I deemed it useless to sacrifice the *Miami* in the same way."[10] With one gunboat already on the river bottom, and no help to speak of on the way, his decision was a sound one; and the *Miami* sped off down river for the safety of the sound and the remaining boats of the Federal flotilla.

Aboard the *Albemarle* Cooke had given orders to fire, and the forward Brooke rifle barked repeatedly at the *Miami* as she fled, but to no obvious effect. The Federal gunboat, now accompanied by the *Ceres* and *Whitehead*, which had just put in an appearance from down river, fled without further molestation, the Federals firing a few parting shots of their own, a sort of defiant pretense of resistance.

The *Albemarle* came about and scoured the waters, picking up eight sailors from the sunken *Southfield* who were swimming forlornly in the middle of the channel, exhausted and numb from the cold. "They were the only Union seamen left alive anywhere in the Roanoke River or the adjacent waters of Batchelor's Bay."[11] While for many of the seamen who had been engaged the encounter probably seemed like an eternity, the actual combat probably lasted little more than ten minutes. Just that quickly the new ironclad had established Confederate naval supremacy on the Roanoke River.

With the sinking of the *Southfield* and the flight of the remaining Federal gunboats, Confederate aspirations for the *Albemarle* had so far been completely fulfilled. With the Rebel ram now in sole command of the waters around Plymouth, Confederate infantry would no longer be subjected to the horrific fire of the Federal flotilla, while the Yankee positions nearest the waterfront could be pummeled into submission by the *Albemarle*'s powerful rifled guns. From that point forward it was only then a matter of concluding the operation, precisely as it had been originally planned.

As the Yankee gunboats fled downriver, Commander Cooke prepared for the second phase of combat. "Satisfied his enemies had retired, Cooke ordered the *Albemarle* anchored about one mile below Plymouth to await further orders from General Hoke. Taking advantage of the enemy's departure, he ordered a damage report. It was found only nine iron plates had been fractured. Still intact was the small boat which had been used to rescue eight crewmen from the sunken *Southfield*."[12] Aboard the ram there had been but one casualty, and that little more than a foolish mistake made by a crewman who had stuck his head out of a gun port to get a better look at the action, only to catch a bullet for his curiosity. Aside from that, all hands were reported safe and sound.

Gilbert Elliott, anxious to get on with the business at hand, volunteered to go ashore and make contact with the infantry. Cooke later reported that "Mr. Elliott again volunteered and took Pilot Hopkins with a boat's crew and proceeded down to the mouth of the river and up a creek in the rear of Plymouth, distant from the boat by water about 12 miles. He communicated with General Hoke and sent me dispatches."[13] Late that evening, and responding to requests from Hoke, Commander Cooke moved the ironclad to a position on the flank of Ransom's Brigade of Hoke's division, and then took up the shelling of Battery Worth near Plymouth, almost two miles distant form the ironclad.[14]

The following day, April 20, the *Albemarle* returned to Plymouth proper, and began a murderous shelling of Fort Williams, a Federal stronghold. Dropping anchor just off the town, the ironclad commenced a withering cannonade of the Federal position, ultimately forcing General Henry Wessells to capitulate."[15]

For the ironclad the effort had been one of simplicity and domination, but not necessarily so for the land assault. As Gilbert Elliott recounts, "Captain Cooke having successfully carried out his part of the programme, General Hoke attacked the fortifications the next morning and carried them; not, however, without heavy loss, Ransom's brigade alone leaving 500 dead and wounded on the field, in their most heroic charge upon the breastworks protecting the eastern front of the town. During the attack the *Albemarle* held the river front, according to contract, and all day long poured shot and shell into the resisting forts with her two guns."[16] Regardless of the price, however, Plymouth was now in Confederate hands, and the surrender proved an impressive one, Rebel forces capturing some 1,600 Federal soldiers, and twenty-five pieces of artillery.[17] More importantly, North Carolina's interior sounds west of Roanoke Island were now once again entirely in Confederate hands — the ultimate goal of the operation.

Across the South the fall of Plymouth was hailed as a major success, and the *Albemarle* lauded for its part in the operation. "The country was thrilled. Davis telegraphed Hoke his congratulations and added: 'You are promoted to be a major-general' as from the date of the battle."[18] Confederate success's during the early months of 1864 had been few and far between, and since the debacle at Gettysburg, the general mood glum. The fall of Plymouth repre-

The CSS *Albemarle* rams the Federal steamer *Southfield* (U.S. Naval History and Heritage Command).

sented a sudden ray of sunshine in what had been a dismal forecast, and buoyed hopes across the South. Perhaps success and independence were still possible after all.

The Confederate Congress voted formal thanks to both Commander James Cooke and General Hoke for their exceptional performances at Plymouth,[19] and for the time being, at least, areas of North Carolina previously under Federal control rejoined their Confederate brethren. At her plantation near Edward's Ferry, Catherine Edmondston was almost overcome with joy and newfound hope upon receiving the news. "How thankful we should be to God for this signal triumph!" she wrote. "Plymouth has been a thorn in our side & the garrison there a perpetual uneasiness to us. Its loss may compel a change in Grant's programme, especially if the Gunboats in the Neuse succeed in joining the Albemarle, as we may then attack Hatteras & flank Norfolk & open the most magnificent trade in Blockade Running yet seen."[20]

In a stunning display of power and seeming invulnerability the Confederate ram *Albemarle* had for the foreseeable future wrested domination of the surrounding waters from the Federal Navy, but it had come at a price no one understood at the time. Lieutenant Commander Charles Flusser, William Cushing's friend and mentor, had been killed in the affair, and that tragedy would stir in the young naval lieutenant a simmering clamor for vengeance. Upon hearing the news of Flusser's death, a stunned Cushing responded with grim determination: "I shall never rest," he vowed, "until I have avenged his death."[21]

And he wouldn't. A death warrant for the *Albemarle* had in a sense been issued by William B. Cushing. It would be a matter only of time and opportunity before it would be served.

CHAPTER 17

Heaven Has Crowned Our Efforts with Success

From Plymouth Federal forces fled as though they had encountered a beast akin in strength and boldness to the ancient leviathan of mythical lore — a force that might perhaps be contained, but surely not provoked, better yet assailed. Union General John Peck, for instance, hearing of the debacle at Plymouth, wrote that "the ram is heavy and formidable, and none of the gunboats here can stand against its power. The *Southfield* is sunk and the rest disabled."[1] The Federal flotilla withdrew to Albemarle Sound, and there contented itself with picketing the mouth of the Roanoke River for any sign of the ironclad's appearance, while making desperate arrangements should that eventuality unfold — which, considering the beast's apparent invulnerability, seemed only a matter of time.

William Barker Cushing, writing years later, summarized the grim situation from the Federal perspective, explaining that "the government was laboring under much anxiety in regard to the condition of affairs in the sounds of North Carolina." This anxiety had been induced when "a rebel iron-clad made her appearance, attacking Plymouth, beating our fleet, sinking the *Southfield*, and killing the gallant Captain Flusser, who commanded the flotilla. General Wessell's brigade had been forced to surrender, and all that section of country and the line of the Roanoke River had fallen again into Rebel hands. Little Washington and the Tar River were thus outflanked and thus lost to us."[2]

Meanwhile across the South there was jubilation. Colonel J. Taylor Wood, who had captured the USS *Underwriter* during the earlier and abortive assault on New Berne and was considered by many one of the Confederacy's most daring officers, openly rejoiced writing to Jefferson Davis: "Heaven has crowned our efforts with success."[3] Secretary of the Navy Stephen Mallory, clearly as moved by the victory at Plymouth as was Wood, wrote that "the signal success of this brilliant naval engagement is due to the admirable skill and courage displayed by Commander Cooke, his officers and men, in handling and fighting his ship against a greatly superior force of men and guns."[4] Success at Plymouth could never make up for failure at Gettysburg, but it certainly represented a bright ray of hope in the blue days of early 1864 for Confederate leadership. And that small but invigorating victory had turned most principally on the dramatic arrival of the *Albemarle*.

At Plymouth the victorious Confederates began inventorying their spoils. Beyond the twenty-five pieces of artillery surrendered with the capitulation of Federal forces were stores of ammunition, food, and other supplies needed to help stock the Rebel cause. In particular, Cooke discovered a ready supply of coal placed in storage there by the Federal Navy that might fuel the *Albemarle* for at least the near future. Additionally, the sunken Union gunboat *Bombshell* had been located at the Plymouth wharf. The small gunboat had been struck by artillery during the Confederate assault on the town and later sank at the wharf, but if raised — in addition to the *Cotton Plant*—might add at least some small measure of additional fire power and maneuverability to Confederate naval aspirations in the area. Cooke, grasping the possibility, at once commenced salvage operations. The greater idea was to gather enough force to remain on the offensive and still secure, if possible, the port of New Bern as originally planned back in January. Now more than ever it appeared entirely feasible for Confederate forces to reopen the sounds, and as a consequence reestablish the back door supply route to Richmond. Such a feat would constitute a major success, and thus a disaster for Federal efforts.

As spring arrived in full blossom, General Hoke was ordered to return to the vicinity of New Bern with his brigade. Hoke, now under the command of General Pierre G.T. Beauregard, the new Confederate commander for North Carolina — and not ordered to return to Lee's Army of Northern Virginia as had been expected, was ordered to begin plans to take the town in cooperation with the navy. The original plan for the capture of New Bern had called for the ironclad *Neuse* to steam down the Neuse River in much the same manner as had the *Albemarle* on the Roanoke toward Plymouth in order to achieve naval superiority and reduce the land batteries that defended the town. But the *Neuse* had failed, and as a result the New Bern operation had been put off indefinitely. Now, however, Beauregard proposed to use the *Albemarle* in place of the *Neuse*, and promptly suggested a detailed plan of action. "In a text book sequence Beauregard planned for the *Albemarle* to sink all gunboats defending

New Bern, destroy all bridges across the Trent river, and 'take such position in the Neuse as to cut off from New Bern all communications from forces north of that river.'"[5] Just as with the successful operation at Plymouth, Beauregard was counting on the *Albemarle*'s fire power and seeming invulnerability to enemy artillery fire, to spearhead the assault.

Whereas, however, the trip for the *Albemarle* from Halifax to Plymouth had been only some seventy miles down river, this new adventure suggested by Beauregard entailed a trip of far greater magnitude. To reach New Bern the *Albemarle* would have to steam down the Roanoke River to Albemarle Sound, cross that sound, then head south across Croatian Sound, pass near Roanoke Island, cross Pamlico Sound, then finally sail up the Neuse River to New Bern — a trip by water of at least 180 miles. And this entire journey would be across waters controlled and patrolled by the Federal Navy, and where their land batteries often lurked in locations unknown. It would require food, fuel, and logistics far more involved than anything before planned or executed, and all in a vessel still largely untested from a mechanical perspective. In short, it was asking a great deal of a new vessel recently hammered together in a cornfield to accomplish.

Yet James Cooke had faith in his new ram and was not about to give up the initiative the Confederacy had gained with the successful capture of Plymouth. On April 29 Cooke again set off in the *Albemarle*, this time on a trip down to the mouth of the Alligator River, bordering the southern shore of Albemarle Sound. His mission was to accompany a captured steamer back to Plymouth. On the way down the ram encountered three Federal gunboats in the waters of the sound. Spotting the hulking form of the new Confederate ironclad heading straight toward them, the Federal gunboats — easily outgunned and outclassed — immediately turned and fled. Cooke gave chase, but the scrappy Federal steamers made better time and outran him, and Cooke eventually called off the pursuit. He then brought the *Albemarle* about, picked up the steamer, and had an uneventful trip back to Plymouth. Yet it was apparent that James Cooke and his ironclad *Albemarle* were now the undisputed ruler of the surrounding waters, and that the Federal flotilla was under orders to avoid the ram at all cost.

But Cooke also knew that occasionally putting his toe in the water of the sounds and crossing those waters with a small flotilla to attack New Bern were two very different propositions. No doubt the Federals would be aware of any large-scale plan to retake New Bern and as he crossed the sounds would thus be waiting for him with anything and everything they had — and willing to attack him with anything and everything they had in the hopes of foiling the operation. Before he could plan the mission, therefore, he required information on the extent of Federal forces in Albemarle Sound. Thus Cooke turned to Frank O'Brien, a known and proven scout.[6] O'Brien agreed to the mission, and with an associate started off by canoe for the waters of Albemarle Sound, as Cooke looked to the salvaging of the *Bombshell* and the fitting out the *Albemarle* and *Cotton Plant* for the anticipated journey.

A few days later O'Brien returned with important news. He had spotted a number of Federal gunboats in the sound guarding the mouth of the Roanoke River, among them the *Commodore Hull* and *Whitehead*. But far more importantly, O'Brien had also uncovered the fact that the Federal authorities were aware of the Confederate plan to seize New Bern, but they expected Cooke to sail a week later than was his real intention. Of even greater significance, O'Brien had discovered that the Federal flotilla on the sound was soon to be augmented by several double-enders, all supposed to be carrying heavy armament. Double-enders were wooden side wheelers, built for speed and maneuverability, capable of going forward or backward with equal facility. They were excellent in narrow, shallow waters, and often packed numerous rifled pieces in their batteries; and more than one might give the *Albemarle* a stern test.[7] Cooke was at first furious, realizing that his plans had somehow been compromised, but then the obvious apparently dawned upon him — if the Yankees thought he was going to sail in a week's time, the time to go was now before they were ready, and before the new double-enders were on hand.

And there were other considerations. If the Federal Navy was already aware of his plans to move on New Bern, there was no telling — despite O'Brien's report — just what sort of trap they might set to ensnare him. All reports indicated that the Federals had no monitors with shallow enough draft to cross over the bar and operate in the sounds, but that was yesterday's news. What if those reports were wrong, or simply outdated? Should his small flotilla en route to New Bern stumble across even a few Federal monitors accompanied by double-enders with heavy batteries, the *Albemarle* might have difficulty escaping, while his other gunboats would be riddled and sent to the bottom in minutes only. So time was suddenly of the essence. At once Cooke ordered his crew aroused and made arrangements to set sail — the *Albemarle*, *Cotton Plant*, and *Bombshell*— for May 5.[8] Cooke then notified Richmond of his change of plans and set about preparing the three vessels for an early launch. The *Cotton Plant* was to carry additional troops for the assault on New Bern, while the *Bombshell* was loaded with extra provisions and coal.[9]

On the morning of the May 5, the small flotilla departed Plymouth on schedule. As Gilbert Elliott wrote, "On May 5, 1864, Captain Cooke left the Roanoke River with the *Albemarle* and two tenders, the *Bombshell* and *Cotton Plant*, and entered the Sound with the intention of recovering, if possible, the control of the two Sounds, and ultimately of Hatteras Inlet."[10] In the early afternoon the Confederate flotilla departed the mouth of the Roanoke River, and almost immediately Cooke spotted a number of Yankee vessels directly in his path including the *Ceres, Commodore Hull,* and *Whitehead*.[11] These were not monitors or double-enders that could spell immediate trouble for the *Albemarle*, but smaller gunboats and transports. From atop the casemate Cooke could see them clearly, and they appeared to be laying torpedoes for defensive purposes. The sudden appearance of the Confederate flotilla had caught them off guard, and noting the *Albemarle*'s approach, all the vessels came about and immediately began heading back up the sound, the small transport *Ida May* streaking ahead to sound the warning.[12]

Cooke decided to give chase. The Federal boats fled east-northeast on a course toward Wade's Point, the three Confederate vessels hot on their tails. Cooke followed easily enough for about sixteen miles[13] when suddenly across the horizon distant some five miles he spotted through his glass the closing silhouettes of three larger vessels. One thing was certain — they were not sister Rebel craft coming to pay their respects. They were Federal vessels, and judging from their size alone, Cooke guessed each sported perhaps as many as twelve guns, and all three were coming straight for him. From a distance they appeared to be the double-enders O'Brien had warned him about, and Cooke immediately gave orders to signal the *Cotton Plant* and *Bombshell* to break off at once and make a hasty retreat for the Roanoke River. The *Cotton Plant* complied, but for some reason the *Bombshell* pressed forward as if oblivious to the message.[14]

Suddenly the four vessels Cooke had been chasing came about and fell into line with the three approaching double-enders. Just like that, the tables had turned — the Yankees were no longer running from the Rebel ram, but aligning for battle. Coming toward the *Albemarle* now in two separate lines running parallel to one another and approximately a half mile apart were seven Federal gunboats, well-armed and obviously with malice in mind. It would be seven against one, but for James Cooke aboard the ironclad *Albemarle*, those odds must have seemed reasonable. "Perceiving the unequal contest in which we were compelled to engage," he later explained in his official report, "I immediately prepared for action."[15]

CHAPTER 18

A Terrific Grand Waltz

Aboard the *Albemarle* Cooke ordered the gun ports opened and the Brooke rifles loaded and run out. From the upper deck of the rapidly closing *Sassacus*, Edgar Holden had a good look at events as they unfolded and recalled clearly that "all eyes were fixed on this second *Merrimac* as, like a floating fortress, she came down the bay. A puff of smoke from her bow port opened the ball, followed quickly by another, the shells aimed skillfully at the pivot-rifle of the leading ship, *Mattabesett*, cutting away rail and spars, and wounding six men at the gun."[1] Seven against one it would be. The fight was on.

The *Albemarle* began a sweeping turn to starboard as the *Mattabesett*, Captain Melancton Smith's flagship, absorbed the first two direct hits. The *Mattabesett* was a well-armed, sturdy ship, a "vessel of 974 tons, she carried four 9-inch Dahlgren smooth bores; two 100-pdr. Parrott rifles; two 24-pdrs.; one 12-pdr. heavy smooth bore; and one 12-pdr. rifle."[2] The seven Federal vessels approached the *Albemarle* on parallel lines, intent on circling the Rebel ram, blasting her with their guns, and either running her down, fouling her propellers, or detonating a torpedo under her bow. Edgar Holden explains: "The Union plan of attack was for the large vessels to pass as close as possible to the ram without endangering their wheels, deliver their fire, and then round to for a second discharge. The smaller vessels were to take care of thirty armed launches, which were expected to accompany the iron-clad. The *Miami* carried a torpedo to be exploded under the enemy, and a strong net or seine to foul her propeller."[3]

The *Mattabesett* avoided being rammed by the *Albemarle*, then rounded the ironclad's bow, followed in turn by the *Sassacus*, which delivered a full broadside of solid shot at very close range. This broadside, however — just as during the previous combat between the *Albemarle*, *Miami* and *Southfield* — did little more than rattle the ironclad. Edgar Holden recalled the futility on the Federal side: "The guns might as well have fired blank cartridges, for the shot skimmed off into the air, and even the 100-pound solid shot from the pivot-rifle glanced from the sloping roof into space with no apparent effect."[4] The seeming invulnerability of the Confederate ram was for the Federal sailors like a potion of doom, and a sense of hopelessness suddenly pervaded the Yankee flotilla — the best weapons they had appeared impotent before the strength of the ironclad. "The feeling of helplessness," Holden later recalled, "that comes from the failure of heavy guns to make any mark on an advancing foe can never be described."[5] A seaman aboard the *Albemarle* affirmed Holden's assessment of the ironclad's strength, recalling that "they steamed right up in line of battle, passing us on the port side firing right into us ... it was the first broadside that knocked a hole in us, but not all the way through, splinters of wood flew about."[6]

All seven Yankee vessels continued their orderly approach, firing away as they did; and the waters of the sound quickly became blanketed in smoke, fire, and flying metal, huge naval shells booming and ricocheting off the ram's casemate like pebbles hurled at a knight's armor. At 4:45 the *Mattabesett* opened with its starboard battery from about 150 yards, firing solid shot, then the Federal double-ender drifted off toward the hopelessly outclassed *Bombshell* that had, for some reason, remained near the *Albemarle*.[7] Around the embattled Confederate ram, the Federal vessels dodged and danced, firing when opportunity presented itself, trying desperately not to hit one another or fall victim to the *Albemarle*'s ram in the smoke and confusion of battle. "To add to the feeling in this instance," Holden recalled years later with vivid clarity, "the rapid firing from the different ships, the clouds of smoke, the changes of position to avoid being run down, the watchfulness to get a shot into the ports of the ram, as they quickly opened to deliver their well-directed fire, kept alive the constant danger of our ships firing into or entangling one another."[8]

The carefully choreographed Federal battle plan had devolved into a hectic, violent bullfight of sorts, seven dodging, frantic matadors trying desperately to land the lethal blow on a single, snarling bull. "The *Wyalusing* and *Sassacus,* having overtaken her, were then steaming around her bow, the latter having given the ironclad a broadside in passing. Moments later the *Mattabesett* was on her quarter with engines stopped. The *Sassacus* was abeam, and off her starboard bow was the *Wyalusing*."[9]

The *Sassacus*, rounding the ram under full steam, came abreast of the forlorn *Bombshell* and immediately delivered a full broadside, ripping the smaller gunboat asunder. The *Sassacus* then moved in for the kill, the captain

The CSS *Albemarle* surrounded by Federal gunboats (U.S. Naval History and Heritage Command).

of the stern pivot-rifle — now shirtless and worked up to a fever's pitch — leaped angrily up onto the railing, waving a pistol in his hand. "Haul down your flag and surrender," he screamed, "or we'll blow you out of the water!"[10] Facing annihilation, the *Bombshell* had but little choice. The flag was lowered at once, and the small Confederate gunboat was ordered to fall out of the fight and drop anchor. She complied.

Meanwhile the *Albemarle* had been surrounded and was taking fire from all sides. She responded as best she could, but two guns were no ordinance match for the thirty odd pieces she faced from the double-enders alone. Inside the ram's casemate the two Brooke rifles were loaded, then run out as the iron port doors were cranked open in order to quickly get off a shot, but often the opportunity the gun crews thought they would be afforded had shifted or moved off, and the ports had to be quickly cranked shut again. Thus the *Albemarle* was forced to respond slowly and methodically to the torrent of shell she was receiving, but virtually every shot fired from the ram would prove both deadly and effective, whereas the torrent of shells hurled from the Federal flotilla was having little if any effect.

The *Albemarle* remained in the center of the storm, for the time being giving far more than she was taking; but James Cooke realized that his ram could not weather such an assault indefinitely. The Federal vessels continued to pound away "and hurled at her their heaviest shot, at distances averaging less than one hundred yards. The *Albemarle* responded effectively, but her boats were soon shot away, her smoke-stack was riddled, many iron plates in her shield were injured and broken, and the after-gun was broken off eighteen inches from the muzzle, and rendered useless."[11]

"Now came the decisive moment,"[12] as Edgar Holden recalled it. For the *Sassacus*, having moved off to engage the *Bombshell*, had in fact distanced itself from the *Albemarle* by a good four hundred yards and, more importantly, due to the ram's maneuvering to avoid the *Mattabesett,* the *Sassacus* had been granted a position broadside the ironclad. P.A. Roe, commanding the *Sassacus*, spotted the opportunity at once and moved to seize the moment. "Crowd waste and oil in the fires," he yelled to the engineer, "and back slowly! Give her all the steam she can carry!" Then he turned to Acting Master Boutelle and ordered him to "lay her course for the junction of the casemate and the Hull!"[13] Roe's intention was clear—his aim was to run the *Albemarle* down, perhaps split her in half, and hopefully send her to the bottom.

"Then came four bells," Edgar Holden remembered, "and with full steam and open throttle the ship sprang forward like a living thing. It was a moment of intense strain and anxiety."[14] Inside the *Albemarle* Commander Cooke spotted the *Sassacus* closing on his starboard beam at high speed, and ordered the ironclad forward at full steam[15] to try and dodge the collision; but the ironclad moved sluggishly, and the crew had to quickly prepare for the impending impact. As the *Sassacus* closed on the *Albemarle*, the other Federal gunboats ceased firing for fear of striking their own comrade, the smoke momentarily drifted away, and a clear view of the impending collision was had by all. "Straight as an arrow we shot forward to the designated spot. Then came the order, "All hands lie down!' and with a crash that shook the ship like an earthquake, we struck full and square on the iron hull, careening it over and tearing away our own bows, ripping and straining our timbers at the water line."[16]

Inside the ram the collision with the *Sassacus* sent men flying every which way. The sounds of wood splintering, iron cleaving, and the great beams trembling filled the vessel as it rocked violently to starboard. Gilbert Elliott recounts the scene as "the commander of the double-ender *Sassacus* selected his opportunity, and with all steam on struck the *Albemarle* squarely just abaft her starboard beam, causing every timber in the vicinity of the blow to groan, though none gave way. The pressure from the revolving wheel of the *Sassacus* was so great that it forced the afterdeck of the ram several feet below the surface of the water, and created the impression on board that she was about to sink."[17] Water poured through the ironclad's open starboard port, and it was at first feared the ram would go down, but the weight of the *Sassacus* could not further depress the *Albemarle*, and the two vessels remained entangled on the water's surface. Many of the seamen inside the ironclad feared for

The Federal gunboat *Sassacus* rams the *Albemarle* (U.S. Naval History and Heritage Command).

the worst, but Commander Cooke, who had himself been knocked down during the collision, had righted himself and calmly addressed his panicked crew. "Stand to your guns," he directed, "and if we must sink let us go down like brave men."[18]

With that the crew of the *Albemarle* quickly recovered from the shock of the moment, and soon had one of the Brooke rifles loaded and run out almost dead against the hull of the *Sassacus*. Edgar Holden, then aboard the Federal double-ender, was at the moment standing a mere ten feet from where the giant Brooke rifle made its appearance. It was a moment he would not soon forget. "My own station was in the bow, on the main-deck, on a line with the enemy's guns. Through the starboard shutter, which had been partly jarred off by the concussion, I saw the port of the ram not ten feet away. It opened; and like a flash of lightning I saw the grim muzzle of a cannon, the straining gun's-crew naked to the waist and blackened with powder; then a blaze, a roar and rush of the shell as it crashed through, whirling me round and dashing me to the deck."[19]

For almost thirteen minutes the *Sassacus* lay across the *Albemarle*'s upper deck, both vessels straining mightily, the *Albemarle* to free herself, the *Sassacus* to drive the ram under. Finally a deft bit of maneuvering by Cooke shifted the weight of the ironclad and freed her from her laboring foe. "Captain Cooke ordered Pilot Hopkins to put his tiller 'hard-a-port.' By that means the *Albemarle*'s stern swung to port, loosening the *Sassacus*' grip, and allowing Cooke to order 'All ahead slow.' The stern's movement had wrenched her free."[20]

Free at last, Cooke at once maneuvered in close for an open shot at the Federal double-ender. The Brooke was at once run out and delivered a murderous shot, again at point-blank range. This shell blew through the side of the Federal vessel, piercing her boilers, and sending scalding steam blasting about the craft. The shot wreaked near chaos aboard the *Sassacus*. Men were down, many scalded and screaming in pain. Small arms fire was snapping all around, and suddenly the double-ender veered hard to port as the water from her boilers poured out. "The ship is sinking," someone screamed. "All hands repel boarders on the starboard bow!"[21]

But the *Sassacus* did not sink, and her crew quickly regained their composure, and continued firing at the ram below them. All the while the seamen aboard the *Sassacus* threw grenades toward the ram's deck hatches, as fire was returned from the *Albemarle* from selected sharpshooters. Aboard the ram Cooke, now flushed with success, ordered men up top to try and board and take the reeling Federal vessel, but thought better of it once the size of the Federal resistance had been determined. Instead he simply continued to pour broadsides into the sinking *Sassacus* until disabled, she drifted off.

With the *Sassacus* drifting away, the contest again became general, all the Federal boats opening once more on the Confederate ram. Watching from his flagship, Melancton Smith later offered this description as the action renewed. "During the contest it was, of course, impossible for the other vessels to fire, but when the *Sassacus* became disengaged and resumed her firing the engagement became general, the smaller vessels firing so rapidly that it was dangerous for the larger ones to approach, and they appeared also to be ignorant of all signals, as they answered without obeying them."[22]

Aboard the damaged *Sassacus* Edgar Holden reported that "at length we drifted off the ram, and our pivot-gun, which had been fired incessantly by Ensign Mayer, almost muzzle to muzzle with the enemy's guns, was kept at work till we were out of range."[23] The double-ender continued to sputter down the sound until its steam gave way entirely. She then dropped anchor and, nearly swamped, was out of action for the remainder of the day.

But that was hardly the case for the other Federal vessels. The *Miami*, mounting a torpedo on her bow, approached the ironclad intent on exploding the device below the water line, but the *Miami* was a vessel that maneuvered poorly, and she could not come close to effectively delivering the device, while taking several shots from the *Albemarle* for her efforts. Melancton Smith wrote of the forlorn effort: "A torpedo was rigged out from the bow of the *Miami* and she was ordered to go ahead and attempt to explode it, but from some cause, yet unexplained, it was not done. She ran up, however, sheered off and delivered her broadside and continued to fire at him rapidly."[24]

By this time the engagement had been ongoing for over an hour and a half. After the *Miami* sheered off, the *Wyalusing* closed and offered a full broadside, once again to little or no effect. Then came the *Commodore Hull* which attempted to drop a seine over the ironclad's stern in order to foul her screw while firing hotly to cover its own move, but this failed also, and the *Hull* had to retire while taking fire from the *Albemarle*.

At about 7:30 P.M.[25] the *Albemarle*, having inflicted far more damage than she had absorbed and now losing steam, finally broke off the engagement and started back for the Roanoke. The ironclad's smokestack had been so riddled with shot that, despite the casemate holding and no shot penetrating the ram, the draft from the smokestack was slowly becoming insufficient to power her engines. Cooke realized that if he lost power entirely, the Federal vessels would simply ram him until the *Albemarle* was submerged, so a fighting withdrawal now appeared in order. In Cooke's words, "The disadvantages under which I labored, from the tiller giving way, and the impossibility of producing steam enough to maneuver the vessel to advantage, prevented me from inflicting much greater damage than we did. The smokestack was riddled to such an extent as to render it useless, and so great was my extremity at one time that I was forced to tear down the bulkheads, throw in all of my bacon, lard, and other combustible matter, to produce steam sufficient to bring me back to the river."[26] But Cooke's extreme action provided the ram at least enough pressure in the boiler to again produce steam, and the *Albemarle* was able to limp back to the mouth of the Roanoke, spitting shots at her pursuers as she did.

Melancton Smith had ordered both the *Commodore Hull* and *Ceres* to trail the ram back toward the river and picket the area if she entered the Roanoke or steamed off toward Plymouth. "The engagement continued," Smith reported, "until about 7:30, when it becoming dark the *Commodore Hull* and *Ceres* were then sent ahead to keep the ram in sight and to remain on picket duty off the mouth of the Roanoke River if she succeeded in entering it, the *Mattabesett, Wyalusing, Miami,* and *Whitehead* coming to anchor in the sound 2½ miles below."[27]

The engagement was over, but for the Federals, the shock was just beginning to set in. The Yankees had brought seven vessels into the contest, bearing a total — as would later be tabulated — of some 60 naval guns firing 557 rounds of ammunition at the *Albemarle*, all from almost point-blank range. The *Albemarle* alone responded with but two guns, firing a total of 27 rounds,[28] yet by far and away the most damage had been sustained by the Federal flotilla. Not one of the Federal vessels escaped undamaged, the "*Sassacus* itself was so badly disabled that it had to return to base for extensive repairs to its boiler and hull, and the six other Union vessels suffered varying amounts of damage, which while not disabling required serious repairs."[29] The *Albemarle*, on the other hand, had escaped with only her smokestack shot up, a few iron plates missing, her port shutter damaged, two timbers cracked, and the tube of one of her Brooke rifles shot away.[30]

For the Confederate ironclad it had been an impressive performance, and a performance that had not been lost on the Federal officers and men who had fought her. Melancton Smith, for instance, after the smoke had cleared, penned a rather sober assessment of the *Albemarle*'s fighting prowess. "The ram is certainly very formidable," he noted. "He is fast for that class of vessel, making from 6 to 7 knots, turns quickly, and is armed with heavy guns, as is proved by the 100-pounder Brooke projectile that entered and lodged in the *Mattabessett*, and the 100 pounder Whitworth shot received by the *Wyalusing*, while the shot fired at him were seen to strike fire upon the casemates and hull, flying upward and falling in the water without having had any perceptible effect upon the vessel."[31]

Melancton Smith now grasped the grim facts. Against the *Albemarle*, almost six hundred shells at close range had accomplished little if anything. Ramming had proved ineffective. The Federal Navy had now both a problem and a question on its hands. The problem was that the *Albemarle* had somehow to be stopped. That question was: how?

CHAPTER 19

Four Miles from Wilmington

WHILE THE SOUTHERN CONFEDERACY was drawing renewed hope and confidence from the sudden success of the *Albemarle*, William Cushing's exploits — most specifically his raid into Smithville, NC — had drawn quiet, but important, approval at the Naval Department in Washington. On April 8, Gus Fox, the Assistant Secretary, wrote to Admiral S.P. Lee, Commander of the North Atlantic Blockading Squadron at Hampton Roads. Fox had become impressed with Cushing's dash and daring and wrote to encourage more of the same. "What I meant about Cushing," he wrote, "was that it was a pity [that] so much luck and dash had not brought fruits equal to the risk. You notice that the Department never finds fault with these exploits. I believe they ought to be encouraged."[1] And encouraged they would be.

On the night of June 23, Cushing slipped away from the *Monticello* with Howorth, Jones, and fifteen handpicked seamen in two cutters once again bound for the interior waters of the Cape Fear River. His mission was to find and cut out the new Rebel ironclad *Raleigh*. Returning from a coaling trip to Beaufort, Cushing had gotten word that the Confederate ironclad had come down the Cape Fear River in the black of night escorting a number of blockade runners and had stormed out amidst the Federal blockading fleet, thus covering the runner's escape. The *Raleigh* had remained at the mouth of the Cape Fear until morning, apparently without challenge; and Will Cushing could not understand how that could have happened. Indeed, he considered it a black mark against the fleet and instantly vowed to make amends for what he considered nothing less than a blatant Rebel insult. "Why she was not attacked I do not to this day know — but as soon as we heard the news, Lt Comdr Braine in the *Vicksburg* and myself in the *Monticello* started down the coast, determined to ram her in company upon sight."[2]

Catherine Edmondston openly rejoiced upon hearing of the *Raleigh*'s success, and filed this delighted report in her journal: "The iron clad built at Wilmington, '*the Raleigh*' bearing the broad person of Com Lynch steamed out of Cape Fear & dispersed the blockading squadron there, much to the astonishment of the Yankees. She thinks she disabled one as a shot struck her fairly. She was out for hours & not a Yankee came in sight after their flight until she was back in the river again."[3]

Yet upon Cushing's return the ram could no longer be located on the open waters off Wilmington, so Will submitted a written application to his senior officer, requesting permission to take a party once again up the Cape Fear — just as he had done in February to Smithville — in search of the *Raleigh*. His intention was to board the Rebel craft, overwhelm her crew, cut the ram out, and sail her back out to the Federal fleet.[4] On this occasion Will had the foresight to send a copy of the application off to Admiral Lee, and in this his judgment would ultimately prove perceptive; for, "as usual, no one would take responsibility excepting myself," Cushing lamented. "I argued that the noses of the squadron had virtually been pulled, and begged permission to go in — promising not to come out alive if I failed. It was of no use."[5]

What his senior, Captain Sands, refused to condone, however, Admiral Lee would rapidly approve, authorizing Cushing to draw whatever men, boats, or equipment he might require for the expedition. For Will Lee's authorization represented a small coup of sorts, and he wasted no time in getting underway. On the evening of June 23 at 8:40 P.M. he headed off in two boats with Jones, Howorth, and fifteen sailors, carrying with them "two days rations — beef, pork, bread, etc.— with 11 revolvers, 7 pistols, 6 Sharps rifles, and ammunition."[6] It was just the sort of exploit Gus Fox had encouraged in his letter to Lee back in April, and just the sort of exploit Will Cushing had developed both a taste and talent for — although Will's initial plan had now been changed just slightly. This trip was to be a reconnaissance to locate the *Raleigh* only. As he later explained it, "I was determined to find the *Raleigh* and having ascertained her berth go out and bring back a hundred men to take her."[7] That, at least, was the plan.

The early portion of the mission proved uneventful. "They rowed past the batteries guarding the western bar on the night of the 23rd,"[8] and slipped through the darkness up toward Smithville. "With muffled oars we proceeded up the stream," Cushing remembered, "keeping a bright lookout for the ironclad and for the guard boats. In passing the town of Smithville, I was nearly run down by a tug that passed on unsuspected."[9] But in the dim light the berth of the *Raleigh* could not be determined, and the two boats continued rowing upriver without discovering the slightest sign of the ram's whereabouts. Unobserved, they pressed onward toward Wilmington, successfully past the first few Confederate forts. But it was a clear night, and the moon suddenly broke out brightly across the river, and some fifteen miles from the mouth of the Cape Fear the small expedition ran into trouble.

Shots rang out, musket balls began thumping the water nearby, and warning fires began to flare up all along the shore. The two boats had been spotted by Rebel sentries along the bank. Cushing notes in his official report that "as we came abreast of Old Brunswick batteries, some 15 miles from the starting point, the moon came out brightly and discovered us to the sentinels on the bank, who hailed at once, and soon commenced firing muskets and raising an alarm by noises and signal lights."[10] The situation was hazardous to the extreme, and required an immediate response. Cushing, almost instinctively, knew just what to do. "It was too near daylight to make my way out, if I desired it, (and I did not) so I determined upon a bit of strategy."[11]

With shouts of "Boat ahoy!"[12] ringing out from shore and bullets plunking the water nearby, Will Cushing immediately had the boats brought about and pointed in the opposite direction so that in the full light of the moon it would appear to the Confederate sentries along the bank as if the Federal boats were making their way back downriver toward the mouth of the Cape Fear. The sailors pulled hard at their oars for some few minutes, cutting obliquely across the water to the far shore as they did, hoping the Rebels would spread the word of their escape downriver, and be on the lookout for them in that direction only. Then Cushing ordered the boats to sheer hard out of the Rebel's line of sight, and Will brought both to a stop in the shadows near the far shore of the channel where they were obscured by the swell.[13, 14] Once out of sight, Will ordered the boats to come about again and to start upriver in the shadows, unseen by the Rebels ashore, pulling slowly away from danger and, as Will phrased it, "leaving them to send their boats and alarm downriver."[15] It was quick thinking, a clever response, and a ploy that worked perfectly. The two boats continued rowing silently upstream as the alarm spread rapidly downriver, as Will would later report "thereby baffling the enemy and gaining [our] safety."[16]

The mission continued unmolested and unobserved until the sun began to crease the eastern horizon, at which time Cushing decided, for obvious reasons, to pull off the river and remain concealed during the approaching hours of daylight. By then they had rowed to within seven miles of Wilmington,[17] but had yet to see anything of the ram *Raleigh*, or even a trace of its berthing point. As activity on the river began to pick up with the arrival of daylight, Cushing headed both boats to shore. "We landed and hauled the boat, by great effort, over a strip of sand into some swamp grass; concealing it with branches of trees; after which we stowed ourselves away in the bushes on the bank, close to the channel and in a fine position to see all movements of vessel [s] in the river."[18]

There they remained all day, carefully watching the comings and goings along the channel. Military movements on the inner portion of the Cape Fear River were a topic of much curiosity for the Federal high command, and Cushing's vantage point proved not only interesting, but significant. Will made careful observations of everything that sailed passed his position. His official report indicates that "steamers soon began to ply up and down, the flagship of Commodore Lynch, the *Yadkin,* passing within 200 yards. She is a wooden propeller steamer of about 300 tons; no masts, one smokestack, clear deck, English build, with awnings spread fore and aft, and mounting only two guns. Did not seem to have many men."[19] The raiding party remained concealed for the daylight hours, getting what little rest they could in the heat of the day, spotting nine steamers on the river, three of which Cushing considered "fine, large blockade runners."[20] But no rams had been spotted, and the location of the *Raleigh* remained a mystery.

Just as the sun began to set, and as the sailors prepared for another night at the oars, two boats came around a nearby bend in the river and appeared headed straight for Cushing's position. Fearing his small party had somehow been discovered and the boats an attack, Will quickly positioned his men under cover behind a log and readied them for the worst, while he strode out openly upon the riverbank—apparently convinced that boldness generally trumped numbers—and demanded the boat's surrender. "This they did," Will reported, "but proved to be a fishing party of white men from Wilmington," and not the Confederate assault he had presupposed. "From them I learned that the *Raleigh* had run upon a bar at high water and that as tide fell, the weight of armor had caused her to split open."[21] So at that moment the *Raleigh,* apparently by means of the inexorable tug of gravity alone, had been deleted from Cushing's short list of targets. He and his small band were now well behind enemy lines, only some seven miles from Wilmington proper yet, beyond his observations of traffic on the river, had achieved little. Now his prime objective had been removed. What to do?

A quick reevaluation was called for. "My next thought," Will Cushing later explained, "was to learn all that was possible about the batteries, roads and obstructions, as I knew that our government soon intended a movement on so important and troublesome a place."[22] But Cushing was in, of course, uncharted terrain from the Federal perspective, and might easily stumble headfirst into serious trouble without better information or at least knowledgeable guidance. Improvising on the spot, this problem Will solved at once. "Taking the fishermen as guides," he wrote, "we moved to the city, examining everything and discovered the nature of the channel and obstructions."[23]

The party soon discovered the fact that the inner defenses of the Cape Fear River were constructed both ingeniously and in considerable depth. For any Yankee flotilla hoping to steam up to Wilmington with the thought of taking the city, they would prove a daunting obstacle. Cushing later reported back to Admiral Lee that three miles from Wilmington he "found a row of obstructions consisting of iron-pointed spikes, driven in at an angle, and only to be passed by going into the channel left open, about 200 yards from a heavy battery that is on the left bank. A short distance nearer the city is a ten-gun battery and another line of obstructions, consisting of diamond-shaped crates, filled and supported in position by two rows of spikes, the channel in this instance being within 50 yards of the guns. A third row of obstructions and another battery complete the upper defenses of the city. The river is also obstructed by spikes at Old Brunswick, and there is a very heavy earthwork there."[24] This intelligence was invaluable, indeed, far more important than the armed destruction of the *Raleigh* would have been, for now serious war planning could begin on one of the most significant ports still available to the Confederacy. From that perspective, Will Cushing had struck gold.

It was now daylight, however, and quickly it became a need of paramount importance to either hide again or get off the river proper. The expedition continued on and soon discovered a creek that led off the river behind the city,[25] and Cushing decided to see where it might lead. "Discovering a creek in the Cypress Swamp," he explained, "we pulled or rather poled up it for some time, and at length came to a road, which upon being explored, proved to connect with the main roads from Fort Fisher and the sounds to Wilmington."[26] Cushing promptly split his command, leaving half behind at the newly discovered road to guard the boats, while leading the other half himself off to see where the road might lead. Some two miles distant they struck another main road, and there in the undergrowth they quickly concealed themselves. "We were just outside the rebel city," Cushing pointed out, "in the midst of swarms of soldiers, and lines of fortifications, and it was policy to keep very quiet, but we were growing hungry and a little cross and did not long suffer people to pass unmolested."[27]

The first traveler who passed their position proved a hunter who was also a local resident who owned a general store not more than a mile distant. He was detained. Then a mail carrier came down the road on horseback; and Cushing quickly, and politely, relieved him of his official burden and suggested he stay. As Cushing later phrased it, "About 11:30 A.M. a mounted soldier appeared with a mail bag and seemed much astonished when he was invited to dismount, but as I assured him that I would be responsible for any delay that might take place he kindly consented to shorten his journey."[28] The mailbags were taken and then carefully sifted through for whatever military information they might reveal, and this proved significant. Much was disclosed regarding the Confederate fortifications in the area and the size of the forces garrisoning them. This intelligence would prove critical for the Federal operation being then planned to take Fort Fisher. Indeed, Will was able to advise Admiral Lee specifically that "there are 1,300 men in the fort, and the unprotected rear that our troops were to storm is commanded by four light batteries."[29]

Cushing then decided to simply sit and wait on the next mail courier who was expected down the road from the other direction. But as this courier was not due for some time, his concern soon turned to securing enough food to sustain his hungry raiding party, which had already devoured all the rations that had been packed and carried with them. A sensible, although somewhat dangerous, plan was devised. Cushing explains: "Mr. Howorth was therefore dressed in the hat and jacket of the Georgia cavalryman; mounted upon his horse, and started off to the store of our captured friend, with a pocket full of confederate money taken from the mail, and the 'brass,' requisite for his dangerous adventure.[30] The requisite "brass," of course, referred to the fact that Howorth would not only have to pass himself off as a Southern cavalryman, but also the danger of being potentially discovered and captured, a danger that would in all probability result in his being hanged as a spy if caught—no petty risk.

But William Howorth, displaying dash and pluck all his own, handled his mission with panache. "This gallant officer returned safely," Will reported, "after mingling freely with soldiers, and having to spin a long yarn to an inquisitive female who had a brother in the place which he named as his home."[31] The chicken and milk acquired by Howorth accompanied by local blueberries picked from the vine provided the basis for a meal that, at least according to Cushing, "could not be improved in Seceshia."[32]

Hunger resolved, Cushing began laying the groundwork for the capture of the last mail rider. He mounted the first mail carrier's horse and posted himself in ambuscade near the road along with a number of his men; but at the last moment he decided to have the majority of the locals he had detained—a group that now numbered over twenty-five—taken back to the boats for safety's sake. Unfortunately, just as his sailors were moving the civilians across the road, the second mail carrier, accompanied by another rider, rounded the bend. They immediately reined in their horses, spooked by the scene before them. "Seeing the blue shirts and carbines they knew at once what had become of the morning courier and instantly wheeled about."[33]

The two riders turned and fled in a burst of flying dust. They would spread the word! Cushing gave his horse the spur and, in hot pursuit, dashed off behind them. But his horse was simply not up to the task, and the two riders pulled away and soon disappeared from view. Cushing had no choice but to stop and head back to his men, a serious problem now on his hands. Some twenty miles or so behind enemy lines, his presence and location had now been discovered by the enemy, and there seemed little doubt that his only realistic route of escape — the Cape Fear River — would now be energetically patrolled and picketed from top to bottom. In short, the Confederates would be looking for him everywhere, and the chances of an effective escape whittled down to somewhere between slim and none. Speed and stealth were now of critical importance. "I now for the first time cut the [telegraph] wires to prevent them from sending a message to Fort Fisher," Cushing explained, "and made for the boat with all speed — placed my prisoners in canoes, took them in tow and moved down toward the river, which we entered at dusk."[34]

But Cushing had been discovered, and the Rebels were soon telegraphing messages of caution up and down the river. On the twenty-fifth of June this message flashed across the line from the Confederate telegraph at Smithville. "About sixteen Federals are said to be on the Cape Fear River, and some think they are yet. Keep a close watch out on the bay."[35] Entering the river, of course — as Will reported he had accomplished at dusk — would be one thing; getting off alive would be quite another.

CHAPTER 20

Captain Cushing's Exploits in the Cape Fear River

For William Cushing, his problems seemed to have suddenly multiplied. He had taken twenty-some odd prisoners, and had kept them close at hand so that they could not escape and sound the alarm. Now that the Confederates had discovered his location, however, and he thus had to make an escape with as much urgency as possible, those same prisoners had become an ungovernable burden. He could not travel with them, yet he could not let them simply walk away freely for fear they would immediately provide the Rebels with much needed information regarding the size of his party, his weaponry, and most of all, his intentions. In the blink of an eye the calculus of command had flipped. What just moments before had represented a crafty advantage had suddenly been transformed into a distinct disadvantage. What should he do?

The prisoners were all noncombatants, detained by his party for no transgression other than being in the wrong place at the wrong time. He meant them no harm, and had no intention of harming them. But by the same token, the prisoners had come now to represent a serious threat to his mission, and William Cushing realized that threats had to be handled with both speed and precision. Cushing, a man who could most definitely think on his feet, rapidly devised a workable plan. "I now determined," he explained, "to place the most of the captured men in the light house on Marsh Island, which had no keeper,"[1] where they would not soon be found. The island was remote and in the dark it was a good bet the prisoners would not be discovered there for at least a few hours, thus he might make good his escape before they could speak to the authorities. Moreover, the island was on his way downriver, thus no time would be lost in disposing of them.

It was a sound plan, and as the island suddenly loomed ahead in the gathering darkness, Cushing ordered the boats to make their way toward the bank. But just as they were about to take the prisoners ashore, fate toyed with his plans yet again. "When the cutter was within a few feet of the island the men saw a steamer shoot around the bend in the river above them and head directly for them."[2] It was the steamer *Virginia*, no doubt loaded with Confederate militia on the lookout for him, and her sudden, threatening appearance represented an immediate dilemma. There was not a second to lose. "I instantly ordered the men to jump overboard," Cushing recalled, "and shove the boats in close to the marsh grass; holding their head below the gunwale; and threatened any prisoner who spoke with immediate death."[3] The steamer came on in the darkness, seemingly headed straight toward them, closing rapidly. No one made a sound. The *Virginia* then passed in the darkness, not ten feet[4] from where Cushing, his party, and his prisoners were huddled in the water, and continued downriver, then eventually off out of sight. Will and his party emerged from the water undetected, but it had been a very close call.

There was no time left now to even take the prisoners ashore, and Cushing, in a rush, struck on a different plan. "As we had more prisoners than we could look out for, I determined to put a portion of them in small boats and set them adrift without oars or sails, so that they could not get ashore in time to injure us. This was done," he went on in his report, "and we proceeded down the river, keeping a bright lookout for vessels in order to burn them, if possible."[5] Not all the prisoners had been set adrift, however. Some, important to the Federal mission, were maintained, in particular a pilot who knew well the river's channel and supposedly the location of the wrecked Confederate ram *Raleigh*. "This pilot came in handy. He was forced at the point of a pistol to lead the cutter to the place where the *Raleigh* had run aground, where Cushing found that the fisherman's story had been correct, and the ironclad was a total wreck."[6, 7]

Cushing and his men then piled back into the cutter and headed once again downriver, fully aware of the fact that the Confederate's garrisoning the forts and redoubts all along the riverfront would be waiting for them. Yet recalling that the colonel who commanded Fort Caswell had cautioned Ensign Jones after the Smithville raid in February that he intended to take steps to insure the fact that Cushing — should he ever be so fool as to try such a venture again — would never be able to repeat his earlier feat, Will directed the sailors to row up to a buoy so that he could affix a note reminding the good colonel that his threat had proven futile.[8] That piece of whimsy accomplished, they pushed off once more, the most dangerous part of the journey waiting directly ahead, not far downriver. Ahead lurked a virtual gauntlet of Confederate naval guns, infantry positions, and picketboats, all of which would have to be run. "We had now to get down by Fort Anderson," Cushing later wrote, "Fort Fisher, the forts on Leeks Island, and batteries Campbell and 'the Mound,' and it was quite certain that their boats would be ready to intercept us at the bar."[9]

Near the forts off the East Bar a boat was spotted, and Cushing ordered it run down. After a brief chase, the boat was captured, and its passengers found to contain "six persons, four of whom were soldiers."[10] Unfortunately, the other two passengers were ladies,[11] and this presented for Will Cushing yet another dilemma. Once again, he could not let them go for, so near the Confederate works, they would obviously sound the alarm, yet he had no desire to drag them into harm's way. Unfortunately, he had little choice, and as Cushing later phrased it, "Taking them all into my boat, I cut theirs adrift, but soon found that 26 persons were more than a load."[12] By careful questioning, it was discovered that the Confederates had in the nearby waters at least one large guard boat on duty with some seventy-five soldiers or militia aboard, this plying "the narrow passage between Federal Point and Zeek's Island."[13] There were also several smaller boats reportedly out patrolling the waters at the mouth of the river.[14] No matter what form the contest was to take, it appeared at that point that the confrontation would be decidedly uneven. But uneven contests seemed not to faze William Cushing.

Will Cushing then made one of the bold, aggressive decisions for which he was becoming famous. Rather than attempting to elude the picketboat — which the Rebels would surely expect — he determined to go straight at it. He would attack![15] Yes, he would go straight after a substantially larger force than his own; still there was method to what initially seemed like madness. "The tide was now in our favor," he pointed out, "and I concluded to pull boldly for the bar — run foul of the guard boat — use cutlasses and revolvers and drift by the batteries in that way, since they would not fire on their own men. It was within an hour of daylight and everything was as bright in the moons rays as if dawn were indeed come."[16]

The two boats with all prisoners aboard continued down the Cape Fear, bound for the fort's big guns and the squadron of patrol boats that were out and on the prowl for Cushing's party. Then suddenly the enemy was spotted. "As we neared confederate point a boat was seen rising and falling with the swell, and our course was at once shaped for it," Will reported. This appeared to be the large vessel containing the armed militia his most recent prisoners had warned of and, as planned, Cushing cut a course straight for it, relishing the thought of such an uneven fight. "My men were eager to commence so unequal a fight," Cushing later boasted, "feeling confidence in themselves, in an encounter with five times their number of soldiers in the water. My orders were to wait for my word, and *then* all but the two bow oars 'trail' and take to their arms while I sheered in and laid our boat aboard. The eight rebel soldiers with us I promised immediate death upon the least sign that they would aid their comrades."[17]

As the sailors rowed hard, the cutter sliced across the water headed straight for the large Rebel vessel, but just as they were prepared to fire a broadside from about twenty yards, the game shifted again. Cushing explains that "as we prepared to sail into her, and while about 20 yards distant, three more boats suddenly shot out from that side, and five more from the other, completely blocking up the sole avenue of escape."[18] The odds had shifted once again, and this time radically. Now he was not only facing some seventy-five militia in the larger Confederate vessel, but an additional eight boats strung across the water directly in his path. The situation appeared almost hopeless, but it was about to get even worse. "I immediately put the helm down," Will said, "but found a large sailboat filled with soldiers windward and keeping us right in the glimmer of the moon's rays."[19] If there was a moment for demoralization or panic, surely this was it, but Cushing had seemingly been born for such moments, and his raiding party handpicked for the task. "None of Cushing's extraordinary little crew became panicky, and all pulled steadily so that each stroke was perfection — this after five hours of rowing and three nights without sleep."[20] As naval professor James Russell Soley, a contemporary of Will's, later observed: "It seemed now that the game was up; but Cushing's never-failing pluck stood by him."[21]

Will Cushing later explained his instantaneous response to a virtually hopeless situation: "At the first glimpse I saw the trap and formed the only plan that hope left me," he said. "With helm hard aport we went short around but only to find a large boat to windward, under canvas. We were now at the junction of the two channels, where the tide splits — one leading down seven miles below to [Fort] Caswell — where I had entered, and the other where I proposed to go out. At the Caswell entrance a south west gale had been blowing, and it was no doubt breaking clear across the bar, besides it would be daylight ere we could have passed Smithville or the forts, so our only chance was at Fisher."[22] In short, Cushing instantly realized that he could not leave through the channel that led down to Fort Caswell due to both the hour and the high seas, but only through the channel that led off to the guns at Fort Fisher. Cushing knew this instinctively because he was an excellent sailor, but he also guessed that the Confederates who were chasing him probably were not, and therefore would not realize that their prey had in fact only one alternative. This one slim advantage, then, was in his favor, and he decided to use it by faking his exit toward one channel, then making a mad dash for the other once the Confederate boats had been committed to the chase.

"Being soldiers," Cushing explained, "they did not take into consideration the facts regarding the impossibility of escape at the west bar: and concluded that I was making for it. The whole line [of Confederate boats] came after, in pursuit, leaving their original station unguarded."[23] The Confederates had swallowed the bait, and Cushing promptly turned once they were committed, and made hard for the sailing vessel that had been trailing him, once again intent on boarding and taking her. "Suddenly turning we approached the sail boat as if to board, when her crew lost their nerve and tried to back. Missing stays [that is, fumbling the sails in the crosswind] they drifted off with the tide, while we shot around the semi-circle and cut under the stem of the line of boats in chase."[24]

The Confederates immediately spotted Cushing's boat on the move, hence their mistake, but they were a heartbeat too late. A hundred yards ahead now, and with his sailors pulling the oars for their lives, the Federal cutter pulled ahead fast toward the ocean. "Then again turning," Will wrote in his official report, "by the extraordinary pulling of my sailors I gained the passage of the island, and before the enemy could prevent, put the boat into the breakers of Caroline Shoals."[25] The Confederate pursuers, not being trained sailors, were incapable at that point of following Cushing's crew into the high surf. The instinctive, coolly executed escape had worked to perfection. Literally surrounded at one moment, then free and running the next, Will Cushing had disappeared from the Rebel trap as if by magic. "The rebels dared not follow, and we were lost to view before the guns of the forts trained on the channel could be brought to bear upon our unexpected position. Deeply loaded as we were, the boat carried us through in fine style, and we reached the *Cherokee* just as day was breaking, and after an absence from the squadron of two days and three nights."[26]

The entry on the *Monticello*'s log for June 26 reads simply as follows: "At 12:20 P.M. the steamer *Cherokee* arrived from the north side, having in tow our first cutter. At 2:20 P.M. first cutter returned to the ship, they having succeeded in getting within 4½ miles of Wilmington. Had possession of the main road Saturday. They captured the mail carrier and mail. Cut the telegraph wire. The prisoners brought to the ship."[27]

Upon receiving news of Cushing's adventure, Gideon Welles, Secretary of the Navy, wrote Will Cushing directly, offering his profound appreciation. "The boldness exhibited by you on this reconnaissance," he penned, "and the success attending it are most gratifying to the department."[28] Admiral David Porter would later write, "There was not a more daring adventure than this in the whole course of the war."[29] News of Cushing's adventure soon flashed across the Northern press, headlined often as "Captain Cushing's Exploits in the Cape Fear River."[30] But perhaps the most telling praise of the expedition would come from none other than General Whiting, then commander of the Confederate Wilmington defenses, who complained in a dispatch to General Hébert at Smithville: "The last exploit of Cushing is pretty strong, *pas trop fort*. What do you think can be done? Can you get any help from the navy? I shall have to have a guard for my house in town."[31]

For his daring Wilmington exploit Will Cushing would receive the official thanks from the Navy Department and, aside from his official report, he would allow only that "in this expedition I did not sleep for sixty-eight hours."[32] Pretty strong stuff, indeed.

CHAPTER 21

Captain Cooke

WHILE WILLIAM CUSHING'S exploits on the Cape Fear River might have been greeted across the North with considerable interest and enthusiasm during the month of June 1864, the truth of the matter was that for the Union, the principle war effort was not going well. On March 3 Abraham Lincoln had ordered Ulysses S. Grant east to take full command of all Federal armies, and on March 8 he met the president for the first time at a reception in the White House.[1] Grant soon developed the sensible strategy of employing all Union armies in concert so as to strain Confederate forces across the board, and ostensibly prohibit them from shifting troops and material from one theater of operations to another to meet disjointed attacks. But so far that strategy — sound though it might have been — had yet to produce substantial results.

In the Eastern Theater, for instance, Grant had accompanied the Army of the Potomac south against Robert E. Lee's Army of Northern Virginia, and throughout the months of May and June vicious fighting had taken place north of Richmond, on a line stretching from the Wilderness near Fredericksburg, south and east to Spotsylvania Court House, then on to Cold Harbor, a country crossroads just east of Richmond. That fighting had cost the Federal Army some 54,000 casualties; yet Lee's army — while most certainly pushed back to the outskirts of Richmond — appeared no closer to defeat than when the campaign had begun. Grant's critics rightly pointed out that 54,000 casualties had brought the new Federal commander no closer to Richmond than McClellan had come in 1862 via a water route and with far, far few casualties; and while McClellan had failed to take Richmond, he also had not lost 54,000 men for nothing. Now Grant's army had stumbled into a siege of Petersburg, a rail junction of critical importance south of Richmond that could have been taken in a day, but was not taken at all.

Federal armies in the Western Theater had fared little better. Sherman's objective had been Atlanta, Georgia, but his army had become stalled far from that objective. For General Grant the picture in all military theaters appeared to be one of endless overestimation and underperformance. The popular mood, which had originally been extremely positive with the promotion of Grant to high command, was starting to turn. Was all this failure the result of Confederate martial excellence or Federal incompetence? People were beginning to wonder, journalists to speculate, politicians to mumble. In the North both Grant's — and as a direct consequence Lincoln's — effectiveness was being increasingly questioned by a public weary of war, enormous casualties counts, and marginal success.

While during this same period the Confederacy could not claim much in the way of military accomplishments for itself, its unique brand of success was, by the summer of 1864, its simple survival. It can be recalled that Robert E. Lee, after his defeat at Gettysburg, had altered his objective from the infliction of a catastrophic defeat upon his Federal adversary — indeed, a defeat that might in a single afternoon secure for the Confederacy its independence — to the frustration of Northern war objectives. It was essentially a Fabian strategy, designed to delay and demoralize an opponent; and while Lee's army had itself suffered significantly during the spring campaign, the Confederacy at least remained intact. If Lee could continue to frustrate Grant's offensive schemes, and the Army of Northern Virginia continue to inflict severe casualties upon its foe, it was hoped that the people of the North would grow increasingly weary of war, and that Lincoln might be rejected at the polls in the coming fall election, and a candidate open to some form of political accommodation with the South chosen in his stead. The Confederacy might then accomplish through negotiation what for years had eluded it on the field of battle. That, at least, was the hope.

Thus as May gave way to June in 1864, a vigorous defense appeared key to Southern aspirations, and in this the success of the *Albemarle* had come to play a new and important role. Now, for instance, it could be genuinely hoped that Confederate forces might soon reopen the North Carolina sounds to Southern commerce, and as a result the backdoor supply route to Richmond — a critical development that might prolong the war effort significantly. More importantly, the *Albemarle*'s dramatic encounter with seven Yankee gunboats had provided a lift to Southern morale far greater than its true strategic significance; and in war morale as a critical factor should never be discounted. More than one historical confrontation has turned on spirit alone, and in the early summer of 1864 the South remained generally both confident and defiant.

After the *Albemarle* had returned to its Plymouth berth, Catherine Edmondston, for instance, offered up this hopeful assessment of the recent naval engagement: "Captain Cooke has had a severe fight with Yankee gunboats in Albemarle Sound. His Smoke Stack was so riddled with shot that he could not burn coal & but for a supply of Lard & Bacon he would have been taken. He kept up his fires with these, however. Sunk two steamers & fought his way back to Plymouth with one gun disabled & her smoke stack with holes in it through which a man might creep. He lost his new tender, the Bombshell. She was sunk & her crew captured. Ten men were killed on the deck of the Albemarle. She engaged eleven boats at once & escaped them all. They threw a net made of Rope over her but the ropes which held it to the steamers parting, it fell harmless off her sides into the water. For her preservation God be thanked.... May we not be ungrateful for the blessings we have enjoyed and in Thy goodness continue them to us O Lord!"[2]

Increasingly the *Albemarle* was being looked upon as one of those blessing. At Plymouth in North Carolina, the *Albemarle* remained fundamentally at her berth, iron once again being the delaying factor. New iron plates could not be readily found to replace the old few that had been shot away; and until the plates that had been damaged during the fighting on the sound could be repaired, the ship was sensibly restrained from further action. While the ironclad remained the toast of the South — and a considerable concern for the United States Navy — her commander, James Cooke, had in the heat of combat, in fact, found her design and function somewhat lacking. An honest appraisal was therefore required, and this Cooke took upon himself on May 8, only days after returning to Plymouth. He took the time to write Stephen Mallory directly, outlining his thoughts as to the ram's deficiencies and what might be done to best resolve the situation. No one knew the *Albemarle* better, and Cooke, in light of his two most recent engagements, had surely earned the right to speak his mind. "The recent fight in the Albemarle Sound with the enemy's boats demonstrated to me," he suggested, "that the *Albemarle* draws too much water to navigate the sounds well, and has not sufficient buoyancy. In consequence, she is very slow and not easily managed. Her decks are so near the water as to render it an easy task for the enemy's vessels to run on her and any great weight soon submerges the decks."[3]

Cooke believed that these defects were so inherent to the overall design of the *Albemarle* they could not be rectified. No repair would do. What was needed, in the commander's opinion, was an entirely new ironclad, built on the Roanoke, and incorporating the improvements he deemed necessary. "It is, in my judgment," he went on, "as I before took the liberty of informing you, of the greatest importance that at least one additional gunboat should be built on the Roanoke River, with the least possible delay, and that the vessel should only draw 6½ feet water."⁴ The iron, Cooke believed, should be switched from one course of two inch iron, to two courses of one inch, the purpose being that one inch iron plates were rolled more compactly, and thus two courses of the one inch would bend rather than break in combat, making the vessel less vulnerable to enemy fire. Moreover, Cooke was emphatic that the new ram should incorporate at least one gun at midships, but preferably two. This would allow for twice the fire power, far more rapid, accurate fire, and greater coverage. "I feel no doubt," he continued, "but that we should have had an entire victory in our late fight if there had been two broadside guns in addition to the two now mounted on the *Albemarele*."⁵

Whether the good commander actually believed that iron enough for a second ram could be easily located and shipped to Halifax is a question of some speculation. That such a craft could be built on short order, as Cooke suggested, when considering the all too obvious fact that the *Albemarle*, in need of only a few iron plates, had yet to be repaired, suggests that the commander — consciously or subconsciously — may as well have been lobbying for a miracle. But whether the suggestion of a second ironclad was fancy, fantasy, or genuine concern, Cooke no doubt realized that if such a recommendation was going to be taken seriously by the powers that be in Richmond, the time to act was now, after the *Albemarle*'s fine showing in the sound, and not some weeks or months later when the fickle gaze of the Confederate government had turned to contemplate a wide range of other accumulating problems. For the time being, however — until repairs to the *Albemarle* could be properly affected — Commander Cooke and his ironclad would remain tethered to their berth in Plymouth, and the prospect of a second ironclad little more than hopeful speculation.

Such was not the case, however, for the Federal Navy. For them fear and worry over the *Albemarle*'s condition and availability spawned any number of schemes to destroy her.⁶ In early May, for instance, after the *Albemarle*'s impressive showing in the sound, a reconnaissance party had been sent up the Middle River. There they landed, marched through the intervening swamp, finally to emerge on the bank of the Roanoke River opposite Plymouth. From there they were able to closely observe the *Albemarle*, her current condition, and what repairs remained incomplete. Returning safely, the party's report indicated that "the ram lying at the coal yard wharf, lower end of the town, with smokestack down and a number of men engaged upon the repairs. The vessel seems to have been lightened, as he appears much higher out of water forward and aft than when we engaged him in the sound, but the sides of his casemates are even now touching the water."⁷ This report, and the ease by which the party had gained access to the Roanoke River opposite Plymouth, suggested an attempt on the ram by means of the same route, and this in fact was carried out on May 25 by a number of daring Yankee volunteers.

The effort was made to swim across the river unobserved and attach torpedoes to the hull of the ironclad below the water line. Two one hundred-pound torpedoes were selected for the task and successfully hauled across the swamp to the northern bank of the Roanoke where their final assembly took place. But while swimming across the river with the torpedo in tow, one of the raiders was discovered by a sentry who promptly opened fire and sounded the alarm, thus derailing the plot. The raiders were able to escape with their lives, however, by making their way once again through the swamp, but having accomplished little more than having placed the Confederate garrison on notice that such torpedo tactics might be expected again in the future — a potential for which the Confederate defenders would now have to prepare a more thorough defense.

The Federals, endlessly wringing their hands over the possible reemergence of the Confederate ram, dusted off every tactic in their book. Torpedoes were laid in the river, gunboats sent up the Middle River to shell Plymouth from afar in the hopes of drawing the *Albemarle* from her berth into a fight on the sound. New gunboat strategies were formulated and put in place should the ram reappear, but all of this to no effect. The *Albemarle* did not budge. The ironclad would apparently remain at Plymouth until repaired, then venture forth when time and circumstance suited her, not her Federal tormenters. The ironclad now reigned supreme, and she alone would call the tune. So for the time being the tactical situation on Albemarle Sound remained an odd sort of standoff, the Federal Navy tied in knots by a vessel that, for the time being at least, refused to confront them; and so it would remain for the undefined future.

This odd situation did not, however, prevent some curious facts from flying about and disturbing the local citizenry, in particular Catherine Edmondston at her plantation home near Edwards Ferry. On May 27, for instance, provoked by a supposed Yankee claim of having disposed of the *Albemarle*, she penned in her journal a critical analysis of this presumed Federal subterfuge. "Have they no shame that they thus persist in telling such lies. Mr. E thinks it is done in order to secure Lincoln's nomination by the political convention which meets on the 7th of June, but they are short sighted if they think so flimsy a tissue of falsehoods will last until then. Even now the truth begins to peep out."[8]

While there may have been some confusion in the Northern press regarding the fate of the *Albemarle* and the true outcome of the May 5 naval engagement on the sound, there was no confusion whatsoever in the South. The *Albemarle* was considered a magnificent vessel, and James Cooke a commander of rare ability. Indeed, so gratified were the powers in Richmond that for his April efforts at Plymouth and his recent fight on the sound, Cooke was promoted to the rank of captain in the Confederate Navy, dated June 10.[9] It was a reward well deserved.

Unfortunately, the pleasure of his promotion and all the excitement attendant his most recent success, could not conceal for Captain Cooke his increasing physical strain. His health had apparently been worsening over a period of time, and that condition could not have been but exacerbated by his most recent trials and engagements. In ill health now beyond his capacity, Cooke submitted a request to be temporarily relieved of command of the *Albemarle* in order to rest and recover. This was granted on June 17.

In Cooke's place Commander John N. Maffitt was ordered to Plymouth to take command of the *Albemarle* on June 9.[10] Maffitt was well-known in the Confederacy, had seen much action as the captain of the CSS *Florida*, a foreign built commerce raider that had claimed some 23 prizes on the high seas. He had developed a considerable reputation for swagger and aggressiveness, but had been brought low by a bout of yellow fever that killed many of his crew.[11] Now recovered, Maffitt was anxious to get back to duty and seemed at first a perfect fit for the *Albemarle* in Cooke's absence, but storming the high seas aboard the *Florida* and command of an ironclad going nowhere at Plymouth were, as Maffitt was soon to discover, two very different things. Indeed, mulling the situation over, Catherine Edmondston hit the nail directly on the head when she observed: "Capt Cooke has at his own request, in consequence of his health, been removed from command of the Albemarle & Capt Maffitt of the Florida memory assigned to the duty. Poor gentleman. I pity him! How he will chafe cooped up in this narrow crooked river after roaming at will the broad bosom of the sea in search of Yankee commerce."[12]

But the Yankees responded with trepidation to Maffitt's new appointment. "Maffitt's assignment as the *Albemarle*'s commander brought with it varying degrees of anxiety. Among Union commanders he was widely known as a wily, aggressive, and successful blockade runner. His being teamed with the feared ironclad had prompted Union commanders to explore every possible way, other than battle, of defeating the *Albemarle*."[13] The Confederate ironclad had to be destroyed, but direct confrontation seemed, at this point at least, a fool's errand. What could be done?

At Hampton Roads Admiral Lee, in command of the North Atlantic Blockading Squadron, pondered the dilemma. The *Albemarle* had somehow to be eliminated before it could wreak havoc on the sounds again. A Federal monitor, he knew, might go toe-to-toe with the *Albemarle*, but he had no monitors, due to their deeper draft, that could cross the bar and operate in the sounds. So that was not an option. He did have gunboats of light enough draft that could operate nimbly in the sounds, but they had already proven incapable of little more than getting themselves blown to pieces when in direct conflict with the Rebel ram. So that approach seemed now imprudent. The solution, by logic, seemed thus to require a new or novel approach, something outside the traditional, naval methodology. Lee also had a young officer — he knew from reading the most recent reports — remarkably capable of bold, novel solutions. It would not take long before Admiral Lee would put two and two together. The answer to his problem was named, of course, William B. Cushing.

CHAPTER 22

David against Goliath

O N JULY 1, ADMIRAL Samuel Phillips Lee sent a message requesting the presence of Lt. William Cushing aboard his flagship, *Minnesota*, in the waters off Hampton Roads, Virginia.[1] "Admiral Lee sat in his cabin on the *Minnesota* reading the report of Cushing's extraordinary reconnaissance in the Cape Fear River.... The admiral laid the paper down and sat, softly humming to himself, smoking a big cigar. He rapped on the table, and an aide appeared. 'Get Lieutenant Cushing. Bring him to me as quick as you can.'"[2] Five days later Will Cushing arrived aboard the *Minnesota*, and was shown the way to the admiral's cabin. Cushing later recalled the situation as follows: "The government had no iron-clad that could cross Hatteras bar and enter the sounds, and it seemed likely that our wooden ships would be defeated, leaving New Berne, Roanoke Island, and other points endangered. At all events, it was impossible for any number of our vessels to injure her [the *Albemarle*] at Plymouth, and the expense of our squadron kept to watch her was very great."[3]

The admiral quickly got to the point. He wanted to know if Cushing had any ideas as to how the Confederate ram could be attacked successfully. As Will later recalled, "At this stage of affairs Admiral S.P. Lee spoke to me of the case, when I proposed a plan for her capture or destruction."[4] Cushing's childhood friend and later biographer, Mary Edwards, described the moment: "Cushing came to deliver the navy from this terrifying *Albemarle*, as David against Goliath, a youth of twenty-one years of age. And he did not rush into the adventure under a quick and effervescent excitement of patriotic fever. He coolly contemplated the importance of the situation with all the details of the circumstances, of the difficulties and dangers and while in command of the Monticello, formulated his plans, two in number, and presented them to Admiral S.P. Lee."[5] Admiral David Porter would also note the fact that, while Cushing's expeditions often seemed perilous almost to the point of recklessness, the organizational detail and coolness with which they were executed were what set them apart. Commenting, for instance, on Cushing's most recent reconnaissance on the Cape Fear River, the admiral remarked, "There were ninety-nine chances in a hundred that Cushing and his party would be killed or captured, but throughout all his daring scheme there seemed to be a method, and, though criticized as rash and ill-judged, Cushing returned unscathed from his frequent expeditions, with much important information."[6]

In short, William Cushing had developed the unique and highly sophisticated ability to conceive and execute missions behind enemy lines involving surprise, stealth, and daring. Indeed, often the element of surprise in his plans was predicated upon little more than the high degree of daring they involved, the sheer boldness of his conceptions calculated to catch his adversaries off guard — which almost always they did. But to either take or destroy the *Albemarle* at her berth in Plymouth was in fact a proposition far beyond anything he had previously contemplated. For this he would require every bit of his well-honed martial aptitude, with a good bit of luck thrown in for good measure.

The two plans Cushing devised and laid out for Admiral Lee were intriguing. His first thought was to employ some 100 sailors on the route utilized earlier during the failed torpedo attempt on the ram. He would carry a number of India-rubber boats across the swamp to a point on the Roanoke across from where the *Albemarle* was berthed. There the boats would be inflated, slipped into the water, and the assault launched — no doubt at night — on the ram. The idea here was to overwhelm the crew, cut the ram out, then sail the ironclad from her berth right back out to the Federal flotilla in the sound.[7] Indeed, if the crew could be quickly overwhelmed, and the ram taken, nothing the Confederate garrison fired would dent the ram, while Cushing might then turn the *Albemarle*'s Brooke rifles on her own defenders. Total surprise was the key element. Reminiscent of a World War II style Ranger raid, or even a modern day special forces operation, Cushing's first idea was bold, original, and entirely workable, yet not quite as good as his second.

In his second plan, as Cushing explained the details, "the offensive force was to be conveyed in two low-pressure and very small steamers, each armed with a torpedo and howitzer."[8] This plan was not designed to cut the *Albemarle* out as before, but rather sink the ram at her berth by means of a torpedo (a torpedo during the Civil War referred to an explosive charge either submerged or on a spar, more akin to what today might be called a depth charge, and not a self-propelled projectile as implied by the modern term). A torpedo would be mounted on the bow of both steamers by means of pole or "spar," extended under the ironclad's water line, then detonated. "In this last named plan (which had my preference)," Will wrote, "I intended that one boat should dash in, while the other stood by to throw canister and renew the attempt if the first should fail. It would also be useful to pick up our men if the attacking boat were disabled."[9]

These two designs were, at least, Will Cushing's initial thoughts regarding a potential assault on the *Albemarle*. Lee heard the young man out, but wanted him to develop a more thoughtful, detailed plan that could be presented to the authorities at the naval department for their approval. "The admiral ordered the lieutenant to draw up his 'mature views' on the subject, and return with them in a day or two."[10] So Cushing took his time and worked his way through the entire mission, step-by-step. When done, he put his ideas down in writing for the admiral to review, and hopefully pass on to the department in Washington. On July 9 he wrote: "Deeming the capture or destruction of the rebel ram *Albemarle* feasible, I beg leave to state that I am acquainted with the waters held by her, and am willing to undertake the task.

"If furnished with three low-pressure tugs, one or more fitted with torpedoes, and armed with light howitzers, it might be effected, or if rubber boats were on hand to transport across the swamp to a point immediately abreast of Plymouth. If detailed for this work, I would like to superintend the outfit of the boats, and would be glad to see Lieutenant Kempff, of the *Connecticut*, in charge of the *Monticello* during my absence."[11]

Admiral Lee read Cushing's plans over carefully then sent them along with their author off to Washington in order to present the proposal in person. "Admiral Lee believed that the plan was a good one," Cushing later wrote, "and ordered me to Washington to submit it to the Secretary of the Navy."[12]

Lee penned a brief note to accompany Cushing. "I concur in Captain Smith's opinion," he stated, "that it would be inexpedient to fight the ram with our long double-enders in that narrow river. I proposed to Lieutenant Cushing a torpedo attack, either by means of the India-rubber boat heretofore applied for, which could be transported across the swamp opposite Plymouth, or a light-draft, rifle-proof, swift steam barge, fitted with a torpedo.... The *Monticello* will return to the blockade as soon as Lieutenant Kempff arrives, who is hourly expected, and Lieutenant Cushing, who desires to superintend the fitting of the boats he may have, is instructed to report to the Department and deliver this communication. I have enjoined secrecy and discretion upon him. He is entirely willing to make an attempt to destroy the ram, and I have great confidence in his gallantry."[13]

Thus was Will Cushing off for Washington to argue on behalf of the proposed assault. There he met with the Assistant Secretary Gus Fox on July 27.[14] Fox was an old navy man who ran the everyday, nuts and bolts operation of the department, leaving Gideon Welles to concentrate on the more political aspects of the job. Fox was both highly efficient and highly effective, and had become, over the wartime years, the operational backbone of the navy. "Forty years old, with a great balding head, he was a man of zealous energy, absolutely unable to sit behind a desk for more than a few minutes. Single-handedly, he plunged into all the duties of what fifty-four years later would be designated the office of the chief of naval operations."[15]

Cushing explained the details of his plan to Fox, but the Assistant Secretary was far from impressed. Will's plan sounded hazardous to the extreme, and fundamentally unworkable. "The work was extremely dangerous, he [Fox] said soberly; it was unlikely that he would return alive; it was equally unlikely that he would be successful."[16] Fox realized, of course, that the Confederates controlled the entire length of the Roanoke River, and that the ram, itself a frightful defensive weapon, would be extremely well guarded. When all the elements were soberly considered, the chance of success for such a mission as described by Cushing no doubt seemed to Fox pitifully low, perhaps even bordering on suicide.

Yet one fact remained unchallenged — the *Albemarle* had to be destroyed, and Gus Fox was painfully aware of that fact. That uncomfortable certainty could not be ignored, and Gus Fox knew that, like it or not, he had few alternatives. Will Cushing's plan may not have appealed to him for any number of reasons, but in the end it was the best the Navy had to offer. Cushing continued to plead his case until Fox ultimately gave in to the young lieutenant's enthusiasm. The Assistant Secretary gave his tacit approval, and passed the order on to Gideon Welles for final authorization. The next day, July 28, Welles wrote William Cushing the following, short order: "Proceed to New York and report to Rear-Admiral Gregory, who will assist you in the purchase of a suitable tug and India-rubber boat."[17]

In April, just three months prior, William Cushing had sworn vengeance upon the *Albemarle*. He would now have the opportunity to make good that vow. With Secretary Welles' one, single sentence, the wheels had been put in motion for what would ultimately prove to be one of the most daring and remarkable missions in the history of American arms.

CHAPTER 23

To Prevent an Impending Calamity

THE CELEBRATED CONFEDERATE RAM *Albemarle* now found itself the unique and surprising victim of its own, sudden success. Having favorably shifted the balance of naval power on Albemarle Sound, many in the Confederate government were suddenly loathe to see the ram placed in any sort of situation where its effectiveness might be compromised. For the time being that meant, therefore, any combat beyond the immediate defense of Plymouth. Designed as a formidable naval weapon, for the immediate future the *Albemarle*, like some mythical beast chained to its lair, would now have to rule through intimidation alone. The Rebel ironclad had become, ironically, too valuable a fighting machine to risk in a fight. It was the *Albemarle*, after all — and the hulking presence of the *Albemarle* alone — that now kept the Federal Navy at bay; thus it had become the critical deterrent to a large-scale Federal offensive that might not only retake Plymouth, but sweep inland up the Roanoke toward the Weldon Railroad. Like the little Dutch boy who had saved the day by sticking his thumb in the dike, the ram had assumed for the Confederacy a position of crucial importance from which it could not be removed. If the thumb were dislodged, the dike might collapse.

This situation did not play well with Commander Maffitt's career goals. The good commander may have ventured to Plymouth with visions of naval victories dancing in his head, but boredom would be his lot. "The months of August, September, and part of October were quiet times for the *Albemarle* and her crew. She remained the captive of political maneuvering. Lethargy permeated the atmosphere around her. Summer's heat, boredom, inactivity, and isolation were relieved only occasionally when brief excursions downriver were ordered to observe the enemy and show the flag."[1]

One of those brief excursions occurred on August 6, when Maffitt took the *Albemarle* downriver to the mouth of the Roanoke. There the ironclad was immediately spotted by Commander A.D. Harrell aboard the Federal gunboat *Chicopee*.[2] Harrell had the *Chicopee* slip its cable and maneuver out to the vicinity of the other Union picketboats, presuming that the Rebel ironclad intended to engage them; but the *Albemarle*, having come to a stop, appeared unwilling to budge from that position. Maffitt, under enormous pressure to refrain from jeopardizing the ironclad, could do little more than wait and watch as the Federal vessels attempted to induce battle. Harrell reported, for instance, "I have to inform you that the ram made its appearance this morning at a few minutes before 4 A.M. It advanced as far as the mouth of the river and halted. I slipped and stood out slowly, with the picket boats, with the expectation that it would follow. It is yet in the river."[3]

Commander Harrell, noting that a large crowd had gathered on a nearby beach, logically presumed that the reason they had appeared was to bare eye witness to another large-scale naval engagement on the sound; and, moreover, that that the crowd of locals must have had, in all probability, some forewarning of an impending clash.[4] The appearance of such a congregation was by no means an everyday occurrence on the banks of the Roanoke, thus Harrell had every right to conclude that the ironclad's sudden emergence signified some form of offensive maneuver on its part. "From the number of people on the beach," the Federal commander sensibly reasoned, "no doubt it was expected that an engagement would ensue."[5] Thus did the Federal commander prepare for action, but his preparations would prove unnecessary. The *Albemarle* simply rested at the mouth of the river, venting steam like a great, surly beast, but venturing no further. "Under the circumstances," Harrell reported, watching closely the ironclad's movements, "I have detained the boats which were to ascend the river until I hear from you. The ram can capture them, should they do so, if she pleases. Besides, the *Ceres* is absolutely necessary here to do duty as picket."[6]

But the *Albemarle* made no aggressive move, indeed no move at all, and after some time Harrell came to the conclusion that the ram had no intention of venturing further. "The ram is now lying in the river blowing of steam," he noted. "I do not think, however, that she will advance. Should she do so, however, I will endeavor to draw her down toward the fleet."[7] But being drawn out into the waters of Albemarle Sound toward the waiting clutches of the Federal Fleet was, however, exactly what was now off limits for the Confederate ram. No doubt Commander Maffitt was chomping at the bit to recreate, or even better, Captain Cooke's successful clash with seven Federal gunboats, but times had changed.

The *Albemarle* sat at the mouth of the river for awhile, providing her Yankee foes a short look at the repair work that had been accomplished to her smokestack, etc., and an even better scare, then simply came about and returned to Plymouth. Then Harrell, apparently aggravated by the gathering of Southern sympathizers nearby, and in what today would no doubt be considered an indefensible, indeed criminal act, decided to humor the gathered civilians along the bank of the Roanoke by paying "my respects to those gentlemen on the beach in the shape of a few shells."[8] Whether any of those gentlemen were injured by the commander's respects was not recorded.

What is recorded, however, and what was becoming increasingly obvious, were the political strings under which the *Albemarle* had now been forced to operate. The ironclad's almost meaningless appearance at the mouth of the Roanoke River on the 6th was symptomatic of her new importance to the Confederacy, thus the increasing reluctance to place the ram in any situation in which she might be seriously damaged or lost. For the *Albemarle*, her newfound importance equated to newfound impotence. Like Gulliver, rendered powerless by the entanglements of his Lilliputian captors, the mighty *Albemarle* had been ensnared in web of military and political misgivings that vastly limited the ram's waterborne use. While Commander Maffitt had received instructions from Secretary Mallory to go after the Federal Fleet in Albemarle Sound, many other knowledgeable military and naval officers, including Captain James Cooke for that matter, had argued against it.[9] Typical of this perspective was General Laurence Baker of the Confederate Army, whose overall command included the area surrounding Plymouth. Aware of Mallory's wishes, yet fearful of the loss of the *Albemarle*, Baker wrote directly to Maffitt to voice his concerns. "I have no doubt," he argued, "that in the event of an attack by you the most desperate efforts will be made to destroy your boat, and thus open the approach to Plymouth and Washington."[10] Colonel George Wortham, the commander of the garrison at Plymouth, went even further, suggesting that the *Albemarle* had to be defended at all costs in order to "prevent an impending calamity."[11]

Baker's views were seconded by many; thus the *Albemarle*, like an actor in a play, remained constrained to little more than the occasional theatrical appearance at the Roanoke's mouth, or even less meaningful duty on the river. Responding to this imposed inactivity, on August 31 Maffitt, apparently casting about for some way to strike at the enemy, or to simply do *something*, issued orders to his pilot, James Hopkins, to strike out with a number of the *Albemarle*'s crew on a clandestine raid of their own.[12] "Commander Maffitt organized a raid to capture the Union mail boat *Fawn*. She routinely made a circuit from Norfolk to Plymouth to Roanoke Island. Besides mail, she also carried paymaster's funds. No doubt the raid was prompted by the boredom of inactivity at Plymouth."[13] Hopkins' orders read as follows: "You will take charge of the party now organized and proceed to the [Dismal Swamp] Canal near Elizabeth City. Capture the mail boat, and if you can not bring her into this port, destroy her by fire and retreat to this place with your prisoners."[14]

On September 9 the raid was carried out, some twenty crewmen from the *Albemarle* successfully gaining access to the mail boat as she slowly negotiated the canal. "All twenty raiders boarded safely, but amid the confusion someone threw mail and other bags into the vessel's furnace. There were seven killed or wounded among the *Fawn*'s passengers and crew. Twenty-nine prisoners were taken, including one colonel, two majors, soldiers, government employees and citizens. The raiders left the burning hulk effectively blocking the canal."[15] The raiding party made a safe return to Plymouth with their prisoners, but this sort of venture, no matter how successful, seemed a poor use for the crew of one of the Confederacy's most formidable ironclads. Moreover, when the party returned they discovered that Commander Maffitt's brief career at the helm of the *Albemarle* had ended. He had been reassigned to take command of the *Owl*, a swift blockade runner, and a job far more suited to his talents than that of counting his fingers and toes in Plymouth.[16]

Lt. Alexander Warley was promptly ordered to Plymouth to replace Maffitt in command of the *Albemarle*; but, just as it had been for Maffitt, it was an assignment with little potential for valor or advancement. A change of command may have taken place, but a change of scene had not. "Politically enforced inactivity, persistent repair difficulties, and the sense of apathy which likely prevailed among the crew affected Warley when he assumed command. The small garrison of troops occupying Plymouth had become dependent on the *Albemarle* for their security."[17] In short, the garrison that was supposed to be guarding the ironclad was in fact being guarded by the ironclad, a situation that could only lead eventually to a false sense of security. And any false sense of security is always ripe for exploitation.

Two things did, however, brighten the picture for the *Albemarle* late that summer. First and foremost, a contract for the new ironclad Captain Cooke had urged upon the Confederate Navy was awarded in late August to Gilbert Elliott & Company. Elliott had returned to the boatyard at Halifax after the *Albemarle*'s maiden journey and engagement about Plymouth in April, and now with new contract in hand, could begin building the ironclad Cooke conceived as virtually invincible for the shallow waters of the sounds. Elliott was contracted to build the boat. The Confederate Navy was to supply the boilers, guns, engines, fixtures, etc., and the vessel was to be completed in a mere six months.[18] Considering the fact that the *Albemarle*, due to the shortage of iron and endless governmental delays, had taken Elliott years to construct, this six-month target date for the new ironclad seems today unrealistic if not fanciful; but if the Confederate Navy could meet their end of the bargain, there was little doubt Elliott would meet his. Perhaps in six months the Confederacy would have a sister ship for the *Albemarle* after all, and a vessel far more potent in terms of its design and function.

The second fortunate development was the return of Captain Cooke to full duty in early September.[19] Having struggled with his health for months, Cooke now returned to the command of the naval defenses in the area, along with the supervision of the boatyard at Halifax where he would once again be able to work directly with Gilbert Elliott, now in the construction of the new ram. Taking into consideration the experiences that both shared while building and fighting the *Albemarle,* the new ironclad should surely benefit from their knowledge of the previous ram's attributes and faults.

Suddenly the focus of Confederate aspirations in and around Plymouth had shifted away from a boring present of meaningless excursions and hot, insignificant days, forward some six months toward a far more tantalizing future. That future now included the expectation — no matter how sanguine — of a second ironclad, a vastly improved model that might sweep, surely in tandem with the *Albemarle,* the Federals right out of the sounds. Such a craft would not simply offer protection to Plymouth and Washington, North Carolina, but hope of recovering most of tidal North Carolina from Yankee occupation. Far more than mere strategic objectives, however, these goals represented truly inspirational ambitions.

Whether these new expectations represented a hard look at a difficult reality or, like spinning castles from cotton, a fantasy bordering upon delusion, remained only to be seen. But in the meantime the status quo would have to be maintained at all hazards and the *Albemarle* protected just as dreams must be guarded, for the ironclad's loss now represented not only the loss of Plymouth, but equally the loss of that shining hope of a successful future; and while the fall of Plymouth might still be endured by a defiant Confederacy, the loss of hope could not.

CHAPTER 24

Send the Boats On

As Confederate interests regarding the role of the *Albemarle* shifted during the late summer of 1864 from those grounded in the present to something planted firmly in the future, so too would Union strategic aspirations alter. Prior to this, of course, Federal hopes had been to somehow engage and destroy the ironclad, perhaps by running her down with numerous vessels on the open waters of Albemarle Sound or, if lucky, sneaking a torpedo up against her hull to sink the ram at her berth in Plymouth. In that those tactical arrangements had proven far more hopeful than realistic, however, Federal planning had ultimately given way to a new approach every bit as ingenious as it was desperate. What admirals could not conceive or accomplish had now been left in the hands of a twenty-one-year-old lieutenant, and there seems little question that, as William Cushing traveled to New York City in search of the proper equipment for his mission, the Federal Navy's fondest desire to destroy the *Albemarle* traveled with him. On August 7, just days after Cushing's meeting with Gus Fox, Secretary Welles sent to Admiral Gregory in New York this simple command: "Fit out as early as practicable two of the picket boats for Lieutenant W.B. Cushing."[1]

While William Cushing had developed a certain reputation for dash, daring, and uncanny success amongst the commanders of North Atlantic Blockading Squadron, the Naval Department in Washington, and even his adversaries along the southeastern coast of the Confederate States, that reputation had apparently not preceded him to New York City. Engineer-in-Chief William Wood, for instance, who was at the time heavily engaged in the construction of Federal ironclads as well as devising new techniques for destroying Confederate ironclads, was present when William Cushing made his initial appearance at the Navy's New York offices; and he seemed, judging by his remarks, somewhat taken aback by the youthful lieutenant who presented himself. "While sitting at my desk," Wood later recalled, "at the ironclad office in Canal street New York (the office of Rear-Admiral F.H. Gregory, the general superintendent), a young man (a mere youth) came in and made himself known as Lieutenant W.B. Cushing, United States Navy." Wood, his curiosity obviously aroused by Cushing's youthful appearance and presumed lack of experience, asked Will to continue. "He stated to me," Wood later recalled, "in strict confidence, that he was North on a secret mission, under the sanction of the Honorable Secretary of the Navy, the object being to cut out or destroy the rebel iron-clad *Albemarle*, then lying at Plymouth, N.C., and he had been looking for small and swift low-pressure tug-boats for the purpose of throwing a force on board, capturing, and cutting her out, and that, should he fail in this object, to destroy her; that so far he had been unable to find just such vessels as he required."[2]

With Wood's assistance Will was finally able to locate several small boats that essentially met his requirements. "Finding some boats building for picket duty," Will later explained, "I selected two, and proceeded to fit them out. They were open launches, about thirty feet in length, with small engines and propelled by a screw."[3] The first object of Cushing's search had been to secure vessels that could carry enough men to either cut the ram out or torpedo it, depending upon circumstances. The second object was, no matter which option he chose — which was something that might come down to a last second decision — to be able to approach the ram as quietly as possible. After locating two boats that appeared to suit his needs, Cushing returned to Wood's office to get more detail on the vessels and make the necessary arrangements. According to Wood, Cushing needed more information concerning the launches and the intended torpedo arrangement, and "called on me to make inquiry as to what was designed to be accomplished by its use, etc." To this request Wood immediately replied in detail. "I gave him all the particulars," Wood remembered, "and urged him to avail himself of the opportunity presented, which he without hesitation did. He sat down at my desk and wrote to the Secretary, stating that he had found what he desired for his purpose, and requested an order from the Department to be furnished with two of the torpedo boats or launches."[4]

The two launches seemed perfect for Cushing's plans. They could carry enough men for either task he chose, and the engine compartments could be muffled to drown the sound of the pistons. Each launch had a howitzer to spray canister, and a spar (or pole) in front upon which the torpedo was attached. "A twelve pounder howitzer was fitted to the bows of each," as Will described the boats, "and a boom rigger out, some fourteen feet in length; swinging by a goose neck hinge to the bluff of the bow. A topping lift to a stanchion inboard; raised or lowered it and the torpedo was fitted into an iron slide at the end. This was intended to be detached from the boom by means of a heel-jigger leading in board; and exploded by another line connecting with a pin which held a grape shot over nipple and cap."[5]

The torpedo and spar combination was a relatively new invention, and its effective use required much practice. Two lines were attached to the torpedo, one to detach the torpedo from the spar, the other to detonate it once it had become lodged near or underneath the intended target. Both lines had to be handled delicately and pulled at precisely the right moment. Much regarding the charges' proper placement and detonation depended upon both feel and experience. Should the torpedo be cut loose too early, it would rise in the water in front of the target and the explosion would lose much of its effect. On the other hand, if the lanyard were pulled too tight, the charge could easily go off prematurely. Indeed, the device was more like playing a temperamental instrument than utilizing a weapon, and Cushing found it touchy and difficult. "The torpedo was, I believe, the invention of Engineer Lay of the navy," Will later wrote, "and introduced by Chief Engineer Wood. It has many defects and I would not again attempt its use."[6]

Far more art than science then, the lines required virtually ideal conditions to function properly; and nighttime raids on the water, Cushing knew only too well, rarely offered those sorts of conditions. That was not going to deter him, however. "He tested it ... exploding several torpedoes in the Hudson River, and found that it could be made to work if one had enough leisure to make sure that the lanyard and trigger line were pulled at exactly the right moments. But he was not overly concerned with the difficulties; there still

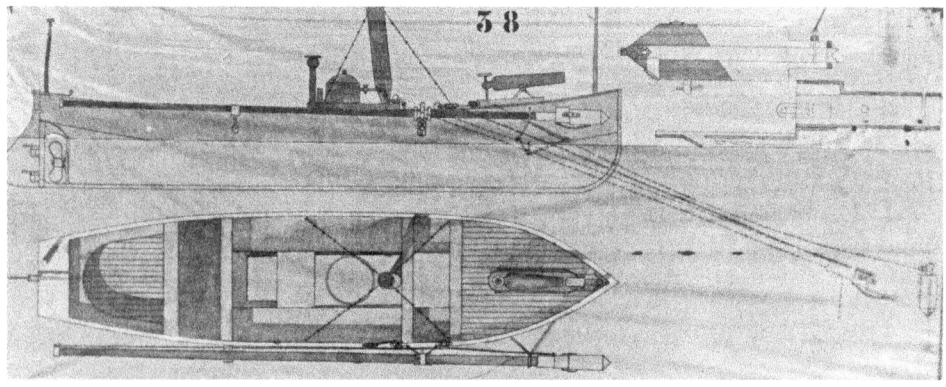

Steam screw launch with spar torpedo (U.S. Naval History and Heritage Command).

lingered in his mind the idea that he might be able to surprise the *Albemarle* and take her by boarding, cutting her out from under the Confederate guns."[7] That thought must have been for William Cushing a guiding light. Immune from Rebel artillery fire once inside the ironclad, Cushing might then simply head the *Albemarle* downriver, at some point hoisting the stars and stripes high above the ram, and sail out to the Federal squadron, his new flag fluttering on the breeze. *That* would be a mission worth remembering!

By mid–September both boats were fitted out, and the practice sessions on the Hudson finally complete.[8] Cushing then, apparently well aware of the fact that any attempt to destroy the *Albemarle* would be far more dangerous than any other he had before undertaken, sought and received permission to have the launches taken to North Carolina by subordinates while he made plans — unknown to the Navy Department — to make a side trip home to Fredonia in order to see his mother, perhaps for the last time. On September 9 Will wrote Gus Fox at Washington: "Can I send the picket boats through the canal to Chesapeake Bay," he inquired, "in charge of their officers, and go myself by the usual route and meet them there? The torpedo is all that detains them now, and that will soon be completed."[9] Cushing's request was, of course, a bit disingenuous in that the "usual route" he intended to use was by way of Fredonia, New York, hardly a direct course down to the Chesapeake Bay. Fox, suspecting nothing unusual was afoot, responded on September 11: "Send the boats on," he agreed. "You can come yourself by rail."[10]

With that William Cushing started north for Fredonia, while the two picketboats headed off for Southern waters, Ensign Howorth in charge of picketboat *No. 1*, Ensign Andrew Stockholm commanding the second. This for Cushing, however, would prove a disastrous mistake. In that neither man was a competent sailor, they should never have been tasked with the mission to begin with. The journey south would prove eventful indeed, and their tribulations would come back, not simply to haunt Will Cushing, but come close to scrubbing the entire *Albemarle* mission.

CHAPTER 25

I Have Undertaken a Great Project

IN LATE SEPTEMBER William Cushing began the trip by rail from New York City north to Fredonia in order to visit his mother, perhaps — as surely he understood it — for the very last time. He would have a few days at home to see some friends then quietly explain the *Albemarle* mission to his mother before heading off to meet Stockholm and Howorth at Hampton Roads. When he arrived the sky was blue, the leaves in full fall color, and Cushing later remarked that "Western New York had never looked so beautiful."[1]

Reasons for destroying the *Albemarle* abounded, no doubt reasons that seemed compelling to a young officer such as William Cushing. "No one in the Union Navy, least of all Will Cushing was unaware of the political as well as the military importance of sinking the ram."[2] As the long summer dragged toward fall, for instance, Abraham Lincoln's chances of again winning the White House appeared to have hit rock bottom right along with the war effort he supervised as Commander in Chief. Grant remained bogged down at Petersburg, Sherman no nearer to taking Atlanta, their combined failures draining the electorate of confidence and the Republican administration of hope. "Defeatism settled across the party that August, as Lincoln's friends and foes alike were certain he could not be re-elected. Weed bluntly told him so; and Swett, Raymond, and Browning all agreed."[3] Typical of this war-weary turn against Lincoln was the editorial writer, Horace Greeley. Writing from New York, Greeley "begged Lincoln to negotiate for peace, arguing that the people wanted the war to end and that 'our bleeding, bankrupt, almost dying' country couldn't stand new conscriptions and 'new rivers of human blood.'"[4]

Indeed, so depressing and seemingly hopeless had the situation become that on August 23, the president virtually gave up any expectation of electoral victory, and privately penned a concession note to General George McClellan who, running on a peace platform, appeared to be the obvious Democratic nominee for president and probable victor. Alone in his office in the White House, Lincoln wrote: "This morning, as for some days past, it seems exceedingly probable that this Administration will not be re-elected. Then it will be my duty to so co-operate with the President elect as to save the Union between the election and the inauguration; as he will have secured his election on such ground that he can not possibly save it afterwards."[5] Lincoln then had each member of his cabinet sign the back of the note — without showing them its contents — which he in turn secreted away in his desk. Thus the election, at that point at least, appeared in its most elemental terms to be a contest between war and peace; the hope of a negotiated settlement, or a war that still appeared mismanaged and utterly unwinnable.

By late September, however, that situation had begun to change if ever so slightly in favor of the president. Military success, the key ingredient for any Republican comeback, finally arrived to bolster Lincoln's cause. In Georgia Sherman had at long last taken Atlanta, one of the key cities in all the South, then in October Phillip Sheridan defeated a Rebel army in Virginia's Shenandoah Valley. But despite those victories, the election still remained very heated and far too close to call. Indeed, one Democratic paper in Wisconsin editorialized with an eerie sense of venom: "If he [Lincoln] is elected to misgovern for another four years, we trust some bold hand will pierce his heart with dagger point for the public good."[6]

It was into this toxic political mix that William Cushing ventured, having completed his work in New York, while preparing to return to North Carolina for his run at the *Albemarle*. And there is little question that Cushing grasped quite clearly the boost a success on his part might provide the president, for "it seems to have been his belief that if he could destroy the *Albemarle* before November the re-election of Lincoln, which with Grant and indeed most members of the armed services he considered essential to the Union cause, would be practically assured."[7] No longer was his contemplated mission against the ironclad merely the completion of the vow he had sworn to avenge Flusser's death, but now a bold strike for Lincoln, union, and country as well.

Meanwhile, as Will Cushing prepared himself to confide in his mother, both Andrew Stockholm and William Howorth were having a difficult go of it on their trip south toward the Chesapeake Bay. By September 25, for instance, neither boat was further along than New Jersey, broken down at New Brunswick near the entrance to the Delaware and Raritan Canal, both launches already in need of repair.[8] Having started off from New York on the

22nd, in three days they had covered barely twenty miles before running aground — hardly an auspicious beginning. Stockholm had spent the better part of two days marooned on a sandbar, while Howorth had managed to damage the hull of launch *No. 1* on some rocks. Repairs were managed quickly, however, and by the evening of the 25th both boats were once again back on the water.[9] Making their way through the Chesapeake and Delaware Canal, eventually to reach the Delaware River, they headed south for Annapolis, Maryland, and arrived on October 5, Howorth towed by Stockholm for much of the journey as launch *No. 1*'s engine had broken down.[10]

The following morning they set off once more, but promptly ran into foul weather and had to put into a small bay on Maryland's Eastern Shore in order to wait out the storm. There Howorth's engine was tinkered with until they got it working again, then both launches headed south down the Chesapeake once the weather had cleared. Arriving off Point Lookout — the southernmost point in Maryland on the western shore of the Chesapeake Bay — Stockholm's engine now began acting up, but Howorth refused to stop, fearful that they had already lost far too much time en route. Stockholm later reported, "I must here state that on the evening of the 7th, when at Point Look-out, I requested Acting Ensign Howorth, commanding picket boat *No. 1*, to remain by me until my repairs were completed, but he declined, he wishing to get to Fortress Monroe as early as possible."[11] Thus Howorth pushed on without Stockholm, while launch *No. 2* put into a river on the western side of the bay for repairs, Stockholm convinced that he was still cruising off the Maryland shoreline.

Unfortunately, Stockholm had radically miscalculated. He was, in fact, now in Virginia waters, and his presence was quickly discerned by the local home guard, which began firing on the boat. "I immediately returned their fire," Stockholm reported, "and fought them until I had expended my last cartridge; previous to which I had slipped my cable, and in trying to get out of the enemy's reach grounded on a sand bar."[12] The small Yankee crew then tossed everything they could manage overboard in the hopes of lightening the vessel, but that proved entirely futile. Stockholm continued: "I destroyed all that I could before surrendering, and set her on fire forward. I also received one shot in the hand and one through the cap. I did all in my power to destroy the engine by breaking and bending it as much as possible.... When I found I could do no more, I surrendered to Captain Covington, of the Home Guard."[13] The Confederates promptly marched their captives off to prison, and burned the boat where it rested. Thus launch *No. 2*, a major key to the operation Cushing had planned and trained for, was gone, neither Howorth nor Cushing having any ideas as to its whereabouts. "This was a great misfortune," Cushing later wrote, "and I have never understood how it occurred."[14]

Howorth ultimately reached the naval base at Hampton Roads in one piece, but behind him launch *No. 2* was nowhere to be found.

At home in Fredonia, William Cushing had, of course, no knowledge of the trials and tribulations his two junior officers were experiencing. For a few days Will had made the rounds, meeting friends, speaking with the editor of the local newspaper, attending several parties, and generally making a good time of it. The ultimate purpose of his visit, however, was to explain to his mother the nature of the mission he had agreed to undertake; and when the day for that explanation finally arrived — cold, dark, windy — William asked his mother to accompany him on a buggy ride away from the house.[15] "In the afternoon he came to her suddenly and said that he must tell her something. He would take her for a ride away from the town where it would be impossible for anyone to overhear them. She was frightened by the urgency in his voice but she went with him to the barn."[16]

He drove her far outside of town to a high point in the Arkwright Hills,[17] and there helped her down from the carriage. They quickly found a place out of the wind below a tree. There he faced her dramatically. "Mother," he began, "I have undertaken a great project, and no soul must know until it is accomplished, but I *must tell you* for I need your prayers."[18] Will then went on to explain the entire mission, from beginning to end, avoiding not even the smallest detail.

When finished, his mother, considering all the facts as he had related them, responded honestly. "My son," she replied, "I believe you will accomplish it, but you cannot come out alive."[19] Then, having already lost one child to the war, she lamented, "Oh, why did they call upon you to do this?"[20]

To this Will responded firmly. "Mother," he said, "it shall be done or you will have no son Will. If I die it will be in a good cause."[21]

The two then kneeled together and prayed for William's success. The following day he was off again for New York by rail, and from there on to Hampton Roads. His mother would later recall that long, painful period waiting for news from Will as fraught with anxiety. "Oh! Those days of suspense shared by no one — every hour an age of agony."[22]

Cushing finally arrived at the naval base at Hampton Roads on October 10 to find Ensign Howorth but, of course, no sign of Andrew Stockholm. Admiral Lee, who had always thought highly of Will Cushing and had firmly backed his scheme to either take or torpedo the *Albemarle*, had unfortunately been transferred, and Admiral David Porter appointed in his place. "Porter, who, unlike Lee, had no high opinion of Cushing and thought of him as a daredevil with more luck than ability, sent the young officer ... out in an army tug to find his second boat."[23] Stockholm could not be located, of course, because the boat had been burned and the crew taken prisoner, but no one

Picketboat #1 with forward howitzer and spar torpedo (U.S. Naval History and Heritage Command).

knew that at the time. Admiral Porter was not pleased by what he considered the negligent loss of navy property, and it required considerable pleading on Cushing's part to finally convince him to allow the mission to continue with but one boat. One day Porter would develop a considerable appreciation for William Cushing, but this episode was long before that day; and Cushing had inadvertently, but obviously, marched his way into the admiral's dog house. There was little for Will to do but swallow his pride and head for the water. "My best boat being thus lost," he wrote, "I proceeded with one alone to make my way through the Chesapeake and Albemarle canals into the sounds."[24]

Yet this part of the journey would not pass without its own unique set of perils. Halfway down the canal Cushing found his route blocked. Fortunately, he was able to locate a small stream that fed off the canal, and he felt his way along this route until he came upon a mill dam that again blocked his way.[25] They waited for high water, took the boat through once it arrived, only to be grounded on the on the other side of the dam. There he "got a flat boat and taking out gun and coal succeeded, in two days, in getting her through."[26] For the remainder of the journey he traveled with his small crew through Rebel territory, exposed to the home guards and militias all along the way, and with no true understanding of exactly where they were, "passing with but seven men through the canal," Will recalled, "where for thirty miles there was no guard or Union inhabitant, I reached the sound, and ran before a gale of wind to Roanoke Island."[27]

At Roanoke Island, due to the proximity of Confederate forces and thus the likelihood of spies and informants, he lied about his true destination, and even made arrangements to take on some passengers to better the ruse. "If any person had known our destination," explained Cushing, "the news would have reached Plymouth long before we arrived to confirm it."[28] Then, in the middle of the night when no one was watching, he quietly got his crew together and pushed off. By daylight they were far beyond Roanoke Island, and hard on their way toward the squadron. "Fifty miles up the sound, I found the fleet anchored off the mouth of the river," Will wrote, "and awaiting the ram's appearance."[29] Thus had William Cushing located the requisite boats, completed his training, and returned with the launch and torpedo necessary for the task of destroying the ironclad. The moment of truth was now rapidly approaching. Eight miles up the Roanoke River the *Albemarle* waited.

CHAPTER 26

You Must Not Hope to Return

WHILE WILLIAM CUSHING had managed to slip away from Roanoke Island unnoticed, he had not departed without misgivings. On the island, for instance, he had learned for the first time of the torpedo attack on the *Albemarle* that had failed in May, and additionally he was shown a recent newspaper article describing a plan to destroy the ironclad.[1] Both bits of information had to have troubled the young lieutenant. While the newspaper article had been incorrect in terms of its details, Cushing knew that Southern military leadership — just as was done in the North — routinely scoured the papers for articles containing troop movements, strategic initiatives, or anything that might prove of value (during the Civil War both sides were notoriously inept at maintaining secrets); and any article, no matter how incorrect, might well arouse suspicions. And aroused suspicions, he knew, would invariably lead to aroused security.

Likewise it was in terms of the failed torpedo attack, for this failure surely had to have sparked concern at Plymouth of a potential similar assault, and thus initiated defensive measures to confound one. These were troubling accounts. The odds, it seemed, of getting to the *Albemarle*— which were already painfully low to begin with — might, because of these two unfortunate circumstances, have been decreased significantly. There was no telling what measures the Rebels might have taken to make the ironclad torpedo safe; and the truth of the matter was, he would probably not know until he actually stumbled upon them at Plymouth — should he be lucky enough to get that far.

But these problems were, for William B. Cushing, of small moment. His confidence was supreme. Nothing was going to stop him. "Thus it seemed impossible to surprise them [the Confederate defenses]," Will readily admitted after reviewing the grim facts, "or to attack with hope of success." Yet where some perceive only failure and potential misfortune, others conceive opportunity. Will Cushing was just such a person. "Impossibilities," he insisted, "are for the timid — we determined to overcome all obstacles."[2]

Upon arrival at the fleet at the mouth of the Roanoke River, Cushing immediately reported to Commander W.H. Macomb, then in command of the squadron in Albemarle Sound, and tasked with the job of containing the *Albemarle*. Will supplied Macomb with his orders and indicated he would require a few more men in order to complete his mission. It went almost without saying that those selected would have to be tough, especially good with cutlass, knife, and pistol. Macomb promptly sent out word to the commanders of the various vessels gathered near. "Quietly, he [Macomb] went to the commanders of the other ships: without stating the duty, ask the various crews for volunteers for an extremely hazardous undertaking, and pick your best men."[3]

The five men who had accompanied Cushing and Howorth south from New York were William Stotesbury, Samuel Higgins, Lorenzo Deming, Henry Wilkes, and Robert King.[4] Will did not know if all five would volunteer for the mission, but suspected they would. During the afternoon an additional seven reported to Cushing aboard Macomb's flagship, the *Shamrock*. These seven were Francis Swan and Charles Steever from the *Ostego*, William Smith, Bernard Harley, and Edward Houghton from the *Chicopee*, John Woodman from the *Commodore Hull*, and lastly Richard Hamilton from the *Shamrock*.[5] These seven had all volunteered for an extremely dangerous mission, not knowing what it entailed, and had been hand-picked from a larger pool of like volunteers. Acting Ensign Thomas Gay would later be added to the expedition at the very last moment.[6] They were, from all reports, the best and toughest men in the squadron.

Up to that point Cushing had told only Howorth — who had accompanied him on many a mission and was to be trusted — of his intended objective, although it is reasonable to assume that many in the fleet had guessed the target what with the arrival of Cushing and the specially rigged torpedo launch. At that time Will decided to gather the men on the deck of the *Shamrock*. There he would explain the purpose of the mission, and allow each man the opportunity to volunteer, or withdraw, should any one of them consider the plan too hazardous.

"Here, for the first time," Cushing wrote, "I disclosed to my officers and men our object, and told them that they were at liberty to go or not, as they pleased."[7] The entire group of volunteers — including those who had traveled with him from New York in picketboat *No. 1*— then gathered on the afterdeck. Will explained the mission in detail, and minced no words concerning the dangers involved. "Not only must you not expect, but you must not hope to return," he counseled sternly. "I can promise you nothing but glory, death or, possibly, promotion. We will have the satisfaction," he continued, "of getting in a good lick at the rebels, that is all."[8] Cushing then asked all those men who were still interested in the mission to take a step forward. Every one of them at once stepped toward him. "I am not surprised,"[9] he said, no doubt pleased with their response. He now had his crew.

Will Cushing then left Howorth to go over all the fine details with the volunteers and to acquaint them with the torpedo launch, while he returned to visit with Macomb in the commander's quarters. There he met with Macomb and Ensign Sommers, who had just that morning returned from an extensive reconnaissance of the *Albemarle* and the local defenses at Plymouth the night before.[10] What Sommers had to tell him was hardly comforting. Sommers' party had been detected, brought under a severe fire, and a number of his men captured. He and the remainder of his party had managed to escape, but they had been thoroughly shot up, and returned early that morning near exhaustion. Yet he had still managed to get a good look at the ironclad and the defenses in place, and his report was of considerable interest.

The security measures employed by the Rebels to safeguard the *Albemarle* appeared not only extensive, but virtually impenetrable. As Cushing later recalled them in his official report, the defenses would present a serious test. "The Roanoke River is a stream averaging 150 yards in width, and quite deep. Eight miles from the mouth was the town of Plymouth, where the ram was moored. Several thousand soldiers occupied town and forts and held both banks of the stream. A mile below the ram was the wreck of the *Southfield*, with hurricane deck above water, and on this a guard was stationed, to give notice of anything suspicious, and to send up fire-rockets in case of attack. Thus it seemed impossible to surprise them, or to attack, with hope of success."[11] Indeed, the entire river was picketed from top to bottom, and any approach might be detected anywhere en route.

The notion that the Confederate defenders might be apathetic due to prolonged inactivity, or incautious in their surveillance had at least twice now been put to rest, once when the prior torpedo attack had been discovered and shot to pieces, and most recently by Sommers' own reconnaissance mission of the night before. There seemed little question the Rebels would be ready and waiting, perhaps now even more so than before due to all the recent activity. Still, after a long discussion and analysis, Cushing decided he could wait no longer. The longer he dallied, the more would the Confederates prepare their defenses. Delay appeared to be a losing formula. The time for the assault had come.

"The sun set behind thick clouds on the night of October 26, and Cushing decided that it would be dark enough for success."[12] Will had picketboat *No. 1* run over to the *Ostego* to pick up the remainder of his crew, and there he encountered Ensign Gay, anxious to come along. Gay later recalled the moment vividly. "On the 26th Of October, 1864," he reported, "Lieutenant Cushing came alongside of the USS *Ostego*, then on picket duty near the mouth of the Roanoke River, with picket boat *No. 1*, to proceed up to Plymouth to endeavor to destroy the rebel ram *Albemarle*. Wishing to be a part of the expedition, I immediately offered my services which were accepted."[13] By Gay's watch the launch shoved off from the *Ostego* around 11:00 P.M., bound for the mouth of the Roanoke.[14]

All critical aspects of the mission appeared ready. The weather had cooperated, the men were set to their tasks, the launch working properly; but fortunately for Will Cushing, on this night his mission would fizzle before hardly getting started. To begin with, Will had misjudged the tide, and soon the launch had run aground almost hopelessly near the mouth of the Roanoke. There the raiding party remained for hours until finally freeing the vessel sometime around 2:00 A.M. Despite the delay, Cushing decided to push on toward Plymouth, but more trouble was encountered directly ahead. "Within five hundred yards a sharp hail ran across the water and the dim shadow of a picket launch loomed out of the darkness."[15] It was a Federal Army picketboat that had clearly heard picketboat *No. 1*'s approach, distinctly picking up the sound of the engine from a distance across the water. Cushing answered the hail, and the crew from the picketboat came close, several men jumping onto the launch with lanterns and guns, the business end of a howitzer trained menacingly on picketboat *No. 1*. Will and his men were soon identified, but it was now too late to begin the mission, and more importantly, a serious problem had been uncovered — picketboat *No. 1* made far too much noise to secretly approach the *Albemarle*. Something had to be done. If the Federal picketboat could pick them out on the open sound so easily, the Confederates would surely detect them on the narrow waters of the Roanoke with even greater ease. They would never get to within a mile of the ironclad!

The launch was brought about and promptly headed back toward the fleet. The mission had not been a failure, simply a postponement, and a postponement for good cause. William Cushing might have been young, fearless, and impatient, but he was certainly no fool. Corrections would have to be made. The mission for October 26 had been scratched. Repairs would be affected to the engine compartment, and they would try again the following night — October 27.

CHAPTER 27

Pick Your Men

At Plymouth, Lt. Alexander Warley, now in command of the *Albemarle*, had his own set of problems with which to contend. To begin with, he had received information that a steam launch had been spotted on the Roanoke River, and it took no great leap of logic to fathom its raison d'être. New troops had also been brought in to garrison the town and nearby forts, and they had to be instructed as to the importance of the ironclad, lest they misconstrue the situation. "On the day of their arrival," Warley noted, referring to the infantry recently arrived, "I heard of a steam-launch having been seen in the river, and I informed the officer in command of the fact, and at the same time told him that the safety of the place depended on the *Albemarle*, and that the safety of the *Albemarle* depended on the watchfulness of his pickets."[1]

Since early September, when Warley had first taken over command of the ironclad, he had been facing an uphill struggle. "I soon found why the very able officer whom I succeeded (Captain J.N. Maffitt) was willing to give up the command," Warley later confided. "There was no reason why the place might not be recaptured any day: the guns commanding the river were in no condition for use and the troops in charge of them were worn down by ague [malaria], and were undrilled and worthless."[2] Meanwhile, he had to contend with constant Federal reconnaissance missions, and the never ending threat of attack, whether by the Federal fleet making a charge up the Roanoke, or perhaps another clandestine torpedo attempt.

Yet the Yankee reconnaissance teams sent to spy on the ironclad could not have determined from a distance what Warley later claimed; that the artillery pieces deployed to protect the ram were in poor condition, the artillerists themselves unskilled and undisciplined. Nor could the Yankee scouts have discerned from the far side of the river the fact that the large infantry garrison in town had been enfeebled by illness. Indeed, more than once Federal missions to Plymouth had been roughly handled by the same garrison Warley later characterized as worthless; and the new garrison, by Warley's own report, had *just* arrived, so how ill could they have been? Twice were Yankee missions quickly detected and rapidly driven off or captured, and in that sense it is difficult to determine whether Lt. Warley's assessment was an accurate reflection of the conditions at Plymouth at the time, or a latter day rationalization.

At any event, immediately upon taking up command, Warley soon discerned the fact that Federal scouts were watching his every move, and he quickly took steps to counter that problem. "On the other side of the river, at pistol range," he reported, "was a low island heavily timbered, and said to be almost impenetrable. As it fully commanded our position, I sent an active officer with a few hardy men to 'explore it.' His report on his return showed that we were under constant espionage. Acting on this information the same officer (Mr. Long), with ten men, ambuscaded and captured a Federal man-of-war boat, and for the time being put a stop to the spy system."[3]

To keep his men fresh, healthy, and to combat the persistent threat of Yankee reconnaissance, Warley also sent out teams drawn form the *Albemarle*'s crew. This, as Warley put it, was done "to break the monotony of life and keep down ague." And these teams proved quite productive. "I had always out an expedition of ten men," he later explained, "who were uniformly successful in doing a fair amount of damage to the enemy. All [the men]" Warley insisted, "were anxious to be on these expeditions to keep out of the hospital."[4] But the demands of constant surveillance proved a task far beyond the capacity of the *Albemarle*'s small crew to handle by themselves. "The crew of the *Albemarle* numbered but sixty, too small a force to allow me to keep an armed watch on deck at night," Warley pointed out, "and do outside picketing besides."[5] For this greater task the Confederate Army had to furnish the manpower, and beyond the normal posting on or near the ram, a forward outpost was eventually established on a schooner anchored downriver near the sunken wreck of the *Southfield*.

In the middle of the channel, the men manning this forward post had an excellent view of the river, thus any craft coming toward Plymouth. "The officer in command of the troops was inclined to give me assistance," Warley admitted, "and sent a picket of twenty five men under a lieutenant; they were furnished with rockets and a field piece. This picket was stationed on board of a schooner about gun-shot below the *Albemarle*, where an attempt was made to raise a vessel (the *Southfield*) sunk at the time of Commander Cooke's dash down river."[6]

Regardless of Alexander Warley's legitimate complaints and concerns, William Cushing's previously detailed evaluation of the Confederate defenses in and around Plymouth seems, even now, fundamentally accurate. At Plymouth the *Albemarle* was moored at the wharf, her guns trained on the river. Around the ram artillery had been unlimbered, the pieces trained on the waterborne approaches to the ironclad. The *Albemarle*'s crew and the local military were involved in constant picket and guard duty. The Roanoke River had picket stations along its entire length from Albemarle Sound to Plymouth, and there were now boats[7] in the water near the wreck of the *Southfield*, one, a schooner, with a field piece and twenty-five soldiers on constant watch. The slightest apprehension on the part of this outpost would send warning rockets high into the air, triggering in turn illumination fires along the riverbanks and, of course, a general notification of the guard. Taken as a whole, these measures seemed a most daunting impediment, indeed, an almost impenetrable defensive screen.

Thus despite Lt. Warley's concerns, constructed in considerable depth from the mouth of the Roanoke to Plymouth, stretched a formidable web of security measures in which any approach might easily be detected, even miles from the ram. Moreover, on the 27th of October, Warley, aware of the presence of a motor launch on the Roanoke, "had the watch on board doubled and took extra precaution."[8] In short, he had reason to believe something serious was afoot, and had taken virtually every precaution he could think of to thwart an attack that night. Even more importantly — and entirely unknown to William Cushing — the *Albemarle* itself, as a deterrent to torpedo attack, now had a log apron extending around it that blocked all waterborne approach. The apron, as Warley described it, was "a cordon of single cypress logs chained together, about ten feet from her side."[9]

Thus what William Cushing did not know as he prepared for his assault — and a crucial piece of information it was — was that, even should he somehow manage to run the prohibitive gauntlet of Confederate defensive measures that protected the *Albemarle*, he would then only run up against the log apron, floating at a distance from the ironclad's hull, a defensive measure specifically designed to prohibit the sort of close approach necessary for a torpedo attack. (It is of interest that on the 15th of October John Woodman of the *Commodore Hull* had performed a reconnaissance on the island across from Plymouth, and had spotted the log apron around the ram. He reported this fact to his superiors aboard the *Hull*. Woodman's report reads "On her port side, which was toward the stream, there are timbers extending from the wharf and lapping on her prow and stern one-quarter her length from each end."[10] But for some odd reason this information appears never to have been shared with Cushing prior to the assault on the *Albemarle*, even though Woodman accompanied Cushing as part of assault the team.) Thus picketboat *No. 1*, even with its spar torpedo, when confronted by the log apron, would be useless against the ram, incapable of gaining the target. By then surely the launch would have been detected, and the Rebels prepared to blow it out of the water. Sitting hopeless and useless in the river near the *Albemarle*, Cushing and his crew would at that most critical of moments find themselves in dire straits, forced to either surrender, or risk being shot to pieces.

Given all the facts, any sober analysis of the situation at the time would surely have deemed the Confederate ironclad virtually impregnable, and Will Cushing's design to destroy her little more than suicidal. But Cushing, of course, did not have all the facts.

* * *

For William Barker Cushing, October 27 arrived with even more unsettling news than had the 26th. Now to be added to Sommers' report of the prior day, for instance, was information gleaned from several runaway slaves who had made their way down to the fleet that morning. At approximately noon the slaves had been spotted trying to swim out to the ships, and were in turn picked up and brought up to the fleet. When it was determined they had recently come from Plymouth and had current information regarding the local defenses, they were brought to the *Shamrock* where they were interviewed by Cushing and Howorth.[11] While Cushing had been aware of the general arrangement of defenses surrounding the *Albemarle*, the twenty-five man detachment aboard the schooner in the channel was news for him, and this obviously represented a grave new danger. The slaves apparently also confirmed at this time that a picket post had been established on what remained of the *Southfield*, this post also capable of firing warning rockets toward the garrison upriver.[12] On the face of these new facts, it surely appeared almost impossible to approach Plymouth undetected, and this information was enough to make Commander Macomb momentarily doubt the mission's feasibility. But Cushing remained steadfast.

Numerous options were discussed and debated between Howorth, Cushing, Macomb, and Lt. Duer, the executive officer of the *Shamrock*. Cushing finally suggested a novel twist to his original plan. He now proposed towing a cutter behind picketboat *No. 1* with an additional ten to fifteen men aboard. These men, like the others already selected, would have to be skilled with the cutlass, for stealth remained a top priority. If necessary, then, this cutter would be cast off as it neared the schooner or the *Southfield*—wherever it was first needed—and the cutter's crew would board and subdue the pickets, hopefully before they could set off a rocket and sound the alarm. Like most of Cushing's plans, this was simple and direct. Macomb remained doubtful, "but Duer was enthusiastic, and Macomb finally concurred."[13]

Yet two important aspects of the mission had still to be resolved. First was the engine noise from the launch that had been detected the night before. This problem had been handed over to the fleet's carpenter, who was in the process of fashioning a wooden box that would cover the engine, hopefully muffling the sound while at the same time not hampering the operation of the engine itself. Added to the sound-proofing was a tarpaulin that was to be wrapped securely around the engine.[14] It was hoped that the two combined would dampen the engine noise to the point that neither the pickets along the river's banks, nor the pickets afloat in the channel, would be able to detect the sound of the launch's engine.

The other unresolved problem was the selection of the additional men now required to fill the second boat. If Cushing was going to make the attempt that night — as was clearly his intention — this would have to be accomplished quickly, for the men would have to prepare and be briefed on their roles — even if the eventual target was still withheld for security reasons. With no time to waste, the entire crew of the *Shamrock*— two hundred and seventy-five men[15] — was promptly ordered to the waist of the vessel, there to await the announcement. In short order Lt. Duer stepped up and addressed them. "I want eleven men and two officers," he said, "to accompany Lieutenant Cushing on a dangerous expedition from which probably none will return. None but young men without encumbrances will be accepted," Duer continued. He then got to the moment of truth. "Those who wish to volunteer," he instructed, "will step over to this side."[16] Cushing, Macomb, Duer and Howorth watched as all two hundred and seventy-five men stepped to the side, in what can only be considered a remarkable testament to William Cushing's hard won reputation. Not one man had balked.

"I thought so," Macomb responded. "Pick your men."[17]

* * *

On October 25, Catherine Edmondston, at her plantation home near Edward's Ferry, North Carolina, noted in her journal that she had just the day before housed her Dahlia roots, and begun planting her hyacinths. This she managed to accomplish despite bristling over the most recent news of the Confederate debacle in the Shenandoah Valley, where Jubal Early's Confederate Army had been defeated and scattered at Cedar Creek. "What a life of uncertainty is ours!" she lamented.[18]

While the Southern war effort dismayed her that day, the truly shocking news had been the reproduction of certain love letters between George Armstrong Custer and his wife, Libbie. Some of these had been captured along with much of Custer's personal baggage during the fierce cavalry engagement at Trevillian Station, Virginia, earlier that summer, and subsequently printed for all to see in the Richmond papers. Obviously meant for no eyes beyond Mr. and Mrs. Custer's, these letters were replete with sexual references and innuendo, and in Richmond, as across the South, they had engendered hyperbolic paroxysms of literary and moral outrage, confirming for all readers their unspoken (or spoken) conviction in the degenerate nature of the Northern invader; truly, now it was clear for all to see, the barbarian was at the gate.[19]

Mrs. Edmondston, scanning one of Custer's letters in the paper for herself, had been shocked almost speechless — almost. "The papers publish a private letter of the Yankee Gen Custer so utterly repulsive," she hissed, "so shocking in all sense of decency or modesty or refinement, that I will not soil my repertory with it & wish I could wipe it from memory as an injury done to my refinement by the knolege even that such things are done in the world & this, 'Fannie,' to whom this shocking letter is written, is an associate of Mrs. McClellan & moves in good Northern society. To what an abyss of corruption are they fallen!"[20]

For months now, since the *Albemarle* had journeyed south from Halifax to Plymouth, the upper reaches of the Roanoke River, which Mrs. Edmondston called home, had fallen under the defensive canopy of the ironclad. As a result, the Edmondstons — like the other residents north of Plymouth — had for a period of time lived a life of relative peace and tranquility, secure in the knowledge that Yankee gunboats could not pass the ram and carry the war further upriver. But that sense of security was about to receive a radical jolt, indeed; an event was about to transpire that would alter the shape of Catherine Edmondston's life forever, and provide a shock for her even more unnerving, if possible, than the intimacies of Libbie Custer's boudoir.

Chapter 28

An Example of Coolness and Skill

ON THE EVENING of the 27th the weather took a turn for the worse. Clouds gave way to bands of cold rain that washed over the treetops along the banks of the Roanoke, obscuring vision and chilling the men as they huddled in both picketboat *No. 1* and the cutter towed behind, all struggling to stay warm.[1] The men in the cutter had been told of the target upon clearing the *Shamrock,* and with them they carried a small arsenal, as Cushing phrased it, of "revolvers, cutlasses, and hand-grenades,"[2] for use if and when necessary. Strict silence was in order. Not a sound could be made, certainly no talking, for even the slightest noise might alert unseen Confederate pickets lurking along the banks of the river. It would be a long, cold, silent run of some two hours duration upriver to Plymouth. And that was if they were fortunate.

At approximately 8:30 P.M. the cutter had been made fast to picketboat *No. 1,*[3] but the two did not arrive at the mouth of the Roanoke until almost 11:30.[4] The two boats then began their mutual trek upriver. The rain, which before had been sporadic, began to fall heavier,[5] making visibility even more difficult and the trip for the crew that much more miserable. But the rain also had the beneficial effect of further dampening the sound of the launch's engine as it puffed its way toward Plymouth, and there was also little doubt that the reduced visibility on the water worked well in their favor — the pickets would have a hard time either spotting or hearing them with the rain lashing the river. All things considered, the weather had turned in their favor; a small but important factor.

William Cushing was standing toward the front of picketboat *No. 1* with most of the officers as they pushed ahead into the darkness and rain. Higgins was at the wheel, Stotesbury working the engine. Howorth was to handle the howitzer once contact with the enemy had been made. Ensign Gay was stationed at the bow, and had been tasked with swinging the boom out and lowering it into position once Cushing had given the order.[6] In order to communicate without speaking, Will held three lines in his right hand: one led to Howorth at the howitzer, a second led to Stotesbury at the engine, and the third was fixed to Gay on the launch's bow.[7] Will had worked out a rudimentary system of pulls and tugs on each line to make his wishes known, and was confident his system would work, even during the stress of combat.[8]

In addition to the three lines in his right hand, in Cushing's left he held two lines that led to the torpedo, which he would have to operate once Gay had placed the boom in the water. While Will had practiced with the apparatus in New York, use of the torpedo remained a dicey proposition. Even under the best of conditions the deployment and firing of the charge was no simple task, as these devices were notoriously unreliable. As J.R. Soley—who was familiar with the torpedo's workings—notes, this aspect of the mission was fraught with uncertainty, for "it must be remembered that nothing short of the utmost care in preparation could keep its mechanism in working order; that in making ready to use it, it was necessary to keep the end of the spar elevated ... and to judge accurately the distance in order to stop the boat's headway at the right point; that the spar must then be lowered with the same precision of judgment; that the detaching laniard must then be pulled firmly, but without a jerk; that, finally, the position of the torpedo under the knuckle of the ram must be calculated to a nicety, and that by a very gentle strain on a line some twenty five or thirty feet long the trigger pin must be withdrawn."[9]

Five separate lines in all would have to be manipulated by Will Cushing with precision. And all of this while quite probably under a severe enemy fire. Yet Cushing remained serene. "He had worked out the manner in which he would, in an emergency, distinguish between the five different lines, and had no doubt that his mind would, at the last moment, be absolutely clear."[10]

"It was a dark, miserable night. The rain was falling and the men shivered with the cold. Upon entering the river it was gloomier still, for the trees growing on both banks densely shadowed the river. The silence also was oppressive, for not a word of conversation, even in whisper, was allowed."[11]

The river slowly narrowed as they made their way toward Plymouth, all the crew shivering and wet, yet constantly aware of every sound that rose up to them. Howorth stood on Cushing's left at the howitzer, prepared to answer any enemy hail with authority if necessary. Woodman sat near the controls, where Higgins worked the wheel. Aside from two firemen in the rear of the launch, the other members of the crew crouched at battle stations, prepared to spring into action at a moment's notice.[12] The entire crew was in for a long, tense trip.

At about 2:30 A.M. Cushing gauged the distance traveled and estimated they would soon be nearing the wreck of the *Southfield*. He signaled back to the men in the cutter to take up their positions at the oars, should they need to make a dash for either the pickets aboard the *Southfield*, or the schooner reportedly anchored nearby. The launch had been making its way along the southern bank of the river, all eyes peeled straight ahead for the first sign of either picket post in the water. The rain continued to fall, but as they had heard neither hail nor sound from shore, Cushing remained confident they had not been spotted. So far, so good. But the first true test would soon be upon them.

Suddenly, out of the vague darkness ahead loomed a murky shadow, unclear at first, then slowly materializing into form—yes, it was the schooner, and it lay dead ahead. On the bow, Gay had spotted it first.[13] The launch was headed dead on, the schooner now clearly visible, no more than fifty yards off their bow. Then the eerie outline of what remained of the *Southfield*'s hurricane deck loomed up from the water like a phantom rising from a watery grave. The two picket posts had emerged from the grayness and rain so suddenly there was almost no time to maneuver, less to calculate a response. The launch chugged on straight toward the schooner. The crew tensed. Would they be spotted? Had they already?

It was clear now that the launch was on a course that would bring it dangerously close to the Confederate vessel, passing, perhaps, with little more than twenty or thirty yards to spare. It seemed too close! Surely the Rebel pickets would hear their engine, no matter how well muffled! Yet there was no time to maneuver, and Higgins headed for that narrow space between the schooner and the riverbank, below the low hanging trees. They were closing now; thirty yards, then twenty, then ten. "There was the sudden soft sound of voices in the night, and then the quick light of a match which flickered and was gone. Fifteen men in the launch and thirteen in the cutter did not draw a breath for a minute, and then they were through, they had passed between the two enemy vessels and had not been seen."[14] Cushing would later report: "A mile below the town was the wreck of the *Southfield*, surrounded by some schooners, and it was understood that a gun was mounted there to command the bend. I therefore took one of the *Shamrock*'s cutters in tow, with orders to cast off and board at that point if we were hailed. Our boat succeeded in passing the pickets, and even the *Southfield*, within 20 yards without discovery."[15]

For a few minutes more the crew held their collective breath, then the little launch puffed its way around a bend, cutter still in tow, and the schooner and *Southfield* disappeared from view. It must have seemed like a miracle. Now all that awaited was the *Albemarle*, and the remaining distance to Plymouth would not take long. "After silently steaming upriver for another ten minutes, the ironclad's dark mass was silhouetted against a distant light. When abeam the shore light they observed the ironclad was then slightly astern. Circling back, the *Albemarle* could be seen moored to a wharf."[16]

It was at this point that Will Cushing believed he might be able to cut the ironclad out, and sail her down stream to the fleet. Surely, it had not been an idle notion on his part, for he had packed a Union flag for just that occassion.[17] In that they had not yet been spotted, the plan made perfect sense. "I now thought that it might be better to board and 'take her alive'—having in the two boats twenty men, well armed with revolvers, cutlasses, and hand grenades. To be sure there were thousands near by, and ten times our number on the ship; but as surprise is everything and I thought if her fasts were cut, at the instant of boarding, we might overcome those on board, take her into the stream and use her iron sides to protect us after, from the forts."[18] Not only would it be a quick and stunning success, but if he could take the ram alive, both his and his crew's chance of survival would be increased considerably, for if he had to go in and torpedo the ironclad, most all of them, he knew, would probably be gunned down, blown-up, drowned, or captured in the effort.

Knowing the layout of Plymouth, Cushing decided to land at the lower wharf, sneak his men around through town, then dash upon the *Albemarle* from the riverbank. In that manner they would be attacking from a direction no one would suspect, thus taking the guards by surprise.[19] He began sheering the launch in toward the wharf in order to do just that, when suddenly there came a hail from a guard on board the ram.

"Who's there? ... Who's there, who goes there?"[20] They had been spotted, and just like that, all bets were off.

Cushing did not hesitate. He turned around and called back to the men in the cutter. "Cast off, Peterkin," he yelled to the officer in charge, "and go down and get those pickets on the schooner!"[21] There was no possibility now of cutting the ram out. Cushing quickly put that thought out of his head, and moved coolly to the next. He would go straight for the *Albemarle* and detonate the torpedo. Ordering full ahead, Will "went at the dark mountain of iron in front of us."[22] Absent now the cutter, the launch accelerated toward the ram, taking a heavy and increasing fire from the riverbank along with the guards onboard the ironclad, who were now alive to his presence.

Events were rapidly accelerating—illumination fires leaping to life along the shore, rifles cracking, men screaming and running—but Cushing kept his wits. There could be no error now, no misjudgment or confusion. Everything relied on Will Cushing keeping his wits about him. "The rebels sprung their rattle," Will recalled, "rang the bell, and commenced firing, at the same time repeating their hail and seeming much confused."[23]

Picketboat *No. 1* barreled in toward the ram, bullets plunking the water and snapping off the launch's stack. The small arms fire was hot and growing hotter. Cushing paid it no mind. He was within mere feet of the ram now, preparing for the attack, when suddenly something totally unexpected was spotted dancing in the water just off their bow. "A large fire now blazed upon the bank and by its light I discovered the unfortunate fact," Cushing later reported with considerable understatement, "that there was a circle of logs around the *Albemarle*, boomed well out from her side, with the very intention of preventing the action of torpedoes."[24] But rather than panicking, Will simply pulled closer and, under a severe fire, studied the arrangement. "To examine them more closely," he wrote, "I ran alongside until amidships, received the enemy's fire, and sheered off for the purpose of turning."[25]

In an instant Will had recalculated the mission, and at that moment he turned the launch out away from the *Albemarle* in a wide circle into the darkness. But Cushing was himself the object now of considerable Rebel fire, and he would not escape unscathed. "As I turned," he reported, "the whole back of my coat was torn out by buck-shot, and the sole of my shoe was carried away. The fire was very severe."[26]

Examining the log apron, Cushing had decided to take the launch out about one hundred yards, turn, then come back upon the apron at top speed. He intended to strike the "booms squarely, at right angles, trusting to their having been long enough in the water to have become slimy — in which case my boat, under full headway, would bump up against them and slip over into the pen with the ram."[27] This was his only real opportunity for success, but even if successful, the launch would be stranded in the pen near the ram, and virtually any chance of survival or escape forfeited. But it did not matter — Will Cushing had come for the *Albemarle*, and he was going to take the *Albemarle* or die in the attempt. "But I was there to accomplish an important object, and to die, if needs be, was but a duty."[28]

The launch came about slowly in the darkness, still taking heavy fire, and began its final run toward the ram. Its speed gradually increased, Stotesbury working the engine with skill. Along the shoreline red bursts of rifle fire flashed and speckled the night like hundreds of fireflies rising on a warm July evening, bullets slapping the launch's sides and thumping in the water. "By this time," Cushing later recalled, "the enemy's fire was very severe, but a dose of canister at short range served to moderate their zeal and disturb their aim. Paymaster Swan, of the *Ostego*, was wounded near me, but how many more

I know not."²⁹ Cushing, at the wheel, was guiding on a spot between two logs, aiming to ride up over the apron, and slide into that thin space adjacent the ram's hull. It was a bold but desperate tactic.

Suddenly the launch struck the apron, there was a terrific jolt, and the men on picketboat *No. 1* went flying. The launch teetered for a moment atop the logs, then slipped forward toward the ram — it had worked! All now was chaos. Cushing looked up: "Ten feet from us the muzzle of a rifle gun looked into our faces, and every word of command on board was distinctly heard."³⁰

There was not a second to lose. Cushing jumped to his feet and called for Gay to lower the boom. Inside the ram the Confederate gun crew was frantically lowering the Brooke rifle, trying desperately to get a shot off before Cushing could trigger his charge. The gaping mouth of the giant gun was only feet from Cushing's face, pointing right at him, but there was no time to worry about that. Bullets were rattling all over the launch, ricocheting off into the darkness. Men were falling, screaming, but in the center of the storm Will Cushing stood now at the bow of the launch, collected and calm. "Four more bullets now plunged through my clothing in quick succession as I stood in the bow; the heel jigger in my right hand and exploding line in my left. We were near enough then; and I ordered the boom lowered until the forward motion of the launch carried the torpedo under the ram's overhang."³¹

It was now a race to see which would be fired first, the torpedo, or the Brooke rifle. He could hear every word uttered by the gun crew, knew it would be only twenty, maybe thirty seconds before the Brooke was properly angled and fired. But the torpedo was in the water now, and slowly he pulled the right hand release line, detaching the torpedo from the spar, allowing it to drift up slowly under the ram. The process could not be rushed. As he waited a bullet cut his hand, another tore away his collar.³²

Will Cushing had waited six months for this moment, had vowed to avenge Flusser's death, and even with bullets hissing in the air all around him, knowing that at any second he might be blown from earthly existence, he would not be rushed. At this extraordinary moment, when, as J.R. Soley would later exclaim, "The naval history of the world affords no other example of such marvelous coolness and professional skill,"³³ William Barker Cushing waited calmly for the torpedo to rise to its proper depth. He counted slowly to five, then, once he felt the trigger line go taught, gave one final, gentle ... tug.

CHAPTER 29

The Fixed Determination to Escape

CUSHING WAS HURLED backward by the enormous concussion then bounced to his knees as the force of two simultaneous explosions slammed the nose of the launch under water like a small cork. It appeared the Brooke rifle and the torpedo had fired coincidentally, the blistering intensity of the cannon shot passing just over the launch's bow, the combined violence of the twin detonations forcing the small vessel's bow to dip underwater.[1] The Rebel gun crew aboard the *Albemarle* had not been able to depress the elevation of the Brooke sufficiently to strike the launch, but the blast and heat had stunned most of Cushing's crew beyond sensibility. Added to that was a volcanic column of water unleashed by the explosion of the torpedo that rose high above the ram, then crashed back down upon the launch like a tidal wave, immediately swamping the small vessel, and washing many of the crew into the river. "The explosion took place," Cushing recounted, "at the same instant that 100 pounds of grape, at 10 feet range, crashed in our midst, and the dense mass of water thrown out of the torpedo came down upon us with suffocating weight. The boat seemed to flatten out like a pasteboard box on the logs."[2]

For a second or two immediately following the twin detonations everything remained quiet, both sides apparently overwhelmed by the shock of the moment, but that lull did not last for long. "In the silence after the gun was fired cries from the ram and from the shore were heard by the men in the launch: 'Surrender, or we will blow you out of the water!'"[3] Within seconds the Rebels opened again, peppering the launch with small arms fire. "The

29. The Fixed Determination to Escape

Picketboat *#1* overrides the log apron and detonates its torpedo against the hull of the CSS *Albemarle* (U.S. Naval History and Heritage Command).

enemy continued to fire at 15 feet range, and demanded our surrender, which I twice refused," said Cushing."[4]

Despite the fact that the launch was swamped — now utterly immovable — his crew shot up and scattered, Will Cushing had no intention of surrendering. No matter the odds, he would attempt his escape. Tossing aside coat, shoes, sword, and revolver, he shouted to his beleaguered crew "Men, save yourselves!"[5] then dove headfirst into the frigid water. "It was cold — long after the frosts — and the water chilled the blood," Will recalled, "while the whole surface of the stream was ploughed up by grape and musketry — and my nearest friend was twelve miles away — but anything was better than to fall into rebel hands."[6]

For the first few yards he remained under water, but then he surfaced and began swimming for the far bank of the river, away from the leaping fires behind the ram, away from the bullets that still ripped the water. Despite his tall frame and slender build, Cushing was a strong swimmer,[7] and it was not long before he had gained the middle of the channel. Here and there bullets

The Brooke rifle on the CSS *Albemarle* fires as the spar torpedo explodes (U.S. Naval History and Heritage Command).

still zipped in the water around him, but for the most part the firing around the *Albemarle* had ended. As the Confederate commander of the ram, Alexander Warley, reported, "By this time I heard voices from the launch — 'We surrender,' etc., etc., etc. I stopped our fire and sent out Mr. Long, who brought back all those who had been in the launch except the gallant captain and three of her crew, all of whom took to the water."⁸

It is constructive to consider at this point the analysis of E.M.H Edwards, one of the first to catalogue Cushing's achievements. "It is well to consider here," the author noted, "just what this act of Cushing's was. The instant of time in which a deed can be done and is done, or not done, marks the difference between great men and ordinary men. Cushing had the faculty of giving his attention to the work in hand. He was as cool in the midst of imminent danger as in ordinary surroundings and able to note unforeseen differences, attending and changing conditions, and he lost no more time in considering what to do when he unexpectedly found the boom of logs around the *Albemarle* than if he had known beforehand that it was there. He saw it and with electrical quickness of thought decided what to do."⁹

There is little question that William Cushing's capacity to quickly grasp a situation and change plans on the fly were, for him, remarkable aptitudes.

29. The Fixed Determination to Escape

Cushing orders, "Save yourselves men!" and leaps into the cold water of the Roanoke River (U.S. Naval History and Heritage Command).

And he would now have to rapidly recalculate his situation once more. Confederate rifle fire may have ceased, but the search for the Federal culprits had not. "The rebels were out in boats picking up my men and one of these attracted by the sound pulled in my direction,"[10] Cushing recalled. They were calling his name, knew — presumably from taking prisoners — that it had been he who had delivered the lethal blow to the ram, and they were out now scouring the river for him. He was cold and losing strength, but he simply refused to be captured. "He held his breath and sank beneath the surface; the boat was coming toward him, but swerved away at the last moment, and he was not seen. Again he struck out for the dark line of the opposite bank."[11]

There in the darkness, however, Will spotted search parties with torches covering the far bank of the Roanoke,[12] and grasped at once the fact that they would be looking for him there as the island opposite the ram had been the means by which previous Federal reconnaissance teams had made their way both to and from Plymouth in the past. Of course they would be expecting him to make good his escape there, which meant he would have to change his plans yet again. Once more, he would have to do the unexpected. Instead of heading across the river to the nearest dry land, he decided to head downriver. It would be a far longer swim to safety, but the search parties did not appear to be out in that direction and he doubted they would be looking for him there. If he could stand the cold and endure the long swim, he just might make it. "I heard my name mentioned," Cushing later wrote, referring to the Rebel search parties that were out calling for him to give himself up, "but was not seen. I now 'struck out' down the stream, and was soon far enough away to again attempt landing."[13]

Will turned south and began swimming with the current downstream, away from the ram, away from the glowing lights behind him. He had no idea what had happened to the other members of his crew, could only hope that some, at least, had made good their escape. The calls from the Rebel search parties slowly began to fade, the river darken, his arms and legs tire. The cold began slowly to numb him thoroughly. "At last he decided that he was far enough downstream and turned out of the current, with some difficulty, for he was very tired, to attempt a landing on the dark, forbidding bank of the river."[14]

Making hard for the riverbank, Will suddenly heard thrashing in the water behind him, and realized that it must have been caused by one of his own men; a compatriot now in trouble. He did not hesitate. "This time," he wrote, "as I struggled to reach the bank, I heard a groan in the river behind me, and, although exhausted, concluded to turn and give all the aid in my power to the officer or seaman who had bravely shared the danger with me and in whose peril I might in turn partake."[15]

Cushing struggled as he swam back against the current, and began losing track as he did of distance and time. He simply made for the sound of the flailing man behind him, stroke after painful stroke. "Swimming in the night, with eye at the level of the water," he recalled, "one can have no idea of distance, and labors, as I did, under the discouraging thought that no headway is made. But if I were to drown that night, I had at least an opportunity of dying while struggling to aid another."[16] Finally coming upon the desperate man, Cushing realized it was John Woodman, and Woodman immediately told Cushing that, utterly exhausted, he could swim no longer.[17] Will promptly took the master's mate in hand, knocked the cap off his head, and *ordered* him to swim. Poor Woodman tried desperately to cooperate, but had no energy left. Offering the junior officer his right arm, Cushing attempted to paddle for them both, trying to keep Woodman afloat as he struggled toward the river's bank.[18] In that both men were nearing total exhaustion, the effort eventually proved impossible. "For ten minutes at least," Will recalled, "I think, he managed to keep afloat, when, his presence of mind and physical force being completely gone, he gave a yell and sunk like a stone, fortunately not seizing upon me as he went down."[19]

Woodman was gone. Indeed, Woodman was dead, swallowed by the cold river; and it is hard to imagine that losing him to the river was not understood by Cushing as a call to rally, no matter how exhausted he might have been. How many of his men had shared Woodman's fate that evening, Cushing did not know, but he was determined not to follow them under. By this point Will Cushing had little left but determination alone, and with that he directed his efforts toward the riverbank. He had to get ashore, he knew, or he too would soon go under. "Again alone upon the water, I directed my course towards the town side of the river, not making much headway, as my strokes were now very feeble."[20] He did not so much swim now as claw his way through the water, the river lapping into his mouth, his soaking garments weighing him down.[21]

Most men would here have succumbed, their bodies failing, their minds numb to fatigue. But William Cushing had the rare capacity it seemed to survive on determination alone, to do with his mind what his body could not accomplish independently. He recounts the moment: "My clothes being soaked and heavy, and little chop seas splashing with a chocking persistence into my mouth every time that I gasped for breath. Still there was a determination *not* to sink: A will *not* to give up, and I kept up a sort of mechanical motion long after my bodily force was in fact expended."[22] Pushing himself beyond physical endurance, he continued to flail his way toward the bank; exhausted, but refusing to give in to exhaustion, an effort, truly, of mind over matter.

On Cushing clawed and flailed and slapped the water, until somehow reaching the lowest reaches of the Roanoke's southern bank. Weakly he grabbed a handful of mud and pulled himself from the water. There he fairly stumbled a short distance up the muddy bank, and collapsed on the shore, by this point insensible. "At last, and not a moment too soon," he recounted, "I touched the soft mud; and in the excitement of the first shock, I half raised my body, and made one step forward; and then remained half in the mud and half in the water until daylight; unable even to crawl on hands and knees — with brain in a whirl and nearly frozen — but with one thing strong in me — the fixed determination to escape."[23]

Chapter 30

No More Gallant Thing

For Alexander Warley, the events of the early morning hours of October 28, 1864, must have seemed like the sudden materialization of his worst nightmare. Not only had not a single picket post along the river spotted the approaching torpedo launch and given warning, but the launch had somehow managed even to slip passed both the schooner and the *Southfield*. Adding insult to injury, the artillery assembled for the defense of the ram had only managed to get off a single round, that misdirected,[1] while the fire from the guards surrounding the ram proved entirely ineffective. Lastly, the torpedo launch was then able to penetrate the log apron—constructed to prevent precisely this sort of an attack from succeeding—and detonate its torpedo below the ironclad's waterline. Somehow, in some way, every preventive measure the Confederate's had taken had been foiled by the Federal torpedo launch as if their defenses had been little more than play things, travel entertainments cleverly arranged for the Yankee's amusement as they steamed their way upriver, and nothing more. All things considered, the picture painted by the *Albemarle*'s destruction was, for Confederate eyes at least, a fiasco in blue.

Warley had been aboard the ram when the attack had struck, the launch so close at that point that there was precious little he could do. The Brooke had been ordered to fire, and the crew "sent to the shield with muskets,"[2] but it was all too little too late. Inside the ironclad, Warley had heard "a report as of an unshotted gun"[3] after which a piece of the ram's wood framing crashed at his feet. Warely, immediately grasping the source and meaning of the explosion, required no explanations. "Calling the carpenter," he stated, "I told him a torpedo had been exploded, and ordered him to examine and report to me, saying nothing to anyone else. He soon reported 'a hole in her bottom big enough to drive a wagon in.'"[4]

The ironclad's commander then went topside and heard the cries of the Federal sailors in the water. Most, overcome by the shock of the explosion and cold of the Roanoke, were hanging for dear life onto the log apron for fear of drowning. Ensign Gay, as an example, had followed Cushing's example and leaped into the water behind him, but due to the frigid water, did not get far. "I had not proceeded far from the boat," Gay recalled, "when I fell in with Acting Ensign William L. Howorth on a log, unable to proceed farther without assistance. Having a life preserver with me, I gave it to him and returned to the boat to procure another, not knowing how far I might have to swim, and at the same time I destroyed two boxes of ammunition and several carbines. I had not gone far the second time when I found myself chilled, and after a severe struggle I regained the circle of logs, where I found several of the crew, with a boat from the ram in charge of Lieutenant Roberts."[5]

Warley then took pains to see to the safety of those members of Cushing's crew who had been taken prisoner.[6] All told, eleven of the crew had been fished from the water. Cushing and Edward Houghton had managed to make good an escape in the river, while John Woodman and Richard Higgins had drowned while attempting to flee, victims of cold and exhaustion.[7] After seeing to his Federal captives, Warley "turned my attention to the *Albemarle* and found her resting on the bottom in eight feet of water, her upper works above water. The very men who had destroyed her had no idea of their success, for I heard one say to another 'We did our best, but there the d — d old thing is yet.'"[8]

With the *Albemarle* lost, Lt. Warley realized immediately that Plymouth lay essentially defenseless; and when the army officer in charge of the local garrison refused to withdraw his troops, he began instituting measures that might in some way impede a naval advance on the part of the Yanks; an advance, he knew, that would come almost as soon as the Yankees got wind of Cushing's success. But Warley had little to work with, and he knew that the troops on the ground could not possibly stand up to a heavy cannonade from the Federal squadron. Warley, after all, was well aware of what the *Albemarle* had done to the Yankee garrison when the shoe had been on the other foot, and had no illusions of what lay ahead. But he did his best. "After her destruction, in failing to convince the officer in command of the troops that he could not hold the place, I did my best to help defend it," he insisted. "Half of my crew went down and obstructed the river by sinking the schooner at the wreck, and with the other half I had two 8-inch guns commanding the upper river put in serviceable order, re-laid platforms, fished out tackles from the *Albemarle*, got a few shells, etc., and waited."[9]

Alexander Warley had been given the thankless job of commanding the *Albemarle* when she could no longer do or accomplish anything of substance, and now he had the thankless and unenviable task of reporting the vessel's demise to his superiors; superiors, he knew, who would not be pleased by the news. The loss of the ironclad was hardly his fault, but he was the one who would have to file the report with naval command in Richmond. On the 28th, when the sun rose on the ironclad sitting on the river bottom for the first time, he sent his official report to Stephen Mallory, hoping, of course, that the blame for the debacle would not be hung singularly around his neck. His report read:

> The night of the 27th instant, a dark, rainy night, I had the watch doubled and took extra precautions. At or about 3 o'clock A.M., on the 28th, the officer of the deck discovered a small steamer in the river, hailed her, received an unsatisfactory answer, rang the alarm bell, and opened fire on her with the watch. The officers and men were at their quarters in as quick time as was possible, but the vessel was so near that we could not bring our guns to bear, and the shot fired from the after gun loaded with grape, failed to take effect. The boat running obliquely, struck us under the port bow, running over the boom, exploded a torpedo, and smashed a large hole in us just under the water line, under a heavy fire of musketry. The boat surrendered and I sent Lieutenant Roberts to take charge of her. Manned the pumps and gave the order to fire up so as to use the donkey engine. The water gained on us so fast that all exertions were fruitless, and the vessel went down in a few moments, merely leaving her shield and smokestack out.
>
> In justice to myself I must say the pickets below gave no notice of her approach, and the artillery which was stationed by the vessel for a protection, gave us no assistance, manning only one piece at too late a time to be of service.
>
> Having condensed this report as much as I could, I respectfully request a court of enquiry, to establish on whose shoulders rests the blame of the loss of the *Albemarle*.[10]

Realizing that Plymouth was soon to be lost, and that the *Albemarle* could not fall into Yankee hands only then to be repaired and ultimately used against Confederate interests on the Roanoke, Lt. Warley had the once formidable ironclad scuttled. This was done by placing an explosive charge in the ram's forward area, which, when detonated, blew the front portion of the ram to pieces.[11] This ignominious action proved the last service the vaunted ironclad would ever see.

Meanwhile, back on the water, John C. Howard had been in the cutter when William Cushing detonated the torpedo under the *Albemarle*, and from his perch behind the motor launch he'd been provided a clear view of the action. "I was sitting in a boat only a few feet away," Howard recalled, "with nothing to do but look, and with a bright light from the shore to enable me to see clearly."

Howard saw Cushing detonate the torpedo, the plume of water rise and descend, and the launch momentarily flattened under its weight. He watched as Cushing "threw off his overcoat and shouted: 'Every man save himself,' and jumped overboard at the same time." Howard continues his narrative: "The air pressure was so great [immediately after the torpedo detonation] that if it had been maintained a few seconds longer, the boat would have filled and gone to the bottom, but as it only lasted the tenth part of a second, no great amount of water came over the gunwales, and the boat came up to her bearings faster than she went down, and slid off the logs uninjured, and the men in her were taken prisoners.... It must be remembered that the troops and the artillery began firing into the bosom of the river immediately after the explosion of the torpedo. The balls pattered on the water like a shower of hail, consequently it was dangerous to venture out into the river."[12]

As will be recalled, Cushing, upon encountering the first hail from the ram, ordered the cutter back downriver to take out the pickets in the center of the channel. John Howard was later part of the crew that accomplished this task, apparently with considerable ease. "Our capture of the pickets on the *Southfield* was quite easily accomplished," he explained. "After the torpedo had been exploded, a battery of artillery and two companies of infantry, who were stationed on the shore to protect the ram, began firing indiscriminately, and at they knew not what. The pickets hearing the uproar, and thinking the town was being attacked and possibly captured, were paralyzed as to their patriotic ardor, upon our sudden appearance over their ship's side and surrendered without a protest."[13]

Thus had the *Albemarle* been destroyed, the pickets subdued and, as Alexander Warley would later put it, "a more gallant thing was not done during the war."[14] The mission, as reconfigured at the very last moment by William Cushing, had been a complete and stunning success.

While Lt. Warley had been clearly impressed by William Cushing's effort to destroy the ram, Catherine Edmondston, on the other hand, would experience only shock and bewilderment. Utterly incapable of crediting the Yanks with any aptitude beyond a highly developed talent for lying, and grasping instantly what the destruction of the formidable ram meant for the Roanoke Valley, she decried the loss of Plymouth, blaming the disaster on ineptitude, cowardice, idleness and — when all those suspects seemed insufficient for her ever blossoming league of culprits — drink. "And so goes all our security & the delightful sense of freedom from the personal presence of our hated enemies," she grieved. "So it all goes & we are once more into the sea of doubt & anxiety which was our position before the fortification of Rainbow Banks, for be it known to you O, Journal, that some Confederate Gen,— Beauregard it is whispered, ordered that strong point to be dismantled, saying that the possession of Plymouth rendered it unnecessary. Yes, but he never dreamed that that strong point would be in such hands as those of Lieut Warley & Gen Lawrence Baker. Gen Baker has known & has spoken of the insufficient guard kept there by one drunken Col Wortham & yet he having the power to remedy it has passively let it go on until the result is seen in drunken worthless pickets who let the Torpedo boat come up and sink what was better than five thousand men to us & open the door to Lieut Warley's hasty act [of scuttling the ram]. The best commentary on the defense is the fact that we lost *three* only killed & fifty prisoners who, being new conscripts from that part of the country, gave themselves up in hope of being released but the Yankees handcuffed every man of them. Perhaps, however, that was for effect. From all we learn now it was a disgraceful piece of business. Plymouth was conquered by Apple Brandy.... This is the verdict of our neighborhood."[15]

After the *Albemarle* had been torpedoed, and the bodies of Woodman and Higgins recovered, it was assumed by the Confederates at Plymouth that William Cushing too had perished in the attack. So Mrs. Edmondston had written just days after the assault upon first hearing the news at her church services.[16] But what Lt. Warley and Catherine Edmondston did not know, what no one in authority could have known, was that William Cushing had survived, indeed had clawed and scratched his way to the river's bank, and on the dawn of the 28th would awake in a pool of muck and mud on the southern shore of the Roanoke, suffering terribly from cold and exhaustion for sure, but prepared, almost miraculously, to resume his escape.

Chapter 31

Dead Gone Sunk

WILLIAM CUSHING AWOKE near dawn, lying at the river's edge in a "thick brake, where bushes and weeds grew luxuriantly,"[1] precisely where he had collapsed the night before. Covered in mud, what clothes he still had on cold and water-soaked, it was astounding he had survived at all.

As will be recalled, Gay and Howorth, for instance, once in the cold water the night before, had not been able to venture beyond the log apron that surrounded the *Albemarle* before finding themselves chilled and incapable of further movement, while both Higgins and Woodman — who had ventured further into the river — had ultimately succumbed to cold and exhaustion, losing their lives in the attempted escape. Yet Cushing had exceeded by far all their efforts then attempted to rescue Woodman before finally managing to struggle to the riverbank south of town. Wet, cold, and working almost beyond exhaustion, it was a wonder he had not died of exposure that evening, yet instead he awoke — even if but vaguely — with the first rays of the new day rising in the east.[2] No doubt the mud in which he had collapsed served to help insulate what little body heat he maintained overnight; but it can be recalled that according to Cushing's own account, he was still half in water when he finally collapsed, thus painfully subject to hypothermia. Regardless of the precise details, his mere survival serves as an amazing tale of endurance.

Fortunately for Will, the day dawned with clear skies, and a warm, rising sun began slowly to restore his vigor. "The sun came out bright and warm," he later wrote, "proving a most cheering visitant, and giving me back a good portion of the strength of which I had been deprived before."[3] But that same sun also began slowly to reveal his position and the discomforting fact that he had managed to swim but only some forty yards below the town of Plymouth and the forts that screened its southern defenses.⁴ The town, he could see from where he lay, was abuzz with angry activity. "Its light [the sun] showed me the town swarming with soldiers and sailors, who moved about excitedly, as if angry at some sudden shock. It was a source of satisfaction to me to know that I had pulled the wire that set all these figures moving (in a manner quite interesting as the best of theatricals), but as I had no desire of being discovered by any of the rebs who were so plentiful around me, I did not long remain a spectator."⁵

With his strength slowly returning, Cushing decided that he had to move or risk detection, for detection meant death as he had made up his mind he would not surrender. "The prospect of drowning, starvation, death in the swamps, all seemed lesser evils than that of surrender,"⁶ he insisted, but grasping the situation he was in as the sun rose over Plymouth, escape, he realized, would be no elementary task.

Not far away stood a Confederate guard post with a sentinel on duty, the sentry walking a post that overlooked Cushing's position. Worse still, Will realized that Plymouth was the home to many free-running dogs, and if he remained in his current location he was certain that one, or many, would find him along the riverbank and tip his whereabouts to the nearby guards.⁷ So it was obvious he had to move, but with the guard watching and the dogs about, it was also obvious that he had to be extremely circumspect in any movement he made — a tricky conundrum to say the least. Moreover, he also knew that Plymouth was home to a large Rebel garrison, and that they would in all probability — with the rising sun — have patrols out searching for any Federal officers or men who might have somehow survived the torpedo attack of the night before.

"My first object was to get into a dry fringe of rushes that edged the swamp," Cushing later explained, thinking his options through, "but to do this required me to pass over thirty or forty feet of open ground, right under the eye of the sentinel who walked the parapet."⁸ Will lay still and watched patiently until the guard turned away, then made his move. He jumped to his feet and raced across the open space toward the cover of the rushes, but had only covered about half the distance when the guard turned abruptly back toward him. Cushing dove immediately to the ground, this time landing between two paths that wound their way up from the village, and a location that was entirely exposed. It was a terrible spot to be in, and under the direct eye of the sentry, he could not so much as flex a muscle.

There, lying on his back in the open, he expected to be spotted at any moment if he had not already, but the sentry continued walking his post as if nothing had happened. "Perhaps I was unobserved," Will suggested, "because of the mud that covered me, and made me blend in with the earth;

at all events, the soldier continued his tramp for some time, while I, flat on my back, awaited another chance for action."[9] But the truth of the matter was, he was worse off by far lying there in the open between the two paths than he had been originally along the riverbank, and it seemed only a matter of time before someone would notice him there. "Cushing lay waiting. His legs were so sore that he did not think it would be a good idea to make another dash across the open space. He began to feel desperate; there seemed no way to escape."[10]

Then it happened — a group of Confederates approached along one of the paths, walking directly toward him.[11] There was nothing he could do but freeze in place and pray that the mud that covered his clothes and skin would conceal him, despite the fact that he lay only feet removed from the walkway. "Soon a party of four men came down the path at my right," Will recalled, "two of them being officers, and passed so close to me as almost to tread upon my arm. They were conversing upon the events of the previous night, and were wondering 'how it was done,' entirely unconscious of the presence of one who could give the information."[12] Incredibly, the Rebels were so involved in conversation that they walked right passed the immobile Cushing without taking notice. But Will realized at once he *had* now to move, for even his good luck could not cover him forever, most certainly while in a position so exposed. Surely, the next Rebel to travel the trail would spot him.

Cushing could not sensibly move forward, thus he decided to go back; to edge his way backward to the swamp along the river from where he had started. He accomplished this slowly, painfully by "sinking my heels and elbows into the earth and forcing my body, inch by inch, towards it. For five hours then, with bare feet, head and hands, I made my way where I venture to say none ever did before, until I came at last to a clear place, where I might rest upon solid ground."[13] The hour was now closing in on noon. The good news for Will Cushing was that five hours of crawling and dragging himself through the mud had removed him from the ready gaze of the sentry; the bad was that to accomplish this feat he had crawled into a cypress swamp that would prove a bloody nightmare. "The cypress swamp was a network of thorns and briers that cut into the flesh at every step like knives, and frequently when the soft mire would not bear my weight I was forced to throw my body upon it at length, and haul it along by the arms."[14] Struggling, crawling, his feet and arms cut and bleeding, he worked his way along the bank toward a clearing downriver. "Hands and feet were raw when I reached the clearing," Will later wrote, "and yet my difficulties were but commenced. A working party of soldiers was in the opening engaged in sinking some schooners in the river to restrict the channel."[15]

The work party Will Cushing had inadvertently stumbled upon was, of course, the men Alexander Warley had sent out earlier that morning, half the *Albemarle*'s crew, ordered to sink the schooner and obstruct the river channel as best they could. Without even the slightest knowledge or attempt on their part, they had managed to create a significant impediment for Cushing's escape. But Will Cushing had not crawled through muck, mud, briers, and swamp for six hours to admit defeat. Taking careful note of the lay of the land, he worked his way around the edge of the swamp to a cornfield. There, carefully crawling down the length of a long furrow, he passed the Rebel work party at a distance of merely twenty yards, and worked his way slowly to a small wood at the end of the field.[16] This accomplished, he disappeared into the darkness of the woods, safe at last, but truly no closer to the fleet than when he had started.

In the cool of the woods Cushing rested briefly, but soon encountered a local black man who was out working the fields, and who inadvertently stumbled upon the weary naval officer. "The man stood still, surprised to see the muddy apparition in front of him, while Cushing got laboriously to his knees and crouched, ready to spring."[17] Naturally enough, the man was taken back by Cushing's mere presence, and hardly knew how to respond; but here, Will quickly reasoned, was an opportunity to solve a problem that still plagued him.

For while Cushing knew he had detonated the torpedo under the *Albemarle*, and he knew as well that he had caused a severe disruption in the port town of Plymouth, he could not be sure if he had, in fact, disabled or perhaps even sunk the ironclad. And this he needed to know. Without this information the success of his mission remained entirely unresolved, and his vow to avenge Flusser's death unfulfilled. While he could not even hope to perform a reconnaissance on the ram himself, the old man, he knew, could easily move in and out of Plymouth without raising an eyebrow. An idea dawned upon him.

Cushing quickly fished twenty wet dollars in greenbacks out of his wallet along with some scriptural texts he had secreted away, and offered them to the man, explaining what he needed to know. The two men reached an agreement, Cushing comfortable enough to state, "I had confidence enough in his fidelity to send him into town for news of the ram."[18] And his confidence was soon rewarded. The man returned and told Cushing exactly what he wanted to hear — the ironclad had been sunk, and was now sitting on the bottom of the Roanoke River.[19] "She is dead gone sunk," the man stated emphatically, "and they will hang you, massa, if they catch you."[20]

While it is not on record, the reception of this information must have been, for Will Cushing, an enormous bounty, and for a man who lived as much on will power as he did the more natural elements of food, water, and rest, a wondrous boost of spirit. Now he knew for certain that he had accomplished precisely what he had steamed up the Roanoke to do, indeed, a task many had considered at the onset nearly impossible. Thanking the old man for his help, Will gathered his strength and moved on.

Cushing had no great sense of where exactly he was, of course, only the course of the Roanoke River—which he had now moved away from—and the sun as natural features to guide him. Keeping those two variables in mind, he stumbled again headfirst into another deep and dark swamp, not sure at all where it might lead him, but hoping to make his way east toward the fleet at the mouth of the river.[21] "I went on again, and plunged into a swamp so thick that I had only the sun for a guide and could not see ten feet in advance."[22] Again tearing his feet and arms to pieces while struggling through thorns and briers, he struggled on for at least another hour, finally emerging along the bank of a flowing creek. "About 2 o'clock in the afternoon," Will later recounted, "I came out from the dense mass of reeds upon the bank of one of the deep, narrow streams that abound there, and right opposite to the only road in the vicinity. It seemed providential that I should come just there, for thirty yards above or below, I never should have seen the road, and might have struggled on until worn and starved—found a never-to-be-discovered grave."[23]

But God, or Providence, or his own remarkable good fortune seemed once again to have served him. Here was a road now for him to trod, and a road, no matter where it might lead, was better by far than the hated swamps; and if his natural luck still held at all, this road might well lead down to the river. Will was worn far beyond simple exhaustion now, hungry and bleeding, but none of that really mattered. Cushing knew he had to push on, so he started hobbling down the road, blood from his damaged feet tracking the dirt behind.

Chapter 32

It Is Done

CUSHING DUCKED AWAY from the road into the dark, shifting shadows of the woods. He moved slowly, tree to tree, inching ever closer to get a better look. Now he crouched down and watched. It was late afternoon, and he was tired and hungry, but his mind remained clear. And here before him now was what appeared to be a great opportunity.

After hours of painful hiking, Will Cushing had at long last reached the Roanoke River, now far downstream from Plymouth. Through a gap in the trees he had spotted a Rebel picket post along the river, seven men it appeared from a distance, but he could not be entirely sure.[1] But what he was sure of was the boat they had tied up in a stream below him, "a little flat bottomed, square ended skiff, toggled to the root of a cypress tree that squirmed like a snake into the inky water."[2] William Cushing wanted that skiff. If he could make off with the boat unseen, he could slip downriver and paddle his way back out to the fleet. Surely it was a long shot, but it was also his best shot — he wanted that boat.

So Cushing sat in the woods and watched the Confederate soldiers as they went about their business, waiting patiently for an opportunity to inch his way down to the creek and untie the boat when no one was watching.[3] There could be no mistakes, he realized. Not now. This might be his only real chance to finally make good his escape, and if only one of the seven Rebels spotted him, he knew, the others would have their rifles trained on him in an instant. So he watched until the sun started to dip behind him in the west, until the soldiers at long last moved off a few yards to enjoy their supper. When he was sure they had all gone off, he made his move.

Quietly as he could manage, he made his way down to the stream, and carefully slipped into the water. Then he swam across, mindful to keep the trunk of a large tree between himself and the Confederate pickets. A few gentle strokes and he was across. "Gaining the bank," Cushing recalled, "I quietly cast loose the boat and floated behind it some thirty yards around the first bend, where I got in and paddled away as only a man could where liberty was at stake."[4]

Around the bend he went and out into the greater Roanoke, the pickets still unaware of their loss. For the first time in almost fifteen hours, he had real hope of returning to the fleet alive. But Will was hardly out of danger or difficulty, for there remained pickets all along the river; and even if not spotted, it would take hours of hard paddling to gain the sound, then more still to locate a friendly vessel. It would be a grinding test of his endurance, no matter the outcome.

"Hour after hour I paddled," Will remembered, "never ceasing for a moment, first on one side, then on the other, while sunshine passed into twilight and that was swallowed up in thick darkness, only relieved by the few faint star rays that penetrated the heavy swamp curtain on either side."[5] He paddled on, never stopping, working until only his arms and mind remained awake, the remainder of his body going almost numb with fatigue.[6] Cushing refused to give in, to surrender to exhaustion; and at long last his efforts were rewarded — there ahead of him finally lay the dark, open waters of the sound. "At last I reached the mouth of the Roanoke, and found the open sound before me."[7]

And here he again encountered good fortune. The rains and storm of the day before had blown through overnight leaving the day calm and the winds and seas light. It was a significant stroke of good luck. "My frail boat could not have lived a moment in the ordinary sea there," Will readily admitted, "but it chanced to be very calm, leaving only a slight swell, which was, however, sufficient to influence my boat, so that I was forced to paddle all upon one side to keep her on the intended course."[8] The stars were out sufficiently for him to guide his course, and he began paddling through the waters of Albemarle Sound to where he hoped the fleet would be located. It required hours of painful labor. "After steering by a star for perhaps two hours for where I thought the fleet might be, I at length discovered one of the vessels, and after a long time got within a hail. My 'Ship ahoy!' was given with the last of my strength, and I fell powerless, with a splash, into the water in the bottom of my boat, and awaited results. I had paddled every minute for ten successive hours, and for four my body had been 'asleep,' with the exception of my two arms and brain."[9]

The vessel Cushing had hailed was in fact the *Valley City*, freshly arrived from Roanoke Island at 9:15 that evening, and having moved off for picket duty at the mouth of the Roanoke River at 10:00 P.M.[10] The fleet was on alert owing to Cushing's torpedo attack, and all vessels were expecting some form of retaliation from the Rebels. Just that morning the cutter with crew had returned to report the detonation of the torpedo, but what all it meant they did not know. No one could say if the Albemarle had been damaged or sunk in the attack. Indeed, the log from the *Shamrock* recorded, "At 6:45 A.M. the second cutter returned with Acting Master's Mate Burlingame and Acting Gunner William Peterkin and 4 rebel prisoners, which they took from the *Southfield*. Reported the steam launch, under Lieutenant Cushing, as having attacked the rebel ram, but what damage to her did not ascertain, as the ram kept up a heavy fire of musketry and artillery for abut ten minutes."[11]

In that manner, Cushing's hail was initially received as a potential threat, and maneuvers taken for immediate defense. Thus when the hail was heard aboard the *Valley City*, the officers "assumed that it must be a torpedo attack by the Confederates, in retaliation for the attack the night before, and the ship's cable was slipped and general quarters sounded. When no attack developed an armed boat in charge of Acting Ensign Milton Webster was lowered and sent to investigate."[12]

Webster located Cushing's small skiff bobbing lifelessly on the calm waters of the sound, and approached cautiously. What he discovered, of course, was an unidentified man lying in the bottom alone, covered in mud, partially clothed, barely conscious. The man displayed no sign to speak of as being a Federal naval officer. While Webster knew Cushing by reputation, he did not know him in person, and had no idea just who, or what, he had found. Indeed, Cushing was then thought to be dead or captured, so Webster, rather unceremoniously, had the body hauled back to the *Valley City* and tossed onto the ship's deck for further appraisal. As Cushing later recalled, "It was some time before they would pick me up; being convinced that I was the rebel conductor of an infernal machine, and that Lieut Cushing had died the night before."[13]

While most of the crew of the *Valley City* could not identify Cushing, the ship's commander, J.A.J. Brooks, knew him well enough to make the identification. Brooks made his way to Cushing's side, leaned over, but could hardly believe his eyes. "My God, Cushing," he exclaimed, "is this you?"[14]

Will heard the question, and struggled to offer a weak reply: "It is I," he answered.[15]

But Brooks had to know if Cushing had destroyed the ram, for it was the one critical piece of the puzzle still missing. Was the *Albemarle* sunk or damaged? Brooks had to know. So he leaned closer and asked. "Is it done?"[16]

Will grasped his meaning at once, and although starving and surely exhausted, answered as readily as he could manage. "It is done."[17]

Remarkably, within hours William Cushing would be on his feet again, and within a day or so write his report of the action for Admiral Porter at Hampton Roads. Concise and to the point, it would begin with this simple statement of fact: "I have the honor to report that the rebel ironclad *Albemarle* is at the bottom of the Roanoke River."[18] It was done.

Chapter 33

Cheer Ship

NOT TERRIBLY LONG AFTER being yanked from the bottom of his skiff by Ensign Webster, Will Cushing stood aboard the flagship *Shamrock* and watched as loud cheers swept from ship to ship across the sound, as rockets hissed skyward, exploding in the air overhead. It was an extraordinary, spontaneous celebration of joy, and an amazing turn of events. Where only hours prior he had been virtually lost and in desperate straits, he was now the centerpiece of a vast celebration. Flares and rockets rose in the air over the dark waters of Albemarle Sound, banging and thumping and cracking like blossoming stars in the heavens, all commemorating Cushing's return to the fleet and the destruction of the *Albemarle*.[1] The good news had been signaled from ship to ship as the *Valley City*, Cushing now aboard, came speeding up the sound, blowing her whistle as she approached. The *Shamrock*'s log recorded the event, noting that at approximately 11:30 P.M. the *Valley City* arrived off its starboard beam, having on board Lieutenant Cushing, who had reported the ram blown up and his launch sunk in the effort. The command was issued to "Cheer Ship," guns were fired, and the celebration begun.[2]

"Peal on peal of cheering rang out over the water as Cushing sat on the deck of the *Shamrock* watching the arching rockets as they flew over the gathered ships."[3] As Will later recorded the moment, "As soon as it became known that I had returned rockets were thrown up and all hands called to cheer ship — and when I announced my success, all the commanding officers were summoned on board to deliberate upon a plan of attack."[4] Goliath had been slain — the *Albemarle* was no more. The impossible had been rendered possible.

On board the *Valley City* Cushing, once recognized, had been given a hero's welcome. He was treated with great care, and given small amounts of brandy and water to help revive him.[5] Then he was rowed over to the *Shamrock* to report to Commander Macomb. Here he met with the commanders of the various vessels to report the results of his mission and provide a rundown of the surrounding defenses.

Commander Macomb immediately set about planning the recapture of Plymouth. On the morning of October 29, the entire blockading fleet — less the *Valley City*—was arranged in battle order (*Commodore Hull* in the lead, followed in turn by *Shamrock, Chicopee, Ostego, Wayalusing,* and *Tacony*) and at 11:45 A.M. began steaming up the Roanoke River toward Plymouth.[6] The passage was uneventful, but after exchanging fire with Confederate batteries established below the town, Macomb discovered that the obstructions sunk by Alexander Warley the day before were entirely effective, and the fleet could not pass the wreck of the *Southfield.* The Federals had no option but to turn around and return to the sound.

The *Valley City*, on the other hand, had been tasked with sailing up the Middle River, bypassing Plymouth, entering the Roanoke at the confluence of the two rivers, and intercepting any Confederate boats fleeing upriver from the town. The *City* accomplished all this, but upon observing the cessation of firing below on the Roanoke, incorrectly assumed that Plymouth had fallen, and eventually desisted in her efforts. Two things of merit were nevertheless accomplished. The first was that on its voyage upriver the *City* had discovered Edward Houghton who, escaping as had Cushing, had swum across the river and hidden in the swamp awaiting discovery.[7] Secondly, the *Valley City*, by simply entering the Roanoke above Plymouth, had demonstrated the fact that the impediments placed in the Roanoke by the Confederates could be bypassed, and the river entered from above the town.

The following morning, October 30, Macomb again placed his vessels in fighting order — with the exception again of the *Valley City* which had been detailed to take Cushing to Hampton Roads — and proceeded up the Middle River. "The expedition threaded successfully the channel, shelling Plymouth across the woods on the intervening neck of land on its way up, until it reached the head of Middle River and passed into the Roanoke, where it lay all night."[8] The following morning the fleet was again arranged in battle order by Commander Macomb then put in motion south toward Plymouth. At around 11:00 A.M. the signal "Go ahead fast"[9] was given, and the fleet was soon hotly engaged with the Rebel defenders. "After a spirited action of an hour at short range, receiving and returning a sharp fire of shell, grape, and canister, the *Shamrock* planted a shell in the enemy's magazine, which blew up, and the Confederates hastily abandoned their works."[10] A Federal landing effort then went ashore, overwhelmed what remained of the batteries and captured the last of the fleeing Confederates. It had been a well conceived and executed mission, its success complete. With only six killed and nine wounded on the Union side, Plymouth had been secured and once again flew the stars and stripes. Additionally, "twenty two cannon were captured, with a large quantity of small-arms, stores, and ammunition."[11]

On November 1 Commander Macomb sat down and penned a short report to Admiral Porter. He provided a brief summation of Cushing's daring assault on the *Albemarle*, then went on to suggest that "he will, himself [Cushing], I suppose, give you the account of his escape, and I shall therefore merely state that he was picked up on the night of the 28th ultimo by the *Valley City*."[12] Cushing was, of course, already en route aboard the *Valley City* bound for Hampton Roads at the time Macomb's description was written, preparing his own report for personal delivery.

Interestingly, after sweeping through Plymouth the Federal forces picked their way through the abandoned spoils of war, including the post office, and there located a letter posted but not yet delivered. The letter had apparently been written by one of the *Albemarle*'s officers and although not clearly identifiable (it was signed simply E.K.L.) provides engaging — and at times humorous — insight into the situation at Plymouth immediately following Cushing's attack.

> Esteemed Friend: I received your kind epistle of the 20th instant, finding me lingering under a severe attack of the fever. I am now up and about again, nearly as well as ever. They are sending out expeditions every now and then. We captured a Yankee yawl boat. It is supposed we killed nearly all of her crew, consisting of about eight men. But the most awful thing of all (perhaps you will hear of it before this reaches you) is that a Yankee torpedo boat steamed up the river Thursday night, and about 3 o'clock Friday morning ran into the *Albemarle*. The torpedo bursting, blew a great hole in her some 6 feet long, sinking her almost instantly. She is now lying at the bottom of the Roanoke River. The crew lost everything they had, bed clothing and everything. Some lost their hats and shoes, and some even came out in their shirts and drawers, barefooted. We are in an awful condition. I believe they are going to hold the place to the bitter end. Captain Warley says he intends to fight as long as there is a man left (this is all gas). I never did witness such an uproar before in my life. Troops were hurrying to and fro, expecting every moment to meet in battle dread. But, fortunately, there has been no attack, though there is no telling how soon we may see a man-of-war steaming up the river, belching forth fury in her mad career, carrying in her front the token of devastation and ruin. We are going to take command of one of the forts on the river. Direct your letter to Plymouth, N.C., care of Captain Warley. I remain, as ever, your sincere friend. E.K.L.[13]

After the Confederates had fled Plymouth, Macomb took the time to make a visual inspection of what remained of the *Albemarle*, and observed in his report that: "On my arrival I found the ram sunk at the wharf as far as her ports, and the top plating of her casemates entirely blown off. I have ordered a survey, and herewith enclose the report."[14]

That survey, conducted by Chief Engineer H.H. Stewart, a sort of technical post mortem of the ironclad, unfortunately provides less insight into the effectiveness of Cushing's torpedo assault than does the description supplied by E.K.L. in his letter. The reason for this is that the damage inflicted by the torpedo could no longer be distinguished from Warley's efforts in scuttling the vessel. "She is sunk at the wharf and heading downstream," Stewart noted, "heeling off shore at an angle of about 10°; the flat part of the casemate on the port side is 22 inches out of the water. We find the entire top of the casemate blown off.... As it is reported that she was again blown up by the rebel authorities after she was sunk by Lieutenant Cushing, it is impossible to say how much of the damage was done by him."[15]

For those members of Cushing's crew who had been taken prisoner by the Rebels at Plymouth, the renewed Federal naval assault proved unfortunate. Rather than risking the loss of these men back to the Yankees, the crew members were hustled off just as the Confederates themselves abandoned the town. Ensign Gay's report provides an interesting account of the hardships they faced once captured, and their treatment, prison to prison, thereafter. "We were all taken on shore and marched to the prison, where we remained until our gunboats made their approach up the river. We were then marched to Tarboro, N.C., a distance of 60 miles, [at] which place we arrived on the 2d of November, being very tired and feet badly swollen. On the 3d we were sent to Salisbury, where we arrived on the 5th. After marching about 2 miles we arrived at the stockade, where we were enclosed with some 10,000 prisoners. Here we suffered immensely for the want of shelter from the inclemency of the weather and also for provisions, as our fare was very poor, being one-half pint of meal per day, which was very inconvenient on account of having no cooking utensils."[16]

From Salisbury the crew was marched to Danville on the 13th, where they were housed in a brick building with another 500 officers. While not providing much for warmth, this facility at least sheltered the men from the cold, rain, and snow. Food, of course, remained meager at best, consisting of one slab of cornbread per day. Finally, the crew was removed to Richmond on the 11th of December. Here they were placed in the famed Libby Prison, where they experienced living conditions essentially similar to those they had left behind in Danville.[17] There they had to settle in for the duration, hopefully awaiting exchange and parole.

For Catherine Edmondston the fall of Plymouth represented the sudden materialization of a nightmare, and she lost no time filling her journal with line upon line of displeasure. But the sparks of sarcasm and anger that had so often filled her pages here gave way to despondency, and this again to a deeper sense of confusion and wonder. Perhaps the dark hand of defeat seemed now to be hovering too dangerously near for her, and that frightening prospect called into question the very nature and meaning of it all. For those, both North and South, who labored in the steadfast attempt to discern God's intent through the ever shifting landscape of war, that divine purpose so assiduously sought after seemed often elusive indeed, and so now it proved for Catherine Edmondston. Had God, for some inexplicable reason, suddenly turned His back on the South? "The capture of Plymouth hangs like a pall on our spirits," she confided. "God's will be done. He exalts & He depresses! Grant us faith to see His hand in it & to know & confess that that state in which He places us is the one in which it is best for us to be. The weather is just into the Yankee's hands for it has rained incessantly since yesterday morning, the very thing for them, for it will raise the river & enable their boats to run up. The river is now & has been for months very low in consequence of unusual dry weather. God knows what is for our best!"[18]

At some primal level Mrs. Edmondston may well have conceived the loss of Plymouth as far more than mere strategic setback or temporary readjustment now required for both her and her beloved Confederacy, but rather a critical step toward something infinitely more cataclysmic — the looming collapse of an entire way of life.

CHAPTER 34

Thanks of Congress

OVERNIGHT WILLIAM B. CUSHING had become a person of such intense interest and importance that the *Valley City* had been detailed for no purpose other than to carry him to Hampton Roads for a meeting with Admiral Porter. Physically, other than his hands and feet, Will reported being "well again in every way,"[1] and had no problem making the journey. Porter, of course, had already received Commander Macomb's brief report of the affair and had sent it on, along with his own comments, to Gideon Welles in Washington. News of the sinking of the *Albemarle* had already been picked up and carried by many newspapers across the North, although Cushing's fate remained initially undetermined.[2] On November 3 William telegraphed his mother from Washington, at long last relieving her intense apprehension. "Mrs. Cushing," he wrote, "Have destroyed the rebel ram *Albemarle*. Am all right. Thanks of Congress, promotion and fifty thousand (50,000) prize money. W.B. Cushing, U.S.N."[3]

Admiral David Porter had experienced, as a result of Cushing's remarkable success, a complete reversal of his opinion of the young lieutenant, no longer dismissing him as a brash daredevil, but rather holding him up now as the very model of the professional naval officer, to be emulated by all concerned. Indeed, so impressed was Porter with Cushing's success that he wrote a general order lauding Will which he had read aloud to the assembled crews of every ship under his command. It read in part:

> It affords me pleasure to inform the officers and men of the squadron under my command that the rebel ram *Albemarle*, which has for so long a time kept a large force of vessels employed to watch her, has been destroyed by Lieutenant William B. Cushing, who, in this hazardous enterprise, has displayed a heroic

enterprise seldom equaled and never excelled. In the face of a watchful enemy, and under a heavy fire of musketry and great guns, he went right into the ram *Albemarle* and blew her up, his own boat being destroyed by one of the enemy's shot. To say nothing of the moral effect of his gallant affair, the loss of this vessel to the rebels cannot be estimated. It leaves open to us all the Albemarle Sound and tributaries, and gives us a number of vessels for employment elsewhere (hitherto kept to watch the ram), which has been a great source of annoyance to vessels in the sound. The gallant exploits of Lieutenant Cushing previous to this affair will form a bright page in the history of the war, but they have all been eclipsed by the destruction of the *Albemarle*.[4]

The response to William Cushing's successful sinking of the *Albemarle*, both professional and popular, was overwhelming. As Will would later write, "I again received the congratulations of the Navy Department and the thanks of Congress of the United States. I was promoted to the grade of Lieut. Commander. The testimonials that I received from Chambers of Commerce, Cities, Union League Clubs &c were numerous and gratifying. I was at the time twenty-one years of age, having had my first command at nineteen. The *Albemarle* was built like the famous *Merrimac[k]* and in her contests with our ships successfully resisted hundred powder Dahlgren and Parrott shot, at ten yards range."[5] Will Cushing had suddenly become a "star" in a country that had very few recognizable stars.

Cushing would soon be invited to speak at Union League events in both New York City and Philadelphia, where his brief comments were greeted with thunderous ovations.[6] "His popularity was universal among the people of the North. There was a craze to get his portrait, and to meet the demand thousands of 'cheap overall cuts and lithographic portraits' were turned out, and were hung in as many parlors, alongside pictures of President Lincoln, and Generals Grant, Sherman and Sheridan. His own account of the destruction of the ram was published in almost every newspaper, and long interpretations were written and published in periodicals. He was even given a nickname, and was known everywhere, and for years afterward in the navy, as 'Albemarle' Cushing."[7]

When the Secretary of the Navy, Gideon Welles, received the report from Admiral Porter of Will's success, he, having stuck by the young officer through many a predicament, responded with profound, personal gratification, sending on to Cushing a congratulatory memo of his own.

> When last summer the Department selected you for this important and perilous undertaking, and sent you to Rear-Admiral Gregory at New York to make the necessary preparations, it left the details with you to perfect. To you and your brave comrades, therefore, belongs the exclusive credit which attaches to this daring achievement. The destruction of so formidable a vessel, which has resisted the continued attack of a number of our steamers, is an important event,

touching our future naval and military operations. The judgment, as well as the daring courage displayed, would do honor to any officer, and redounds to the credit of one 21 years of age.

On four previous occasions the Department has had the gratification of expressing its approbation of your conduct in the face of the enemy, and in each instance there was manifested by you the same heroic daring and innate love of perilous adventure — a mind determined to succeed, and not to be deterred by any apprehensions of defeat.

The Department has presented your name to the President for a vote of thanks, that you may be promoted one grade, and your comrades shall receive recognition.

It gives me pleasure to recall the assurance you gave me at the commencement of your active professional career that you would prove yourself worthy of the confidence reposed in you, and of the service to which you were appointed. I trust you may be preserved through further trials, and it is for yourself to determine whether, after entering upon so auspicious a career, you shall by careful study and self-discipline be prepared for a wider sphere of usefulness on the call of your country.[8]

Soon Will would receive a copy of the president's response to Welles' request, signed by Abraham Lincoln himself. "In conformity to the law of the 16th July, 1862, I most cordially recommend that Lieutenant William B. Cushing, U.S. navy, receive a vote of thanks from Congress for his important, gallant, and perilous achievement in destroying the rebel ironclad steamer *Albemarle* on the night of the 27th October, 1864, at Plymouth, N.C. The destruction of so formidable a vessel, which has resisted the continued attacks of a number of our vessels on former occasions, is an important event touching our future naval and military operations, and would reflect honor on any officer, and redounds to the credit of this young officer and the few brave comrades who assisted in this successful an daring undertaking."[9]

In early November Will Cushing was granted an extended leave — his feet and hands were still giving him trouble, and he had now developed a serious pain in his back — and he began the journey north from Hampton Roads to Fredonia in order to visit with his mother and family, and recover from his ordeal. All along the way he was stopped and congratulated by people on the street who suddenly recognized him from his picture in the papers, and the trip, while exciting and certainly gratifying, proved long and tedious.[10] Thus no one in Fredonia knew when they might actually expect him, and when he finally did arrive many of the townsfolk were engaged in one of a series of war meetings in the town's Concert Hall.

Will arrived by rail one evening, only to find the meeting ongoing, and many of his friends and relatives so invovled.[11] So he headed up to the Concert Hall himself, surely not to create a stir, only to greet friends and family. But what he experienced as he entered the hall may well have eclipsed all the other letters and honors that had been showered upon him in light of his success; for while no one in town knew when to expect him, everyone was aware of what he had accomplished.

The Concert Hall was packed when he arrived, everyone listening to the speaker on stage. Cushing entered quietly from the rear, and began walking up the center aisle. Mary Edwards describes the response: "As soon as he entered the door he was observed and recognized, and a ripple of excitement instantaneously passed over the assemblage, and by the time he had gone halfway up the aisle the entire audience had simultaneously risen, and cheer after cheer pealed through the large auditorium. The president of the meeting descended from the platform to meet him, and from every side the people crowded about him and fairly carried him to the platform, where he made a brief speech of grateful acknowledgment of the greeting. Then the cheers rang out again, and everybody hurried forward to shake his hands and to embrace him, the Fredonia boy, who had gone out from among these citizens for only a brief space of time, and within that limited period had become a world-renowned hero, and now had come back to his mother and his home friends. The greeting given to him was such as could only be bestowed upon a hero by the hero's own appreciative townspeople."[12] Will Cushing had finally come home.

CHAPTER 35

The Cost of the Nation's Unity

WILLIAM CUSHING RETURNED to active duty in late November, promoted to the rank of Lieutenant Commander, and now assigned to command the *Malvern*, Admiral Porter's flagship.[1] It was a somewhat "cushy" position for an officer who lived on daring, and it would not be long before Cushing volunteered to return to the fray.

By December 1864 the Confederacy, although emitting neither the slightest outward nor inward murmur of defeat, in fact displayed many signs of the dying patient. In the East, for instance, Ulysses Grant remained locked in siege before Petersburg with Robert E. Lee's Army of Northern Virginia; and while for some it appeared a siege that might never end, Grant had in fact managed to stretch Lee's capacity to resist nearly to the breaking point. By continuing to expand his lines south and west, Grant was forcing Lee to overcommit everywhere across his front; a situation that, unless radically reinforced, simply could not go on forever. So far Lee — indeed, brilliantly at times — had been able to discern Grant's gambits and shift troops to meet most Federal offensive initiatives; but clearly food, ammunition, men, and time were, for Lee and his army, running out.

In the West Sherman had taken Atlanta in the fall, and over the course of the winter had begun his famous march across Georgia. As he marched his army seemed to disappear from the map, and for a period remained completely out of touch with Washington, cutting a wide swath across the Southern state. Both North and South hung on every news report, waiting for some confirmation of Sherman's whereabouts, anxious to determine, not only where he was, but exactly where he might be headed.

At Scotland Neck, Mrs. Edmondston, watching closely as events unfolded and wringing her hands in anticipation, reacted with increasing anxiety. "Have been for the last week on such a qui vive of expectation, expectation each day disappointed & hope deferred until the next, that I have not cared to write until I had something definite to say of Sherman & even now all I can say is that he is still in Georgia, devastating & burning as he goes. Our troops have concentrated there & the papers bid us be of good cheer & assure us that the War Depart has cheering news which for the present it is best not to publish."[2]

That "cheering news" for Southern ears was not to be, however, as in early December Sherman reappeared on the Eastern Seaboard near Savannah, his army having subsisted on foraging while en route. Sherman then took Savannah, reestablished a waterborne supply route, and turned his force north on a course bound for South Carolina, North Carolina, and eventually Virginia. For any sober analyst at the time, as Sherman turned north — a course that would over time bring him to Grant's assistance and virtually double the Federal force opposing Lee — the days may well have appeared numbered for the Southern Confederacy.

But all of that is, of course, hindsight. At the time few were betting against Robert E. Lee and his army, and at Richmond Jefferson Davis remained defiant to the point of denial. The war effort went on, and in the East for the Union that still meant securing the ports of entry on the Atlantic Seaboard. By December only one significant port remained open to any great extent, and that was Wilmington, NC, on the Cape Fear River. Thus was a combined land and sea effort organized in early December to try and force the forts at the mouth of the river that guarded the town. Fort Fisher, guarding New Inlet, was naturally first on the Federal list, and a combined assault launched on Christmas Eve 1864. The land portion of this operation fell to General Benjamin Butler, a political appointee of Lincoln's who was high on political ambition, but painfully short when it came to military aptitude. The naval part of the campaign fell to Admiral David Porter and, naturally enough, wherever Porter went so went his flagship, and wherever the *Malvern* was to be found, so too was William B. Cushing.

Despite considerable animus between the high commanders of the operation, by December 24 all was in place and the naval bombardment of Fisher began on schedule. "Five commodores led the divisions, and each commanding officer had his own copy of the position and target charts, printed on the *Malvern*'s lithographic press. In a great crescent, no more than a mile to sea, overlapping Fort Fisher from the northeast bastion to the mound battery; more than fifty ships, mounting 580 guns, moved with the precision of a ponderous ballet."[3] For five hours the bombardment continued, and some 2,500 troops landed for the assault — about one third of the entire attacking force. But when the smoke finally cleared, and it was determined that the naval bombardment had not sufficiently enfeebled the fort's defenses to allow for a direct assault, the army refused to budge. What now?

The force already landed was not considered capable to taking the fort, yet Butler did not want to land more men while Fisher's guns remained lethal. General Butler then asked Porter if the Navy could not simply storm passed Fisher up the channel and take the fort in reverse. "Porter knew that was out of the question. The wrecks of blockade runners and sunken hulks on the unmarked bar had altered its whole formation, obliterating the original channel."[4] The Navy could only proceed if a new channel could in some manner be determined and marked below Fort Fisher, but how in the world might that be done in the midst of a hot campaign? Was there someone brave enough to navigate the channel directly below those booming guns, and hopefully find and mark a new channel? There was. His name was, of course, William Cushing.[5]

As Cushing would later recall it, after the troops had been stranded on shore, "I took my gig and went in on the bar to sound and put down buoys. I was six hours upon this dangerous duty; and congratulate my self that we were not blown out of the water."[6] Will Cushing was now a Lieutenant Commander, however, and on this occasion he dressed the part, virtually waving a red bandana in the bull's face above on the battlements. "He wore every bit of gold braid to which he was entitled and his boat carried the blue and white pennant of a commanding officer. He sat coolly in the stern directing the leadsman's activities."[7]

The Confederate gunners, apparently stunned by this brazen act, indeed initiated almost in contempt of their guns, did not open fire for almost ten minutes; but then, apparently realizing what Cushing was up to, threw almost everything at him they could load into their barrels. "Round shot, shell and shrapnel ploughed around us every moment," Will later recalled, "and I actually had to bail out the water that was thrown into the boat by them. A cutter assisting us was sunk by the severe fire."[8] The day proved a typical case of Cushing's cool under fire. "Cushing's boat drew so close to the shore that 'a biscuit might be tossed from the boat to the beach;' at this point Cushing ordered his men to stop rowing and stood up in the stern of his frail craft and took a cool and deliberate survey of the fort."[9]

Exposed to this heavy fire for six hours in a small cutter, Cushing still managed to sound out a narrow channel, and mark it appropriately, but Will determined that the channel was too narrow for the Navy's use, and Admiral Porter advised General Butler promptly that the back door to Fort Fisher, for the time being at least, remained closed. Butler then, almost inexplicably, pulled some of his troops off the landing area but, leaving behind almost six hundred men on the beach, hauled anchor and made sail for Hampton Roads. Butler later claimed that he could not recover the remaining troops due to a rising tide; but the damage had been done, and the professional soldiers and sailors associated with the effort were naturally incensed.[10] "The indignation of army and navy at this inexcusable conduct of Butler's was openly and loudly expressed,"[11] Cushing would write, and Admiral Porter raged at the general's conduct. Two days later the Navy successfully removed the stranded soldiers, but there was little question by then that the first attempt to take Fort Fisher had ended in self-inflicted fiasco.

Another assault was then in the planning stage, but in the interim, Will was given back command of the *Monticello*, a fighting position on a real fighting ship; and it would not be long before Cushing was once again on the prowl. "The day after the withdrawal of the troops," Will explained, "a volunteer Lieut, commanding an armed prize, came around from the western bar and reported that he had been chased away by a rebel privateer loaded down with men and protected by cotton bales."[12] Hearing of the lieutenant's report, Admiral Porter at once thought of Cushing, and it was then that Porter granted Cushing command of his former ship, with the understanding he would run the Rebel down.

"Steaming around the shoal as rapidly as possible," Will later reported, "I found the vessel described, at anchor inside the bar under the guns of Fort Caswell, and fired a blank cartridge as a challenge. This did not draw her out, nor did the subsequent destruction of a large blockade running steamer, which I drove ashore under the batteries, in her attempt to get in. In this service my ship was hulled six times. The *Chickamaugua* would not fight, and probably suspecting some Yankee trap — whereas nothing was desired by us but a fair field and no favor," Will insisted. "With her extra men aboard she was much stronger and might better have finished her career in a gallant action on the ocean; than in the way she did — sunk by a retreating crew in Cape Fear River."[13]

Serious action, however, was but days ahead. On January 13, 1865, the Federal assault was renewed against Fort Fisher, and in this Will Cushing would become intimately involved. General Alfred Terry had been selected by General Grant to replace Butler, and an additional brigade of infantry added to the landing force.[14] "At first light, January 13, the fleet opened a deliberate, concentrated, all-day barrage. At 8:30 A.M., the first wave of Terry's troops pulled for the beach well north of the land face."[15] The landings were made successfully, and all the troops moved ashore where they dug in along the beach.

Admiral Porter, however, not wanting the Navy to miss out on the glory of the assault and the capitulation of Fort Fisher, had assembled a "naval brigade of 1,400 sailors and marines,"[16] organized to land along the beach opposite the army troops, and take the fort by storm. But the assault was mishandled, the men put ashore in the wrong location, forcing the assault to tra-

35. The Cost of the Nation's Unity

The Federal fleet bombards Fort Fisher. Note the mound battery in the center background (U.S. Naval History and Heritage Command).

verse a long beach before approaching the walls of the fort, thus depleted through exertion and strung out upon finally gaining the objective. Armed for the most part with but cutlass and pistol, the sailors were no match for the well armed and determined defenders waiting for them atop the works. The assault quickly devolved into chaos, and Will Cushing, not to be denied, was out front in the thick of it.[17]

"About two in the afternoon I landed with forty men to join the assaulting body of sailors and marines," Cushing declared, "who were to storm the sea front of the fort. These were fourteen hundred in number; the officers all in uniform, bright with gold lace and every man dressed as for inspection. All were armed with cutlass and revolver alone, excepting the marines who carried muskets and were to cover us in scaling the works."

"Wheeling from column into line, we marched up by the flank to within four hundred yards of the frowning fort and lay down under the slope of sand beach until the signal for assault should come from the army — who were to advance from the other side."[18]

When the signal finally came all Rebel eyes had seemingly shifted to the seawall, however, and the defenders were waiting upon the naval brigade as it assaulted up the beach in the middle of the afternoon straight into the strength of the Confederate position. The Yankee sailors were greeted with a

Union monitors move in to provide covering fire for the assault on Fort Fisher (U.S. Naval History and Heritage Command).

hail of lead, and promptly slaughtered for their efforts. The white beach ran red with blood. Cushing was out in front, leading the sailors on. "The beach to be gone over was level white sand," he recalled, "into which we sank ankle deep, and which in the bright sunlight made targets of us all from contrast. The rebels meanwhile were not idle, but thinking ours the main storming party, massed against us and sent a staggering fire into our ranks that ploughed through with deadly effect; and never ceased for an instant. We gained the palisades only to find further advance impossible and all were brought to a halt."[19]

Cushing, seeing what he conceived as an opening, dashed up the palisades toward the Confederate gunners, but turning, noticed that no one had followed his lead, and thus beat a hasty retreat back down into the sand with the rest of the troops. Behind him the naval brigade, still receiving a withering fire, began to break and retreat, men stumbling and running away from the metal conflagration ahead. The Navy would suffer a horrific price for Admiral Porter's grasp for glory. Over 300 men lay dead on the beach, the brigade simply shot to pieces.[20] "The retreat was a fearful sight," Will recalled afterward. "The dead lay thickly strewn along the beach, and the wounded falling constantly, called for help to their comrades, and prayed to God that they might not be left behind. I saw the wounded stagger to their feet all weak and bloody, only to receive other and more fatal wounds and fall to rise no more."[21]

Yet the debacle had one important unintended effect — the Confederates, thinking the naval brigade's assault the main attack, failed to check the Federal infantry on the far wall; and when that attack eventually was launched, was entirely successful. Thus the naval assault had proved a terrible and bloody diversion, but a diversion at least that worked. The Union infantry came at that moment storming over the walls of Fort Fisher, and the fighting became fierce and man-to-man. "The battle degenerated into a hand-to-hand, bayonet and grenade alley fight — battery to battery, traverse to traverse, trench to trench. The *New Ironsides*, whose shooting was particularly accurate, dropped shells into individual rebel positions, blasting the defenders into the open killing ground."[22]

The fighting here was particularly fierce, the Confederates fully aware that if Fisher fell, Wilmington could not stand for long. A reporter for *Harper's* wrote of the struggle: "The guns of the fleet were turned upon the traverses, while the brave men of Terry's command fought their way from traverse to traverse, overpowering the garrison, and driving it back to the Mound Battery."[23] At 10:00 P.M. the last of the Confederates finally surrendered and the fighting ceased. Fort Fisher was now in Union hands, but it had come at the grim price of over 1,000 dead and wounded on the Federal side, most of those killed in the naval brigade.[24]

Will Cushing had been on the beach through it all, from the initial assault to the final surrender, and personally observed both the success of Federal arms, and the resultant carnage. It was something he would not soon forget. "At 10 that night the entire rebel force surrendered. In the intermediate time, between the assault and the surrender, the tide had risen and drowned many of our wounded who fell upon the beach; and swept off into the remorseless ocean the hero clay of many a gallant sailor. How few realize at what a cost our Nation's unity has been *purchased*!"[25]

With the fall of Fort Fisher, Federal forces were one step closer to finally closing the port of Wilmington. But only one step. The Confederates still had much of the length of the Cape Fear River defended, and Fort Anderson on the river blocked access directly to Wilmington.[26] If Fisher had been an example of what might be expected of Confederate resistance, Porter realized that Anderson would not fall without exacting a heavy toll in Union lives.

But it was not to be. By ingenuity alone Anderson would be taken, a ruse played on the Confederate defenders that would have them fleeing in the dark of night, and a ruse played by none other than William B. Cushing. It was a stunt that would delight his compatriots, please Admiral Porter no end, and cause Abraham Lincoln to howl with glee.[27]

Chapter 36

Blind to the Facts

THE FALL OF FORT FISHER, like a string of fire crackers popping, caused in turn a series of Confederate reverses around the port city of Wilmington. Because New Inlet entered the Cape Fear River considerably upriver from a number of Confederate bastions — and New Inlet had now fallen under the control of the Federal Navy — all these positions were as a result now untenable in terms of their defense. The Federals could simply steam up New Inlet, for instance, cut the Rebels off, and ultimately attack the defenses from the rear. Fort Caswell, Fort Johnston, and Smithville were all as a result abandoned by the Rebels, who were forced to draw their defensive perimeter in toward Wilmington proper. Fort Fisher had been the key to the outer defenses of the city, and Fort Fisher now flew the stars and stripes. The cornerstone had been removed from the wall and without so much as an additional push, the remainder had simply crumbled.

The critical nature of these setbacks had hardly been lost on Catherine Ann Edmondston who, despite catastrophic difficulties of her own, was still able to find time to dish out a literary paddling to the floundering Confederate leaders whom she deemed responsible for the debacle. "On Tuesday we heard that the Yankee fleet had returned & recommenced a furious assault on Fort Fisher," she wrote. "[General] Bragg telegraphs that 'there is no cause for alarm, that all goes well, Whiting in command,' that he has repulsed a vigorous assault, etc., etc., but adds PS by which we learn that fort Fisher has fallen."[1] Mrs. Edmondston, no fool when it came to intelligently deciphering the drift of events, immediately grasped what the fall of Fisher meant for the Confederacy. "We since hear that Ft. Caswell has been blown up & abandoned, the fall of Fisher having made it untenable. So we fear it will soon be with Wilmington, tho now troops are hurried & and a determination 'to hold it at all hazards.' Too late in the day I fear. Fort Fisher was the key and that has been thrown away.... Out on Bragg the unlucky & out on Mr. Davis for maintaining him in command!"[2]

Indeed, events for Catherine Edmondston appeared to be cascading rapidly out of control. Sherman had turned north and was rumored to be moving through South Carolina bound for the North Carolina line, Lee still clung desperately to his lines about Petersburg but without reinforcement could not possibly hold forever, and now Wilmington appeared near collapse. Added to the discouraging war news was the fact that a new dam along the Roanoke had given way due to heavy rains and rising waters and flooded Conneconara, one of her farms along the river. Like the biblical plagues of old, all now that must have seemed missing were the locusts.

"A terrible break [to the dam] had taken place above the house & the river was rushing in with tremendous fury carrying everything before it," she recorded in her journal. "The stable was gone, not a vestige of it being left. Father with his own hands released the horses about midnight! The bank had slipped behind the kitchen & it was expected every moment that it, too, would go & the house itself stood in a strong current, the water being within two inches of the sills! & seemed in imminent danger of settling."[3]

Between the depressing news at home and the dismaying dispatches from the various fronts, it appeared Mrs. Edmondston had little choice but to pray for the best while expecting the worst. The war for her had begun in a burst of worry and trepidation, and so too would it end. On April 13, 1861, for instance, upon hearing the news that the Confederate batteries had fired upon Fort Sumter in Charleston harbor, she had anxiously written, "I burst into tears & Patrick entering at the moment I threw myself into his arms & wept like a child! Yes, it is done! Who can tell what will be?"[4]

Well, it would in fact be four terrible, bloody years of conflict in which over 620,000 Americans would lose their lives, a nation would be torn apart, and the Southern infrastructure wrecked for a half century. Reflective of this terrible, suddenly looming reality, Mrs. Edmondston's last entry for January 22, 1865, suffers in anticipation of a world turned upside down. "The discontent with the Government increases. Revolution, the deposition of Mr. Davis, is openly talked of! Who can tell how it all will end? Vain are our conjectures. We wait with folded hands what is in store for us. God grant that it be neither Emancipation or Subjugation; be it what it will, may we see His hand in it all."[5]

In late February Will Cushing had been removed from duty at Wilmington and detailed to Norfolk. Still in command of the *Monticello*, he reported there to the navy yard in order to have a torpedo applied to the vessel.

Word had been received that the Confederates had obtained a new ironclad in France, and that the ironclad — named the *Stonewall*— was soon bound for the East Coast of the United States in hopes of breaking the blockade.[6] Leaving the *Monticello* in the shipyard, Cushing headed up to the Navy Department in Washington to hand deliver some dispatches regarding the fall of Wilmington. There he met Gideon Welles who was just on his way across the street to a meeting with the president, and Welles asked if Cushing would like to join him. Will, of course, accepted.

"The two men — the slim naval officer and the old white-bearded Yankee politician — walked to the White House, where they found General Hooker and secretary of State Seward already with the President. Seward was 'imposing,' Cushing felt; Hooker he had met before, at the review of troops in the summer of 1862."[7] According to Gideon Welles, the president that day was in a very good mood.[8] And why not? While the past two months for Abraham Lincoln had been exhausting, they had also been productive. In January the great fight over emancipation had come to a head, and on the 31st — and validating one of Mrs. Edmondston's worst fears — the House voted on the emancipation amendment Lincoln had proposed.[9] The galleries were reportedly overflowing that day in anticipation of a vote that might literally change the fundamental structure of the nation. Lincoln had remained in the White House, slogging through reams of paperwork, anxiously awaiting the result. Then he got the final count, 119 yay, 58 nay — the 13th Amendment had passed. "At once a 'storm of cheers' broke out among the Republicans, who jumped around, embraced one another, and waved their hats and canes overhead. There were shouts and applause in the galleries, too, where women's handkerchiefs were fluttering in the air."[10] The amendment would have to go before the people for ratification, of course, but for Lincoln his part of the great task had been accomplished.

All this had come about because Abraham Lincoln had managed to win the fall election. By January of the new year the president had traveled a considerable distance in terms of his popularity since that day in August when he had penned his speech theoretically conceding the election to George McClellan. On November 8 Lincoln had won the election over McClellan rather handily, thumping his former general in the electoral college to the tune of 212 to 21.[11] To most that seemed an overwhelming victory, and so it was proclaimed, but the numbers regarding the popular vote were equally instructive. In that count, indeed in a popular vote numbering almost four million, Lincoln had managed to secure approximately 56 percent of the vote to McClellan's 44 percent share; a decided victory, but hardly the overwhelming mandate suggested by the electoral tally. Quite a few citizens had voted for the other ticket. Yet the victory had given Lincoln the opportunity to pursue the war to its rightful conclusion — to steer the nation toward emancipation, no matter how unpopular the idea remained — and for the president the election results had been heartfelt. Not long thereafter a group of citizens had gathered below his window, and Lincoln had gone out to read them a speech concerning just what the election had meant to him. "It meant above all that America's free institutions could work, that the country could carry out a free canvass in the middle of civil war.... And he was glad, he said, that most people had voted for him, the one candidate most dedicated to the Union and opposed to treason."[12]

But still the war raged on, and daily men on both sides were losing their lives in a contest that increasingly appeared a foregone conclusion. The Southern Confederacy could not last much longer — that much appeared clear. But would they ever stop fighting? That was the question.

In late December Federal General George Thomas had virtually destroyed the Confederate Army in the Western Theater near Nashville, Tennessee; and now Lee in the East surely appeared doomed, caught between a hammer and an approaching anvil — Sherman closing from the south, which appeared now only a matter now of weeks. To try and forego further bloodshed, in early February Lincoln had traveled to Hampton Roads to take part in a peace conference with chosen representatives of the Confederacy. If lives could be saved, why not make the attempt? Nothing came of it, however; Jefferson Davis was still spouting victory and independence, and Lincoln would have none of it.[13] The Rebel leadership simply refused to see the writing on the wall. "The Confederacy was about to tumble," as Will Cushing phrased it, "but they were blind to the fact."[14] Indeed, so blind were they to that rapidly approaching reality that "upon the return of the Confederate commissioners a great meeting was held to revive the drooping spirits of the Confederacy, and it was unanimously resolved that the conditions of peace offered by President Lincoln were a gross and premeditated insult to the Southern people."[15] So war it was they unanimously approved, thus war it would be to the bitter end.

Thus had events turned since the previous August for the president, and in that sense Abraham Lincoln — despite the serious work of peace and reconstruction that still lay ahead — had every right to be in good spirits as Welles and Cushing entered his office that day in February. Lincoln recognized Cushing and congratulated him on his promotion to Lt. Commander, and for his daring assault upon the *Albemarle*.[16] That attack had taken place just days before the fall election, and while the destruction of the ironclad had hardly pushed Lincoln over the top, it certainly did not hurt his electoral chances. The conversation then turned to the recent fall of Wilmington, and Cushing reportedly humored the group with the story of how he had helped force the capitulation of Fort Anderson.[17]

"In consequence of a formidable line of obstructions," Will explained, "and a quantity of torpedoes in front of this fort, it was decidedly unsafe to attempt running the fleet by its guns and until that *should* be done it had free communication with the city above. Our army was closing in upon its rear but could not command the river; and it became necessary for the Navy to act. I therefore proposed to Admiral Porter the construction of a mock *Monitor* such as used by him upon the Mississippi River — and at once proceeded to construct it out of an old flat boat and some canvas."[18] The point was to try and construct a vessel that looked from a distance exactly like a real Federal ironclad then somehow drift the boat passed the fort so that the Rebels would believe their escape route upriver had been cut off. With the river above and below now in Federal hands, and Yankee infantry closing rapidly from the rear, Fort Anderson would be in danger of being entirely cut off and forced to capitulate. Rather than fall headfirst into such a dilemma, it was hoped the Confederates — upon seeing the fake monitor pass by in the river — would simply abandon the position and retreat to safer ground.

Cushing's project progressed nicely. "When complete," he wrote, "it was not possible to distinguish between it and the real one near by; at two hundred yards distance."[19] The fake monitor was then towed into position near the fort where it could not be seen by the garrison. The Cape Fear did the rest. "The tide there runs about five knots speed," Will explained, "and it was to be the motive power. Weighting one end of my iron clad much heavier than the other so as to take it straight up with the tide, I towed her up to within two hundred yards of the opening of the obstructions and cast adrift.

"Up the river with the flood tide, she went, apparently steaming in spite of everything passed successfully.

"The consequence was that the commanding confederate, knowing that the army was closing in behind him, and thinking a *Monitor* in the river above — evacuated in such haste as to leave the fourteen heavy guns unspiked, and the magazine intact.

"We took possession the next morning. Confederate officers told me afterwards that this was the true reason for their retreat, and swore like pirates at the imposition."[20] The president was said to have "laughed heartily"[21] over Cushing's tale, and Hooker and Seward no doubt enjoyed it too. For Will Cushing it proved a moment of intense emotion, and he left the meeting flushed with affection for the president, and hoping for more opportunities to display his loyalty.[22]

But that was not to be. Work on the *Monticello* dragged, the *Stonewall* never made an appearance along the Eastern Seaboard of the United States, and in late February Will was detached from the vessel he had commanded with such skill and bravado. For awhile he remained in Washington, traveled briefly to Boston, but he was weary and in need of rest. In late March he returned home to Fredonia.[23] "Cushing had never enjoyed a hearty constitution. He was subject to severe cold and grinding headaches.... Since the night he'd spent hours in the cold river after sinking the *Albemarle*, he'd been troubled by bouts of pain in his back. He needed rest and recuperation."[24]

Will Cushing had tempted the fates of war so many times no doubt it was good fortune that sent him home to recover this one last time with no new assignment to accomplish. Thus would end one of the more remarkable tales of the American Civil War. William Barker Cushing and the *Albemarle* he vowed to destroy would from that moment forward be forever locked in a dance of mutual recognition; no discussion of the ironclad would ever make sense without a mention of Cushing, while Will Cushing's entire career seemed to revolve around the destruction of the ram.

The *Albemarle* had been destroyed, and Will Cushing had lived to tell the tale. Those twin successes were no small accomplishment, and by late March 1865, after four long years of bitter warfare, for most men that would certainly have seemed career enough. As Will traveled home to Fredonia in late March — for a man just turned twenty-two years of age and with his entire life still reaching out before him — surely spring must have seemed in the air.

Epilogue

On April 2, 1865, only six weeks after Abraham Lincoln's last meeting with William Cushing, Robert E. Lee's thin defensive lines surrounding Petersburg, Virginia, collapsed. Fleeing west in the desperate hope of locating a rail line south to evacuate his army, Lee was forced to abandon the Confederate capital at Richmond. Federal forces under Ulysses S. Grant moved rapidly, cutting off Lee's march and eventually surrounding his force at Appomattox Court House, Virginia. There on April 9, out of both rations and options, Lee surrendered the much depleted Army of Northern Virginia to Grant, effectively ending the American Civil War.

Abraham Lincoln rejoiced at the news of Lee's surrender, but would have little time to enjoy the victory. On April 14, only five days after the surrender, Lincoln was assassinated by John Wilkes Booth at Ford's Theatre in Washington, D.C. Lincoln's body lay in state in Washington where thousands paid tribute to their fallen leader. His body was then removed by train to Springfield, Illinois, as millions of mourners lined the tracks, where he was laid to rest beside the body of his young son, Willie. Abraham Lincoln, perhaps the most admired president in American history, would not live to see his ideas of peace and reconstruction enacted, and the nation, particularly the South, would pay a bitter price for that loss.

On April 7, as Federal forces approached, Captain James Wallace Cooke fired the new ram that he and Gilbert Elliott had under construction at Edward's Ferry, North Carolina, then disappeared from public life.

The *Albemarle* would be partially repaired and raised by the Federal Navy, then towed to Norfolk, Virginia, where it would remain moored in ordinary storage for years. In 1867 the vessel was auctioned for sale. Of the *Albemarle* only her forward Brook rifle remains, on display today at the Norfolk Naval Base.

The captured crew members of picketboat *No. 1* remained in Libby Prison, Richmond, until February 21, 1865. On that date they were paroled, removed to Cox's Landing where upon the steamer *New York* they enjoyed their first good meal in months. From that point the men traveled home. The war, for them, was over.

Frank Aretas Haskell's stirring account of the Battle of Gettysburg would be published in 1881 to national acclaim. He would not survive to enjoy it, however. Leading an infantry regiment at the Battle of Cold Harbor, Haskell was killed on June 3, 1864.

Gilbert Elliott, builder of the *Albemarle,* married shortly after the war, raised a family, and worked as an attorney in a number of locations across the country. In 1892 he moved his family to New York City, where he died suddenly on May 9, 1895, at the age of 51. He was buried in the Green-Wood Cemetery, Brooklyn, New York.

Upon hearing the news of Lee's surrender, and grasping that it meant the imminent collapse of her beloved Confederacy, Catherine Ann Edmondston displayed all the classic symptoms of severe depression. "Since we heard of our disaster," she wrote, "I seem as tho' in a dream. I go about in a kind of *'drowsy dream.'* I sleep, sleep, sleep endlessly; if I sit in my chair for ten minutes, I doze. I think of it, but I cannot grasp it or its future consequences. I sit benumbed."[1] She would survive, however, and live to January 3, 1875, still refined, but never reconstructed. She was buried at Trinity Episcopal Church, Scotland Neck, North Carolina.

On February 24, William Cushing received orders detaching him from the *Monticello,* and he would see no further action during the short remainder of the war. After the war's end Cushing remained in the navy, eventually rose to the rank of commander (the youngest ever to achieve that rank), married, and fathered two daughters. During his short, remaining naval career, Cushing traveled the world where his wartime exploits had achieved international renown. Thus it was that "Albemarle" Cushing — as he would come to be known — was often recognized and honored in ports as far distant as China and Japan.

Unfortunately, the wounds and physical hardships of the Civil War would plague William Cushing's postwar career. He would suffer from increasing pain and illness until his untimely death in 1875 at the age of only thirty-three, and his remarkable exploits on the rivers of North Carolina would fade, by and large, from public memory. Yet none less than Admiral David Farragut — who once had himself lashed to the rigging of his flagship as he steamed toward the torpedo strewn waters of Mobile Bay, and thus knew something of heroism himself— had once remarked that "young Cushing was the hero of the war." William Barker Cushing is buried at Bluff Point, the cemetery for the United States Naval Academy, Annapolis, Maryland.

Chapter Notes

Preface

1. Robert L. O'Connell, *Of Arms and Men* (New York: Oxford University Press, 1989), 31–32.

Prologue

1. E.M.H. Edwards, *Commander William Barker Cushing of the United States Navy* (New York: F.T. Neely, 1898), 24–25.
2. Ibid.
3. T.W. Haight, *Three Wisconsin Cushings* (Madison: Wisconsin History Commission, 1910), 20.
4. Ralph J. Roske and Charles Van Doren, *Lincoln's Commando: The Biography of Commander W.B. Cushing* (New York: Harper, 1957), as quoted, 39.
5. Edwards, *William Barker Cushing*, 25.
6. Ibid., 25–26.
7. Robert G. Elliott, *Ironclad of the Roanoke: Gilbert Elliott's Albemarle* (Shippensburg, PA: White Mane, 1999), 14–15.
8. William B. Cushing, *The Sea Eagle: The Civil War Memoir of Lt. Cdr. William B. Cushing*, ed. Alden R. Carter (Lanham, MD: Rowman & Littlefield, 2009), 6.
9. Roske and Van Doren, 41.
10. Edwards, *William Barker Cushing*, 20.
11. Roske and Van Doren, 42.
12. Edwards, *William Barker Cushing*, 22–23.
13. Cushing, *Sea Eagle*, 8.
14. Haight, 27.
15. Ivan Musicant, *Divided Waters: The Naval History of the Civil War* (Edison, NJ: Castle, 2000), 137.
16. Roske and Van Doren, as quoted, 88.
17. Ibid., 89.
18. Robert G. Elliott, 14.
19. Wagner, Gallagher, and Finkelman, 185.
20. Musicant, 137.
21. Ibid., 67.
22. Robert G. Elliott, 14.
23. U.S. Naval Department, *Official Records of the Union and Confederate Navies in the War of the Rebellion* (hereinafter abbreviated as ORN), Ser. 2, vol. 2, Washington, D.C.: Government Printing Office, 1894–1924, 51.
24. Musicant, as quoted, 136.
25. Edwards, *William Barker Cushing*, 89.
26. Roske and Van Doren, as quoted, 303.

Chapter 1

1. Musicant, 85.
2. Alfred H. Guernsey and Henry Mills Alden, *Harper's Pictorial History of the Civil War* (New York: Fairfax, 1866), 244.
3. Rush Hawkins, "Early Coast Operations in North Carolina," in *Battles and Leaders of the Civil War*, vol. 1 (New York: Century, 1888), 640.
4. Cushing, *Sea Eagle*, 123.
5. Robert G. Elliott, 64.
6. Catherine Edmondston, *Journal of a Secesh Lady: The Diary of Catherine Ann Devereux Edmondston, 1860–1866*, ed. Beth G. Crabtree and James Welch Patton (Raleigh, NC: Division of Archives and History, 1979), 420–421.
7. Musicant, as quoted, 83.
8. Hawkins, 640.
9. Musicant, as quoted, 124.
10. ORN, Ser. 1, vol. 11, 553.
11. Musicant, 127.
12. Guernsey and Alden, 246.

13. Roske and Van Doren, 125.
14. Guernsey and Alden, note 1, 240.
15. ORN, Ser. 1, vol. 11, 622–623, full inventory and description of the captured Confederate vessels.
16. Musicant, as quoted, 131.
17. Guernsey and Alden, note 1, 240.
18. Ibid., 240–241.
19. Edmondston, 116.

Chapter 2

1. Edwards, *William Barker Cushing*, 114.
2. Ibid.
3. Haight, 59.
4. Cushing, *Sea Eagle*, 26.
5. Roske and Van Doren, as quoted, 128.
6. Cushing, *Sea Eagle*, 20.
7. Roske and Van Doren, 110–111.
8. Haight, 38.
9. E.M.H. Edwards, as quoted in letter from Will Cushing to the author, 112.
10. Ibid., 115.
11. Roske and Van Doren, 128.
12. Cushing, *Sea Eagle*, 27.
13. Guernsey and Alden, note 1, 246.

Chapter 3

1. Musicant, 67.
2. Ibid., as quoted, 68.
3. Ibid.
4. Guernsey and Alden, 258.
5. Musicant, as quoted, 69.
6. Robert G. Elliott, 18.
7. William Francis Martin Papers (# 493), Southern Historical Collection, Wilson Library, University of North Carolina, Chapel Hill.
8. Robert G. Elliott, 25.
9. Ibid., 26.
10. Martin Papers.
11. Ibid.
12. Ibid.
13. Wagner, Gallagher, and Finkelman, 554.
14. Robert G. Elliott, 15.
15. Musicant, 396.
16. Ibid., 397.
17. Wagner, Gallagher, and Finkelman, 554.
18. *Civil War Naval Chronology, 1861–1865*, 1961–1966 ed., Washington, D.C.: Government Printing Office, 143.
19. Martin Papers.
20. Ibid.
21. Robert G. Elliott, 53.
22. Ibid., as quoted, 59.
23. Charles V. Peery Collection (# 470), Special Collections Department, J.Y. Joyner Library, East Carolina University, Greenville.

Chapter 4

1. Edwards, *William Barker Cushing*, 116–117.
2. Ibid., 117.
3. Haight, 60.
4. Roske and Van Doren, as quoted, 133.
5. Ibid., as quoted, 133.
6. J.T. Headley, *Farragut and Our Naval Commanders* (New York: E.B. Treat, 1867), 384.
7. Cushing, *Sea Eagle*, 29.
8. Roske and Van Doren, 134.
9. Haight, 61.
10. Roske and Van Doren, as quoted, 136–137.
11. Headley, 384.
12. Roske and Van Doren, as quoted, 137.
13. Ibid.
14. Cushing, *Sea Eagle*, 30.
15. Roske and Van Doren, 138.
16. Cushing, *Sea Eagle*, 30.
17. Headley, 385.
18. Haight, as quoted, 61.

Chapter 5

1. Robert G. Elliott, 70.
2. Peery Collection.
3. ORN, Ser. 1, vol. 8, 844.
4. U.S. War Department, *War of the Rebellion: The Official Records of the Union and Confederate Armies* (hereinafter referred to as ORA) Ser. 1, vol. 18, Washington, D.C.: Government Printing Office, 1880–1901, 777–778.
5. ORN, Ser. 1, vol. 8, 849–850.
6. Peery Collection.
7. Martin Papers.
8. Peery Collection.
9. Gov. Zebulon Vance Letter Book (GLB 50.1), North Carolina Division of Archives and History, Raleigh.
10. Ibid.
11. Robert G. Elliott, as quoted, 80.
12. Ibid., as quoted, 81.
13. Peery Collection.

Chapter 6

1. Edwards, *William Barker Cushing*, 121.
2. Ibid., as quoted, 121–123.
3. Roske and Van Doren, 123.
4. Haight, 32.
5. Ibid.
6. Guernsey and Alden, 159.
7. Roske and Van Doren, 110.
8. Ibid., 121.
9. Ibid., as quoted.
10. Haight, 42.
11. Roske and Van Doren, 121.
12. Stephen W. Sears, *Landscape Turned Red: The Battle of Antietam* (New Haven: Ticknor & Fields, 1983), 361.
13. Edwards, *William Barker Cushing*, as quoted, 121.
14. Cushing, *Sea Eagle*, 32.

15. Headley, as quoted, 386.
16. Ibid.
17. Cushing, *Sea Eagle*, 33.
18. Ibid., 33–34.
19. Edwards, *William Barker Cushing*, as quoted, 122.
20. Ibid., as quoted, 98.

Chapter 7

1. Edwards, *William Barker Cushing*, as quoted, 131.
2. Cushing, *Sea Eagle*, 35.
3. Edwards, *William Barker Cushing*, as quoted, 119.
4. Stephen W. Sears, *Chancellorsville* (Boston: Houghton Mifflin, 1996), 36.
5. Edwards, *William Barker Cushing*, 130.
6. Cushing, *Sea Eagle*, 35.
7. Haight, as quoted, 64.
8. Edwards, *William Barker Cushing*, as quoted, 130–131.
9. Headley, 386.
10. Ibid., as quoted, 132.
11. Roske and Van Doren, as quoted, 154.
12. Headley, 386.
13. Edwards, *William Barker Cushing*, as quoted, 133.
14. Headley, 387.
15. Cushing, *Sea Eagle*, 36.
16. Ibid.
17. Roske and Van Doren, 160.
18. Cushing, *Sea Eagle*, 38.
19. Sears, *Chancellorsville*, 96.
20. Ibid., as quoted.
21. Edwards, *William Barker Cushing*, as quoted, 127.

Chapter 8

1. Robert G. Elliott, 84.
2. ORN, Ser. 1, vol. 8, 859.
3. Gilbert Elliott, "The Career of the Confederate Ram *Albemarle*," *Century Magazine*, July 1888, 42.
4. Robert G. Elliott, 89.
5. Ibid., as quoted, 87.
6. Roske and Van Doren, 193–194.
7. Edmondston, 374.
8. Gilbert Elliott, 420–421.
9. Ibid., 420.
10. Ibid., 421.
11. Edmondston, 394–395.
12. Robert G. Elliott, 103.

Chapter 9

1. Roske and Van Doren, as quoted, 164.
2. Ibid.
3. Stephen B. Oates, *With Malice Toward None: A Life of Abraham Lincoln* (New York: HarperPerennial, 1994), 347–348.
4. Ibid., as quoted, 348.
5. Edwards, *William Barker Cushing*, as quoted, 127–128.
6. Ibid., as quoted, 128.
7. Roske and Van Doren, 166.
8. Stephen W. Sears, *Gettysburg* (Boston: Houghton Mifflin, 2003), 59.
9. Roske and Van Doren, 171.
10. Sears, *Gettysburg*, 85.
11. Ibid., as quoted, 86.
12. Ibid., 123.
13. Haight, 44.

Chapter 10

1. Fairfax Downey, *The Guns at Gettysburg* (New York: Collier, 1962), as quoted, 170.
2. Ibid., 169.
3. Edward Porter Alexander, *Military Memoirs of a Confederate* (New York: Da Capo, 1993), 419.
4. Haskell, 100.
5. Ibid., 102–103.
6. Downey, as quoted, 162.
7. Sears, *Gettysburg*, as quoted, 403.
8. Noah Andre Trudeau, *Gettysburg* (New York: HarperCollins, 2002), as quoted, 478.
9. Haskell, 112–113.
10. Roske and Van Doren, 170.
11. Haight, 42.
12. Roske and Van Doren, 172.
13. Ibid., as quoted 173.
14. Ibid.
15. Ibid., as quoted.
16. Haight, 45.
17. Downey, as quoted, 141.
18. Alexander, 422.
19. Haight, 46.
20. Sears, *Gettysburg*, as quoted, 436.
21. Haskell, 113.
22. Downey, 171.
23. Sears, *Gettysburg*, 419.
24. Ibid., 421.
25. Ibid., as quoted.
26. Downey, 172.
27. Ibid., as quoted.
28. Haight, 48–50.
29. Roske and Van Doren, 178.
30. Haight, as quoted in a letter from Sergeant Fuger, 54–55.
31. Ibid., as quoted, 50, 54–55.
32. Shelby Foote, *Stars in Their Courses: The Gettysburg Campaign, June–July 1863.* (New York, Modern Library, 1994), as quoted, 233.

Chapter 11

1. Guernsey and Alden, 513.

2. Trudeau, as quoted, 550.
3. Ibid., as quoted, 551.
4. Sears, *Gettysburg*, as quoted, 500.
5. Edmondston, 428.
6. Trudeau, 551.
7. Cushing, *Sea Eagle*, 39.
8. Ibid.
9. Ibid.
10. Trudeau, 551.
11. Robert G. Elliott, as quoted, 110.
12. Roske and Van Doren, 194.
13. Robert G. Elliott, 111.
14. Ibid., 115.
15. Gilbert Elliott, 420.
16. Edmondston, 474.
17. Gilbert Elliott, 421.
18. Ibid.
19. Robert G. Elliott, as quoted, 117.

Chapter 12

1. Roske and Van Doren, 183.
2. Edwards, *William Barker Cushing*, 127.
3. Haight, 66–67.
4. *Civil War Naval Chronology*, 131.
5. Headley, 132.
6. Cushing, *Sea Eagle*, 40.
7. *Civil War Naval Chronology*, 132.
8. Haight, 67.
9. Cushing, *Sea Eagle*, 41.
10. Ibid.
11. Roske and Van Doren, as quoted, 188.
12. Cushing, *Sea Eagle*, as quoted, 42.
13. Roske and Van Doren, 189.
14. Ibid.
15. Garry Wills, *Lincoln at Gettysburg: The Words the Remade America* (New York, Simon & Schuster, 1992), 24.
16. Ibid., 32.
17. Ibid., 33.
18. Roske and Van Doren, 190.
19. Wills, as quoted, 263.

Chapter 13

1. Robert G. Elliott, 137.
2. ORA, Ser. 1, vol. 33, 1061.
3. Douglas Southall Freeman, *Lee's Lieutenants: A Study in Command*, vol. 3 (New York: Charles Scribner's Sons, 1944), 335.
4. Ibid.
5. Robert G. Elliott, 118.
6. Edmondston, 482.
7. Vance, 373.
8. Gilbert Elliott, 421–422.
9. Ibid., 421.
10. ORA, Ser. 1, vol. 33, 1101.
11. Robert G. Elliott, as quoted, 148.
12. Edmondston, 526.

Chapter 14

1. ORN, Ser. 1, vol. 9, 511, Cdr. Cushing's official report.
2. Ibid., 512.
3. Roske and Van Doren, 191.
4. Cushing, *Sea Eagle*, 43.
5. Ibid.
6. James Russell Soley, *The Blockade and the Cruisers* (New York: Charles Scribner's Sons, 1883), 94.
7. Cushing, *Sea Eagle*, 43.
8. ORN, Ser. 1, vol. 9, 511.
9. Cushing, *Sea Eagle*, 43–44.
10. Ibid., 44.
11. Soley, *Blockade*, 95.
12. Cushing, *Sea Eagle*, 44.
13. Roske and Van Doren, 10–11.
14. Ibid., 11.
15. Cushing, *Sea Eagle*, 44.
16. Ibid.
17. Ibid.
18. Ibid.
19. Roske and Van Doren, 12.
20. Cushing, *Sea Eagle*, 44.
21. Roske and Van Doren, 12.
22. ORN, Ser. 1, vol. 9, 511.
23. Ibid., 512, as recorded in the ship's log.
24. Cushing, 45.
25. Roske and Van Doren, 13.
26. Cushing, *Sea Eagle*, 45.
27. Ibid., 46.
28. Roske and Van Doren, 13.
29. Ibid., 14.
30. Ibid., 13–14.

Chapter 15

1. Robert G. Elliott, as quoted, 166.
2. Ibid., 165.
3. ORN, Ser. 1, vol. 9, 656, Cdr. Cooke's official report.
4. Robert G. Elliott, as quoted, 167.
5. Gilbert Elliott, 422.
6. Musicant, as quoted, 411.
7. Ibid., 167.
8. Ibid., 168.
9. Ibid.
10. ORN, Ser. 1, vol. 9, 656.
11. Gilbert Elliott, 422.
12. Ibid.
13. Ibid.
14. Ibid., 422–423.
15. Robert G. Elliott, 171.
16. Gilbert Elliott, 423.
17. Robert G. Elliott, 171.
18. Musicant, 412.
19. Ibid.
20. Ibid., as quoted.
21. Robert G. Elliott, 177.
22. Gilbert Elliott, 423.

23. Robert G. Elliott, as quoted, 178.
24. Ibid.

Chapter 16

1. Robert G. Elliott, 179.
2. Gilbert Elliott, 423.
3. Ibid.
4. Musicant, 412.
5. ORN, Ser. 1, vol. 9, 657.
6. Roske and Van Doren, 199.
7. Gilbert Elliott, 423.
8. Roske and Van Doren, 198–199.
9. Robert G. Elliott, 181.
10. Gilbert Elliott, as quoted, 425.
11. Roske and Van Doren, 199.
12. Robert G. Elliott, 183.
13. ORN, Ser. 1, vol. 9, 657.
14. Robert G. Elliott, 184–185.
15. Guernsey and Alden, 723.
16. Gilbert Elliott, 425.
17. Guernsey and Alden, 723.
18. Freeman, as quoted, 336.
19. Ibid.
20. Edmondston, 551.
21. Edwards, *William Barker Cushing*, as quoted, 138.

Chapter 17

1. ORN, Ser. 1, vol. 9, 648.
2. William B. Cushing, "The Destruction of the *Albemarle*," *Century Magazine*, July 1888, 432.
3. ORN, Ser. 1, vol. 9, 658.
4. Ibid., 658.
5. Robert G. Elliott, 188–189.
6. Ibid., 189.
7. Edgar Holden, "The *Albemarle* and the *Sassacus*," *Century Magazine*, July 1888, 427.
8. ORN, Ser. 1, vol. 9, 770.
9. Ibid.
10. Gilbert Elliott, 425.
11. Ibid.
12. Robert G. Elliott, 195.
13. Gilbert Elliott, 425.
14. ORN, Ser. 1, vol. 9, 770.
15. Ibid.

Chapter 18

1. Holden, 428.
2. Robert G. Elliott, 196.
3. Holden, 427–428.
4. Ibid., 428.
5. Ibid.
6. Robert G. Elliott, as quoted, 197.
7. ORN, Ser. 1, vol. 9, 747.
8. Holden, 428.
9. Robert G. Elliott, 198.
10. Holden, as quoted, 428.
11. Gilbert Elliott, 425.
12. Holden, 428.
13. Ibid., as quoted.
14. Ibid., 428–429.
15. Robert G. Elliott, 202.
16. Holden, 428.
17. Gilbert Elliott, 425–426.
18. Ibid.
19. Holden, 429–430.
20. Robert G. Elliott, as quoted, 204.
21. Ibid., as quoted, 205.
22. ORN, Ser. 1, vol. 9, 734.
23. Holden, 431.
24. ORN, Ser. 1, vol. 9, 734.
25. Ibid.
26. Ibid., 770.
27. Ibid., 734.
28. Robert G. Elliott, 212.
29. Roske and Van Doren, 206.
30. Ibid.
31. ORN, Ser. 1, vol. 9, 734.

Chapter 19

1. ORN, Ser. 1, vol. 9, 589.
2. Cushing, *Sea Eagle*, 46.
3. Edmondston, 560.
4. Cushing, *Sea Eagle*, 46.
5. Ibid.
6. ORN, Ser. 1, vol. 9, 206, ship's log.
7. Cushing, *Sea Eagle*, 46.
8. *Civil War Naval Chronology*, pt. 4, 82.
9. Cushing, *Sea Eagle*, 46.
10. ORN, Ser. 1, vol. 10, 202.
11. Cushing, *Sea Eagle*, 47.
12. Ibid., 46.
13. ORN, Ser. 1, vol. 10, 202.
14. Cushing, *Sea Eagle*, 47.
15. Ibid.
16. ORN, Ser. 1, vol. 10, 202.
17. Ibid.
18. Soley, *Blockade*, 95.
19. ORN, Ser. 1, vol. 10, 202.
20. Ibid.
21. Cushing, *Sea Eagle*, 47.
22. Ibid.
23. Ibid.
24. ORN, Ser. 1, vol. 10, 202.
25. Soley, *Blockade*, 96.
26. ORN, Ser. 1, vol. 10, 202.
27. Cushing, *Sea Eagle*, 47.
28. ORN, Ser. 1, vol. 10, 202.
29. Ibid.
30. Cushing, *Sea Eagle*, 48.
31. Ibid.
32. Ibid.
33. Ibid.
34. Ibid., 48–49.
35. ORN, Ser. 1, vol. 10, 206.

Chapter 20

1. Cushing, *Sea Eagle*, 49.

2. Roske and Van Doren, 24–25.
3. Cushing, *Sea Eagle*, 49.
4. Ibid.
5. ORN, Ser. 1, vol. 10, 203.
6. Roske and Van Doren, 25.
7. Soley, *Blockade*, 96.
8. Cushing, *Sea Eagle*, 49.
9. Ibid.
10. ORN, Ser. 1, vol. 10, 203.
11. Roske and Van Doren, 26.
12. ORN, Ser. 1, vol. 10, 203.
13. Ibid.
14. Roske and Van Doren, 26.
15. ORN, Ser. 1, vol. 10, 203.
16. Cushing, *Sea Eagle*, 49.
17. Ibid.
18. ORN, Ser. 1, vol. 10, 203.
19. Ibid.
20. Roske and Van Doren, 27.
21. Soley, *Blockade*, 97.
22. Cushing, *Sea Eagle*, 49–50.
23. Ibid., 50.
24. Ibid.
25. ORN, Ser. 1, vol. 10, 204.
26. Ibid.
27. Ibid., 206, ship's log.
28. Ibid., 205.
29. *Civil War Naval Chronology*, 84.
30. Roske and Van Doren, as quoted, 28.
31. Ibid., as quoted, 29.
32. Cushing, *Sea Eagle*, 50.

Chapter 21

1. Horace Porter, *Campaigning with Grant* (New York: Konecky & Konecky, 1992), 18.
2. Edmondston, 556.
3. ORN, Ser. 1, vol. 10, 627.
4. Ibid.
5. Ibid.
6. Robert G. Elliott, 222–227.
7. ORN, Ser. 1, vol. 10, 49–50.
8. Edmondston, 569.
9. Robert G. Elliott, 228.
10. ORN, Ser. 1, vol. 10, 687.
11. Wagner, Gallagher, and Finkelman, 564.
12. Edmondston, 578–579.
13. Robert G. Elliott, 231.

Chapter 22

1. Robert G. Elliott, 234.
2. Roske and Van Doren, 208–209.
3. Cushing, "The Destruction of the *Albemarle*," 432.
4. Ibid., 432–433.
5. Edwards, *William Barker Cushing*, 143–144.
6. *Civil War Naval Chronology*, pt. 4, 83.
7. Cushing, *Sea Eagle*, 51.
8. Cushing, "The Destruction of the *Albemarle*," 433.
9. Cushing, *Sea Eagle*, 51.
10. Roske and Van Doren, 209.
11. ORN, Ser. 1, vol. 10, 248.
12. Cushing, "The Destruction of the *Albemarle*," 433.
13. ORN, Ser. I, Vol. X, 247–248.
14. Roske and Van Doren, 210.
15. Musicant, 58.
16. Roske and Van Doren, 210.
17. ORN, Ser. 1, vol. 10, 315.

Chapter 23

1. Robert G. Elliott, 237.
2. ORN, Ser. 1, vol. 10, 339.
3. Ibid., 339–340.
4. Ibid., 340.
5. Ibid.
6. Ibid.
7. Ibid.
8. Ibid.
9. Robert G. Elliott, 231.
10. ORN, Ser. 1, vol. 10, 718.
11. ORA, Ser. 1, vol. 40, pt. 3, 751–752.
12. ORN, Ser. 1, vol. 10, 736.
13. Robert G. Elliott, 243.
14. ORN, Ser. 1, vol. 10, 736.
15. Robert G. Elliott, 244.
16. ORN, Ser. 1, vol. 10, 739.
17. Robert G. Elliott, 246.
18. Ibid., 242.
19. ORN, Ser. 1, vol. 10, 741.

Chapter 24

1. ORN, Ser. 1, vol. 10, 340.
2. W.W. Wood, editor's note on "The Destruction of the *Albemarle*," *Century Magazine*, July 1888, 438.
3. Cushing, *Sea Eagle*, 51–53.
4. Wood, 438.
5. Cushing, *Sea Eagle*, 53.
6. Ibid.
7. Roske and Van Doren, 210.
8. Ibid.
9. ORN, Ser. 1, vol. 10, 448–449.
10. Ibid., 459.

Chapter 25

1. Roske and Van Doren, 215.
2. Ibid.
3. Oates, 395.
4. Ibid., as quoted.
5. Paul M. Angle and Earl Schenck Miers, *The Living Lincoln* (New York, Barnes & Noble Books, 1992), 616.
6. Oates, as quoted, 396.
7. Roske and Van Doren, 215.
8. ORN, Ser. 1, vol. 10, 483, Capt. Boggs report.

9. Ibid.
10. Ibid., 539, Ensign Stockholm report.
11. Ibid., 540.
12. Ibid.
13. Ibid.
14. Cushing, "The Destruction of the *Albemarle*," 433.
15. Edwards, *William Barker Cushing*, 147.
16. Roske and Van Doren, 217.
17. Edwards, *William Barker Cushing*, 147.
18. Ibid.
19. Ibid.
20. Ibid.
21. Ibid.
22. Ibid., 148.
23. Roske and Van Doren, 218.
24. Cushing, "The Destruction of the *Albemarle*," 433.
25. Cushing, *Sea Eagle*, 53.
26. Ibid.
27. Cushing, "The Destruction of the *Albemarle*," 433.
28. Cushing, *Sea Eagle*, 53.
29. Cushing, "The Destruction of the *Albemarle*," 433.

Chapter 26

1. Roske and Van Doren, 220.
2. Cushing, *Sea Eagle*, 55.
3. Roske and Van Doren, 221.
4. A.F. Warley, note on "The Destruction of the *Albemarle*," *Century Magazine*, July 1888, 439.
5. Ibid.
6. ORN, Ser. 1, vol. 10, 613.
7. Cushing, "The Destruction of the *Albemarle*," 433.
8. Roske and Van Doren, as quoted, 222.
9. Ibid., as quoted.
10. Ibid.
11. Cushing, *Sea Eagle*, 55.
12. Roske and Van Doren, 223.
13. ORN, Ser. 1, vol. 10, 613.
14. Ibid.
15. Roske and Van Doren, 223–224.

Chapter 27

1. Warley, 439.
2. Ibid.
3. Ibid.
4. Ibid., 440.
5. Ibid., 439.
6. Ibid., 440.
7. ORN, Ser. 1, vol. 10, 611.
8. Ibid., 624, Lt. Warley's report.
9. Warley, 439.
10. ORN, Ser. 1, vol. 10, 557.
11. Roske and Van Doren, 225.
12. Cushing, *Sea Eagle*, 55.
13. Roske and Van Doren, 225.
14. Robert G. Elliott, 250.
15. Edwards, *William Barker Cushing*, 152.
16. Ibid., as quoted.
17. Ibid., as quoted, 153.
18. Edmondston, 626.
19. Eric J. Wittenberg, *Glory Enough for All* (Washington, D.C.: Brassey's, 2002), 114.
20. Edmondston, 627.

Chapter 28

1. Edwards, *William Barker Cushing*, 153.
2. Cushing, "The Destruction of the *Albemarle*," 434.
3. Roske and Van Doren, 225.
4. Robert G. Elliott, 250.
5. Roske and Van Doren, 225.
6. Ibid., 227.
7. J.R. Soley, editor's note on "The Destruction of the *Albemarle*," *Century Magazine*, July 1888, 436.
8. Roske and Van Doren, 226.
9. Soley, editor's note, 436–436.
10. Roske and Van Doren, 226.
11. Edwards, *William Barker Cushing*, 153.
12. Roske and Van Doren, 227.
13. Robert G. Elliott, 251.
14. Roske and Van Doren, 228.
15. ORN, Ser. 1, vol. 10, 611.
16. Robert G. Elliott, 251.
17. Ibid.
18. Cushing, *Sea Eagle*, 55.
19. Ibid.
20. Roske and Van Doren, as quoted, 230.
21. Ibid., as quoted, 230.
22. Cushing, *Sea Eagle*, 55.
23. ORN, Ser. 1, vol. 10, 611.
24. Cushing, "The Destruction of the *Albemarle*," 434.
25. Ibid., 434–435.
26. Cushing, *Sea Eagle*, 55.
27. Cushing, "The Destruction of the *Albemarle*," 435.
28. Cushing, *Sea Eagle*, 55.
29. ORN, Ser. 1, vol. 10, 612.
30. Cushing, "The Destruction of the *Albemarle*," 435.
31. Cushing, *Sea Eagle*, 56.
32. Roske and Van Doren,, 232.
33. Soley, editor's note, 436.

Chapter 29

1. ORN, Ser. 1, vol. 10, 612.
2. Edwards, *William Barker Cushing*, 157.
3. Roske and Van Doren, 232–233.
4. ORN, Ser. 1, vol. 10, 612.
5. Ibid., 613, Ensign Gay's report.
6. Cushing, *Sea Eagle*, 57.
7. Roske and Van Doren, 233.

8. Warley, 439–440.
9. Edwards, *William Barker Cushing*, 157–158.
10. Cushing, "The Destruction of the *Albemarle*," 436.
11. Roske and Van Doren, 233.
12. Ibid.
13. Cushing, "The Destruction of the *Albemarle*," 436.
14. Roske and Van Doren, 234.
15. Cushing, *Sea Eagle*, 57.
16. Ibid.
17. ORN, Ser. 1, vol. 10, 612.
18. Cushing, "The Destruction of the *Albemarle*," 436.
19. Ibid.
20. Cushing, *Sea Eagle*, 57.
21. Ibid.
22. Cushing, "The Destruction of the *Albemarle*," 436.
23. Cushing, *Sea Eagle*, 57.

Chapter 30

1. ORN, Ser. 1, vol. 10, 624.
2. Warley, 440.
3. Ibid.
4. Ibid.
5. ORN, Ser. 1, vol. 10, 613.
6. Warley, 440.
7. Ibid.
8. Ibid.
9. Ibid.
10. ORN, Ser. 1, vol. 10, 624.
11. Robert G. Elliott, 259.
12. Edwards, *William Barker Cushing*, 183–184.
13. Ibid., 184–185.
14. Warley, 440.
15. Edmondston, 632–633.
16. Ibid., 628.

Chapter 31

1. Edwards, *William Barker Cushing*, 159.
2. Cushing, *Sea Eagle*, 57.
3. Cushing, "The Destruction of the *Albemarle*," 436.
4. Ibid.
5. Ibid., 436–437.
6. Cushing, *Sea Eagle*, 57.
7. Ibid.
8. Cushing, "The Destruction of the *Albemarle*," 437.
9. Ibid., 437.
10. Roske and Van Doren, 239.
11. ORN, Ser. 1, vol. 10, 612.
12. Cushing, "The Destruction of the *Albemarle*," 437.
13. Ibid.
14. Cushing, *Sea Eagle*, 58.
15. Ibid.
16. Cushing, "The Destruction of the *Albemarle*," 437.
17. Roske and Van Doren, 240.
18. Cushing, "The Destruction of the *Albemarle*," 437.
19. ORN, Ser. 1, vol. 10, 612.
20. Edwards, *William Barker Cushing*, as quoted, 160.
21. Cushing, *Sea Eagle*, 58.
22. Cushing, "The Destruction of the *Albemarle*," 437.
23. Ibid.

Chapter 32

1. Cushing, *Sea Eagle*, 59.
2. Cushing, "The Destruction of the *Albemarle*," 437.
3. Ibid.
4. Cushing, *Sea Eagle*, 59.
5. Ibid.
6. Ibid.
7. Cushing, "The Destruction of the *Albemarle*," 437.
8. Ibid.
9. Ibid.
10. ORN, Ser. 1, vol. 10, 621.
11. Ibid.
12. Roske and Van Doren, 242.
13. Cushing, *Sea Eagle*, 59.
14. Edwards, *William Barker Cushing*, as quoted, 161.
15. Ibid.
16. Ibid.
17. Ibid.
18. ORN, Ser. 1, vol. 10, 611.

Chapter 33

1. Cushing, *Sea Eagle*, 59.
2. ORN, Ser. 1, vol. 10, 621.
3. Roske and Van Doren, 243.
4. Cushing, *Sea Eagle*, 59.
5. Cushing, "The Destruction of the *Albemarle*," 437.
6. Soley, editor's note, 438.
7. Ibid.
8. Ibid.
9. Ibid.
10. Ibid.
11. Ibid.
12. ORN, Ser. 1, vol. 10, 615.
13. Ibid., 615–616.
14. Ibid., 615.
15. Ibid., 616–617.
16. Ibid., 613–614.
17. Ibid., 614.
18. Edmondston, 634.

Chapter 34

1. Cushing, "The Destruction of the *Albemarle*," 438.
2. Roske and Van Doren, 245.
3. Edwards, *William Barker Cushing*, 149.
4. ORN, Ser. 1, vol. 10, 614, General Order # 34.
5. Cushing, *Sea Eagle*, 60.
6. Roske and Van Doren, 249–250.
7. Ibid., 250.
8. ORN, Ser. 1, vol. 10, 619.
9. Ibid., 619–620.
10. Edwards, *William Barker Cushing*, 161.
11. Ibid., 162.
12. Ibid., 162–163.

Chapter 35

1. Cushing, *Sea Eagle*, 60.
2. Edmondston, 641–642.
3. Musicant, 424.
4. Ibid., 426.
5. Cushing, *Sea Eagle*, 61.
6. Ibid.
7. Roske and Van Doren, 258.
8. Cushing, *Sea Eagle*, 61.
9. Roske and Van Doren, 258.
10. Musicant, 426.
11. Cushing, *Sea Eagle*, 61.
12. Ibid.
13. Ibid., 61–62.
14. Musicant, 427.
15. Ibid.
16. Guernsey and Alden, 732.
17. Cushing, *Sea Eagle*, 62.
18. Ibid.
19. Ibid., 63.
20. Guernsey and Alden, 732.
21. Cushing, *Sea Eagle*, 63–64.
22. Musicant, 429.
23. Guernsey and Alden, 732.
24. Ibid.
25. Cushing, *Sea Eagle*, 64.
26. Guernsey and Alden, 732.
27. Cushing, *Sea Eagle*, 69.

Chapter 36

1. Edmondston, 657.
2. Ibid.
3. Ibid., 655–656.
4. Ibid., 48.
5. Ibid., 658.
6. Cushing, *Sea Eagle*, 69.
7. Roske and Van Doren, 267.
8. Ibid.
9. Oates, 405.
10. Ibid.
11. Ibid., 401.
12. Ibid., 402.
13. Guernsey and Alden, 669.
14. Cushing, *Sea Eagle*, 66.
15. Guernsey and Alden, 669.
16. Roske and Van Doren, 267.
17. Cushing, *Sea Eagle*, 69.
18. Ibid., 66.
19. Ibid.
20. Ibid., 67.
21. Roske and Van Doren, 267.
22. Ibid.
23. Ibid.
24. Cushing, *Sea Eagle*, 70.

Epilogue

1. Edmondston, 695.

Bibliography

Books

Alexander, Edward Porter. *Military Memoirs of a Confederate*. New York: Da Capo, 1993.

Angle, Paul M., and Earl Schenck Miers. *The Living Lincoln*. New York: Barnes & Noble, 1955.

Cushing, William B. *The Sea Eagle: The Civil War Memoir of Lt. Cdr. William B. Cushing*. Edited by Alden R. Carter. Lanham, MD: Rowman & Littlefield, 2009.

Downey, Fairfax. *The Guns at Gettysburg*. New York: Collier, 1962.

Edmondston, Catherine. *Journal of a Secesh Lady: The Diary of Catherine Ann Devereux Edmondston, 1860–1866*. Edited by Beth G. Crabtree and James Welch Patton. Raleigh, NC: Division of History and Archives, 1979.

Edwards, E.M.H. *Commander William Barker Cushing of the United States Navy*. New York: F.T. Neely, 1898.

Elliott, Robert G. *Ironclad of the Roanoke: Gilbert Elliott's Albemarle*. Shippensburg, PA: White Mane, 1999.

Foote, Shelby. *Stars in Their Courses: The Gettysburg Campaign, June–July 1863*. New York: Modern Library, 1994.

Freeman, Douglas Southall. *Lee's Lieutenants: A Study in Command*. Vol. 3. New York: Charles Scribner's Sons, 1944.

_____. *R.E. Lee: A Biography*. New York: Touchstone, 1997.

Grant, Ulysses S. *Personal Memoirs of Ulysses S. Grant*. New York: Barnes & Noble, 2003.

Guernsey, Alfred H., and Henry Mills Alden. *Harper's Pictorial History of the Civil War*. New York: Fairfax, 1866.

Haight, T.W. *Three Wisconsin Cushings*. Madison: Wisconsin History Commission, 1910.

Haskell, Frank Aretas. *The Battle of Gettysburg*. Madison: Wisconsin History Commission, 1908.

Hawkins, Rush, "Early Coast Operations in North Carolina." In *Battles and Leaders of the Civil War*. Vol. 1. New York: Century, 1888.

Headley, J.T. *Farragut and Our Naval Commanders*. New York: E.B. Treat, 1867.

Keegan, John. *The American Civil War: A Military History*. New York: Alfred A. Knopf, 2009.

Musicant, Ivan. *Divided Waters: The Naval History of the Civil War*. Edison, NJ: Castle, 2000.

Oates, Stephen B. *With Malice toward None: A Life of Abraham Lincoln*. New York: Harper-Perennial, 1994.
Page, Dave. *Ships Versus Shore: Civil War Engagements Along Southern Shores and Rivers*. Nashville: Rutledge Hill Press, 1994.
Porter, Horace. *Campaigning with Grant*. New York: Konecky & Konecky, 1992.
Roske, Ralph J., and Charles Van Doren. *Lincoln's Commando: The Biography of Commander W.B. Cushing*. New York: Harper, 1957.
Sears, Stephen W. *Chancellorsville*. Boston: Houghton Mifflin, 1996.
———. *Gettysburg*. Boston: Houghton Mifflin, 2003.
———. *Landscape Turned Red: The Battle of Antietam*. New Haven: Ticknor & Fields, 1983.
Soley, James Russell. *The Blockade and the Cruisers*. New York: Charles Scribner's Sons, 1883.
Trudeau, Noah Andre. *Gettysburg*. New York: HarperCollins, 2002.
Wagner, Margaret E., Gary W. Gallagher, and Paul Finkelman. *The Library of Congress Civil War Desk Reference*. New York: Simon & Schuster, 2002.
Wertz, Jay, and Edwin C. Bearss. *Smithsonian's Great Battles & Battlefields of the Civil War*. New York: William Morrow, 1997.
Wilber, Ken. *Integral Psychology: Consciousness, Spirit, Psychology, Therapy*. Boston: Shambhala, 2000.
Wills, Garry. *Lincoln at Gettysburg: The Words That Remade America*. New York: Simon & Schuster, 1992.
Wittenberg, Eric J. *Glory Enough for All: Sheridan's Second Raid and the Battle of Trevilian Station*. Washington, D.C.: Brassey's, 2001.

Official Documents, Reports

Civil War Naval Chronology, 1861–1865. 1961–1966 ed. Washington, D.C.: Government Printing Office.
U.S. Naval Department. *Official Records of the Union and Confederate Navies in the War of the Rebellion*. Multiple vols. Washington, D.C.: Government Printing Office, 1894–1924.
U.S. War Department. *The War of the Rebellion: A Compilation of the Official Records of the Union and Confederate Armies*. 70 vols. Washington, D.C.: Government Printing Office, 1880–1901.

Articles

Cushing, William B. "The Destruction of the *Albemarle*." *Century Magazine*, July 1888.
Elliott, Gilbert. "The Career of the Confederate Ram *Albemarle*." *Century Magazine*, July 1888.
Holden, Edgar. "The *Albemarle* and the Sassacus." *Century Magazine*, July 1888.
Soley, J.R. Editor's note on "The Destruction of the *Albemarle*." *Century Magazine*, July 1888.
Warley, A.F. Note on "The Destruction of the *Albemarle*." *Century Magazine*, July 1888.
Wood, W.W. Editor's note on "The Destruction of the *Albemarle*." *Century Magazine*, July 1888.

Collections

Martin, William Francis, Papers # 493. Southern Historical Collection. Wilson Library, University of North Carolina, Chapel Hill.
Peery, Charles, Collection #470. J.Y. Joyner Library, East Carolina University, Greenville.
Vance, Gov. Zebulon, Letters and Papers GLG 50.1, GP 173, GP 177. North Carolina Division of Archives and History, Raleigh.

Index

Albemarle, CSS: construction 60–64; defeats seven Federal gunboats on Albemarle Sound 119–126; defeats *Southfield & Miami* 108–113; launch 81–84; in Norfolk, VA 225; Plymouth assault 102–107; praise 141–142; winter offensive 92–95
Albemarle Sound 14
Atlanta, CSS 30–31

Brooks, J.A.J. 200
Burnside, Ambrose 15, 18, 66
Butler, Benjamin 13

Cambridge, USS 22
Cape Fear River 60, 96–101, 133, 212
Charleston Mercury 79
Chicago 5–11
Commodore Barney, USS 53–59, 65–68, 85
Commodore Perry, USS 20–25
Cooke, James Wallace 14–19, 33, 34, 44, 61–64, 81–84, 92–95, 102–107, 108–113, 116, 117, 118, 119–126, 142, 145, 155, 225
Cushing, Alonzo 8, 11, 47–52, 68–69, 70–78
Cushing, William Barker: aboard *Ellis* 34–40; and Albemarle Sound 193–197; assault on Fort Fisher 211–217; captains *Shokokon* 86–87; commands *Monticello* 88; on *Commodore Perry* 20–25; escapes from Plymouth 182–187; Federal Fleet 198–201; at Gettysburg 80; on Little River 50–52; mission against *Albemarle* 147–150, 166–169, 174, 176–181; on Nansemond River 53–59; post war career 226; and President Lincoln 65–69, 221; on Smith Island 96–101; thanks of Congress 207–210; torpedo boats 156–165; visit to brother 47–52; Wilmington expedition 127–139; as youth 8
Custer, George 174

Davis, Jefferson 10, 26, 60, 91, 212

Edmondston, Katherine 19, 79, 95, 128, 142, 144, 174–175, 191–192, 205–206, 211–212, 218–219, 226
Edward's Ferry, North Carolina 19, 60
Elliott, Gilbert 28, 31, 41–46, 61–64, 81–84, 92–95, 102–107, 108–113, 225, 226
Ellis, CSS 14–19, 33
Ellis, USS 34

Flusser, Charles 10, 106, 109, 113
Fort Bartow 17
Fort Fisher 213–217, 218
Fox, Gus 88, 150
Fredonia, New York 7–9

Gettysburg Address 89
Gettysburg, Battle of 70–78
Grant, Ulysses S. 140, 211

Haskell, Frank 70, 71, 76, 226
Hoke, Robert 92, 111, 115
Holden, Edgar 120–122
Hooker, Joseph 66
Howorth, William 97, 98, 127, 132, 159, 160–165, 167, 189
Hunt, Henry 71

239

Jones, J.E. 97, 101, 127

Lake Michigan 5
Lamson, R.H. 54
Lee, Robert E. 79, 91, 94, 140, 211, 225
Lincoln, Abraham 65–69, 88–89, 160–161, 209, 220–223

Macomb, W.H. 167–169, 173, 174, 204, 207
Maffitt, John N. 145, 151, 152, 153, 170
Mallory, Stephen 10, 11, 26, 29, 34, 41, 93, 142
Malvern, USS 211
Martin, William 28
Mattabesett, USS 119–126
McClellan, George 23, 48, 140, 220
Miami, USS 106–107, 119
Minnesota, USS 11, 12, 21, 147
Monitor, USS 22
Monticello, USS 88, 96–101, 127, 138, 219
Mosquito Fleet 13, 18, 27
Mount Washington, USS 53–59

New River 34–40

Picketboat *No. 1* 176–181
Porter, David 138, 148, 201, 207, 214
Porter, John Luke 28

Raleigh, CSS 127–130, 135
Roanoke Island 14

Sassacus, USS 120–126
Shamrock, USS 167, 202
Shokokon, USS 86
Southfield, USS 106–107, 114, 171, 178, 191
Stockholm, Andrew 159, 160–165

Tredegar Ironworks 27

United States Naval Academy 9

Valley City, USS 199, 200, 202
Vance, Zebulon 42, 92
Virginia, CSS 22

Warley, Alexander 154, 170–172, 184, 188–191
Washington, D.C. 7
Webb, Alexander 75, 78
Weehawken, USS 30–31
Wells, Gideon 10, 53, 65, 81, 87, 150, 208, 220
Westpoint 8
Wilmington, North Carolina 60, 96, 127, 212–217
Wood, John 60, 92
Woodman, John 186–187
Wyalusing, USS 120–126

www.ingramcontent.com/pod-product-compliance
Ingram Content Group UK Ltd.
Pitfield, Milton Keynes, MK11 3LW, UK
UKHW041941140426
5217IPUK00014B/601